D1563883

CAPTIVES &

THEIR SAVIORS

IN THE

MEDIEVAL CROWN

OF ARAGON

CAPTIVES &

THEIR SAVIORS

IN THE

MEDIEVAL CROWN

OF ARAGON

Jarbel Rodriguez

THE CATHOLIC UNIVERSITY
OF AMERICA PRESS
Washington, D.C.

LIBRARY OF CONGRESS CATALOGING-IN-
PUBLICATION DATA
Rodriguez, Jarbel A., 1971–
Captives and their saviors in the medieval crown
of Aragon / Jarbel Rodriguez.
p. cm.
Includes bibliographical references and index.
ISBN-13: 978-0-8132-1475-7 (cloth : alk. paper)
ISBN-10: 0-8132-1475-0 (cloth : alk. paper)
1. Slavery—Islamic Empire—History. 2. Spaniards—
Islamic Empire—History. 3. Ransom—Islamic
Empire—History. 4. Ransom—Spain—Aragon—
History. 5. Aragon (Spain)—Relations—Islamic
Empire. 6. Islamic Empire—Relations—Spain—
Aragon. 7. Freedmen—Spain—Aragon—Social
conditions. I. Title.
HT1315.I78R63 2007
306.3'62094655—dc22
2006006396

CONTENTS

ACKNOWLEDGMENTS

The writing of any large scholarly work is typically a group effort, and although the author does the bulk of the labor, without assistance from institutions, colleagues, friends, and family, the work would never come to fruition and the pleasures of undertaking it would be considerably diminished. This book is no different. Over the last years, I have come to know some remarkable individuals and have received help from unexpected quarters, which it is now my pleasure to acknowledge. Even with all this assistance, readers will still find errors or omissions in the following pages; these are solely my responsibility.

Princeton University, the history department in particular, was incredibly generous in funding and overall academic assistance, ranging from my graduate fellowship to funds from the Hanna Grant to the always welcomed summer stipend given by the graduate school. Money from the Mellon Foundation, the Rollins Prize, the Princeton University Center for Human Values, and the Mrs. Giles Whiting Foundation has also been very helpful. A Fulbright Fellowship, supplemented by a research grant from the Spanish Ministry of Culture, allowed my wife and me to spend a wonderful year in Spain doing the bulk of the archival research. My current institution, San Francisco State University, has also been very kind in its financial assistance with numerous course release grants. I would also like to thank the University of Miami (Florida), where I received my first graduate degree—as well as undergraduate—for its support while I was a student there. The staffs at Firestone, John Paul Leonard, and Richter libraries as well as the archivists at the Arxiu de la Corona d'Aragó, the Arxiu Diocesà de Barcelona, the Arxiu Històric de la Ciutat de Barcelona, and the Arxiu Històric de Protocols de Barcelona were always courteous, professional, and efficient, and through their competence and expertise my job was made much easier. I would also like to thank David McGonagle, Theresa Walker, Robin DuBlanc, and the staff at the Catholic University of America Press for their assistance.

This book has been considerably enriched by the input and advice of William Bonds, James Brodman, Sarah Curtis, Andrew Graybill, Father Joseph Gross, Richard Hoffman, Barbara Loomis, Christopher MacEvitt, Jaclyn Maxwell, Kevin Mummey, Eva Sheppard-Wolf, David Silverman, Larry Simon, Jules Tygiel, Kevin Uhalde, Amanda Wunder, and the anonymous readers who have read parts or all of this manuscript. I have been incredibly fortunate to have come under the tutelage of some magnificent teachers: Peter Brown, Ken Mills, Guido Ruggiero, Teo Ruiz, and Hugh Thomas. Echoing the words of his other students, it is impossible to quantify what William Jordan has taught me, first as my advisor and now as my friend, but the careful reader will recognize his suggestions, influence, and supervision in the pages that follow.

Finally, this book would have never been started, much less finished, without the love, sacrifice, and encouragement of my family and friends. My parents, siblings, grandparents, in-laws, friends, and my family in Spain have always been there to remind me that I am a very fortunate person and that there is an exciting, fulfilling, and love-filled world beyond research, writing, and teaching. In particular, my life has been enriched by the love and support of two remarkable women: my mother, Mariblanca, and my wife, Claudia. Their sacrifices for this book have been greater than mine, and it is to them that I dedicate it.

An early draft of chapter 6 first appeared in *Medieval Encounters* 9 (2003) as "Financing a Captive's Ransom in Late Medieval Aragon." It was originally published by Koninklijke Brill N.V. and is reprinted with permission.

INTRODUCTION

A curious transaction took place in the spring of 1998 in the Sudan. Two men, one dressed in a long white robe and a turban and another in jeans and a T-shirt, sat across from each other, their faces betraying their intense negotiation. Around them, over two hundred men, women, and children waited patiently as the two haggled. A deal was eventually reached, and the one in the jeans and T-shirt handed over "thick wads of tattered banknotes" that amounted to a sum of about 17,000 dollars. He had just purchased 235 of the bystanders for about 72 dollars each. The buyer, a Christian missionary, had bought each person's freedom for the price of two cows in the African nation, releasing them from the life of slavery that awaited them—part of the human cost of the Sudanese civil war that has pitted the Muslims in the north of the country against the Christian and Animist tribes that comprise the southern part and which in recent years has reached genocidal proportions.[1]

Some six hundred years earlier, in 1388, an eerily sim-

---

1. "New Face of Slavery Flourishes in Sudan," *Toronto Star,* Jun 13, 1998. This story was first reported by two reporters from the *Baltimore Sun,* Gilbert Lewthwaite and Gregory Kane, who in the spring of 1996 entered Sudan illegally and purchased two boys, ten and twelve, for 500 dollars each and then returned them to their families. *Baltimore Sun,* June 16–18, 1996.

ilar transaction took place in the North African city of Bougie, where, like their modern counterparts, two men, one Muslim, the other Christian, likely also sat across from each other and bargained over how much a human being was worth. In this case, the Christian friar, a member of a religious order dedicated specifically to ransoming Christians who had fallen into captivity in Muslim lands, was able to liberate thirty-eight people and return with them to the eastern Spanish kingdom of Aragon. He paid the equivalent of two horses for each captive.[2] This book is about the earlier group of Christian captives, although the later group serves to remind us that history, even medieval history many years removed from us, can inform our present condition.

HISTORICAL BACKGROUND

By the time the redemption in Bougie took place, captivity was an ancient problem in the Iberian world in general and in the Crown of Aragon in particular.[3] The Muslim invasion of Spain in 711 was the first act of a long struggle as Christian and Islamic forces fought each other for control of the Peninsula.[4] The years between the eighth and tenth centuries were bleak ones for the Christian kingdoms that had survived the initial invasion and occupation. Politically and militarily weak, these small kingdoms managed to hang on while witnessing the high

2. Millán Rubio, *La Orden de Nuestra Señora de la Merced,* 344.

3. The Crown of Aragon was a confederation of individual polities ruled by one king, the king of Aragon, but each with its own respective ruling elites, representative assemblies, and laws. To the original union of the Kingdom of Aragon and the County of Barcelona (Catalonia) were added significant territories over the course of the thirteenth, fourteenth, and fifteenth centuries. These included the Kingdom of Valencia on the mainland as well as Mediterranean conquests in the Balearics, Sardinia, Sicily, parts of southern Italy, and the duchies of Athens and Neopatria in Greece.

4. For the reader interested in a fuller account of the Spanish Reconquest, medieval Iberia, or the Crown of Aragon, see any of a number of excellent sources including Bisson, *Medieval Crown of Aragon;* Lomax, *Reconquest of Spain;* O'Callaghan, *Medieval Spain.*

point of Muslim culture in Spain, the Caliphate of Cordova. The decline of the caliphate and its eventual fragmentation after 1031 into petty lordships, known as *taifas*, gave the Christian kingdoms the opportunity they needed to begin their crusades to reconquer the Peninsula. Over the next four centuries the power of the Christian kingdoms, notably Castile, Portugal, and Aragon, continued to grow, while that of the Muslim states weakened. By the end of the thirteenth century, the political situation in the Peninsula had shifted decidedly in favor of the Christian powers. Granada, the last remaining Muslim kingdom, precariously held on with some support from the Muslim polities of North Africa. It was at this point, with the conquest of the whole Peninsula seemingly within the grasp of the Christian kingdoms, that the push to drive the Muslims out of Iberia faltered. Portugal and Aragon had lost their land frontiers with Granada and with them much of the impetus for further conquests in Iberia, instead turning their attentions to the Atlantic and the Mediterranean respectively. The weight of the crusade fell on Castile's broad but fragile shoulders, and as Castile suffered through numerous disasters and weak leadership through the fourteenth and fifteenth centuries, thoughts of crusade and reconquest were often replaced by more pressing needs. When the Castilians were able to launch invasions against Granada, they typically accomplished little. A stalemate ensued that would persist for over two hundred years.

Neither the lack of shared land frontiers with Granada nor the near absence of large-scale military campaigns spared the Crown of Aragon from the ongoing struggle. Instead of massive invasions and protracted wars, low-level warfare, so common in the history of the Mediterranean and characterized by piracy and raiding, became endemic in the border regions. The Crown of Aragon's close proximity to Granada (separated only by a narrow strip of land), its extensive coastline, its dependence on maritime trade, and the crown's often aggressive policy vis-à-vis its Muslim neighbors brought its citizens into the forefront of this conflict and constantly placed them in danger of falling into captivity. Soldiers, sailors, and other individuals who worked or lived along the frontiers and seacoasts were prime targets, but so were travelers, pilgrims, and merchants, who sometimes found themselves captured while in Muslim territory simply because they were Christians or were Aragonese subjects.

As the enduring struggle stimulated the ongoing warfare and the taking of thousands of captives on both sides, it also animated efforts to get them back, notably on the Christian side. The advancing Christian frontier, which created new towns to mark and safeguard newly conquered territories, placed an increasing number of civilians on the front lines. These new towns were chartered with extensive obligations and privileges, most notably the obligation of military service for townsmen and the expectation of ransom for those who were captured by Muslim forces. It is clear that by the 1130s town militias had become an integral and active part of the Iberian Christian armies, including those of Aragon.[5] Not surprisingly, the first *fueros* (town charters) that address the issue of ransoms and prisoner exchanges also date from the 1130s. The fuero that Alfonso I of Aragon granted to the town of Calatayud in 1131, for example, gave the parents of captives the right to purchase any available Muslim slave in the settlement "if such a slave could then be used in a redemption."[6] In effect, it was the importance of these citizen-soldiers in Iberian armies that made ransoming a possibility, even a necessity, in Spain, while it was still widely disdained in most other western European armies, in which chivalric notions of honor and courage presented the captive, especially if he was not of the nobility, as a coward and an object of scorn.[7] Iberian monarchs and their nobles could not afford

5. Powers, *Society Organized for War*, 27.

6. Brodman, "Municipal Ransoming Law," 319–20; Powers, *Society Organized for War*, 179.

7. For a full discussion, see Friedman, *Encounter between Enemies*, ch. 3.

to observe these chivalric sensibilities. They did not have the luxury of looking at war as solely the province of the aristocracy, nor could they show the same disdain for commoners in the military found elsewhere in Europe. Needing every possible soldier that they could command, Christian kings in Spain had to extend certain privileges to their nonnoble soldiers, namely the town militias, if they expected extended and reliable service from them. Ransoming was one of these privileges.

Towns and townsmen were not the only ones concerned with the problem of captivity and ransoming. Royal ransomers, known as *exeas* or *alfaqueques*, began appearing in the sources as early as 1126. These men, mostly merchants or Jews, ventured back and forth between the Muslim and Christian regions ransoming captives for both sides. Joining them in their ransoming efforts were lay confraternities and even religious military orders, which at the behest of Spanish kings founded or administered numerous ransoming hospitals, including the hospital of the Holy Redeemer founded in 1188 in Teruel in the Crown of Aragon.[8] Consequently, by the early thirteenth century, Aragon had created or experimented with several different ransoming methods and an embryonic, if haphazard, ransoming system was clearly developing. This process continued in the early thirteenth century with the creation of the ransoming orders, the Trinitarians and Mercedarians. The Mercedarians especially, being a native Catalan order patronized by the king, suggested the growing concern in the kingdom over the fate of captives. Thus, by the time Pope Innocent III (r. 1198–1216) began to put the institutional weight of the church behind ransoming efforts in the Holy Land in 1212 and 1213, the Crown of Aragon already boasted numerous options to help its captured subjects, with more to come.[9]

8. Brodman, "Military Redemptionism," 24–25; Brodman, *Ransoming Captives*, 10–14.

9. For Innocent's letters and bulls relating to captives, see Bolton, "'Perhaps You Do Not Know?'"

Innocent's appeal helped to confirm the place of captives among the needy of Christ and this, in turn, ensured the flow of charitable donations so necessary for the ransoms. By the 1230s, for example, the Mercedarians were routinely receiving alms from faithful Christians to support their efforts.[10] This process continued throughout the century as Christian donors increasingly set aside money for captives in their wills and in their charitable donations. The growing economic importance of Barcelona and other cities in the kingdom also had an impact on captives as merchants became increasingly involved in their releases. Merchants had always played a role in ransoming, as their early involvement as exeas and alfaqueques can attest. This role, however, increased in the thirteenth century as Christian merchants, including many from the Crown of Aragon, began to actively trade with and travel to the Muslim kingdoms of Granada and North Africa. This increased their access to Christians held in those kingdoms, making them ideal middlemen to handle negotiations, but it also increased their exposure to captivity themselves. This last may explain why merchants donated so charitably to captives, always knowing that they could very easily suffer a similar misfortune.

Royal, municipal, and ecclesiastical assistance to captives also increased during the thirteenth century. Royal patronage of the military orders and their hospitals and later the ransoming orders are but two examples and stand in stark contrast to the deeds of Christian kings in the Crusader kingdoms—the other active military frontier against Islam—where monarchs had little responsibility to ransom their captured subjects.[11] Even more striking was the growing willingness of Aragonese monarchs to use diplomatic tools to appeal to Muslim rulers for the

10. By 1235 the Mercedarians had founded three alms centers, in Barcelona, Palma, and Gerona, to facilitate the collection of funds. Brodman, *Ransoming Captives*, 17–18.

11. Friedman, *Encounter between Enemies*, 83.

release of captives. This starts to become common toward the end of the century and is routine by the 1300s. Royal lieutenants and town councils emulated their monarch as they, too, took an interest in the release of local captives and pleaded on their behalf or facilitated negotiations and sometimes ransoms. The church also focused more efforts on captives, exemplified by the numerous grants of indulgence approved by thirteenth-century popes for those who gave money to captives.

As the fourteenth century began, the Crown of Aragon had become, to borrow a phrase from Elena Lourie, a society organized for ransoming, as the resources, privileges, networks, and social outlook that facilitated the assistance of captives were clearly in place.[12] Additionally, these ransoming efforts were not reserved for the elites or for soldiers but were available to everyone, and it was mostly poor sailors, fishermen, and frontier dwellers who benefited from them. If for no reason other than this remarkable social conscience, the experience of Aragon demands further scrutiny.

This ransoming society and its efforts to redeem its captives are the focus of this book, which addresses three main questions. First, how was this ransoming society strengthened and perpetuated over the course of the fourteenth and into the fifteenth century? Part one argues that the threat of piracy and raiding, the living conditions under which captives suffered, and the fear that they could convert to Islam served to increase efforts to liberate captives, maintain awareness of their plight, and generate revenues for their ransoms. The second question asks how this ransoming society functioned. Part two takes an in-depth look at how families, the crown, the ransoming orders, municipal officials, and the church all worked in a complementary fashion to help captives gain their freedom. Finally, is it possible to reconstruct the experience of captivity for both the captives

12. Lourie, "A Society Organized for War."

and the families, friends, and society they left behind, and does this experience help us better to understand Muslim-Christian relations in the later Middle Ages? This question is answered throughout the book as part one follows captives from the time they were taken and into their imprisonment in Granada and North Africa. Part two reminds us that captivity was not suffered only by the captives but also by their families, their communities, and even their country, as the focus in this section shifts to the home front. The epilogue returns to the captives as they gain their freedom and try to restore their shattered lives.

HISTORIOGRAPHY AND SOURCES

The work of many scholars has influenced my approach in this book. In 1915, José María Ramos y Loscertales published *El cautiverio en la Corona de Aragon durante los siglos XIII, XIV y XV*, the first modern work on captivity. *El cautiverio*, somewhat dated by now, remains a useful introduction to the topic, presenting many of the themes that have come to dominate captivity historiography: piracy and raiding, the captive as slave, the ransoming orders, and ransoming and redemption, among others. Numerous scholars have followed in Ramos's wake, creating a long historiographical tradition numbering scores of articles and a handful of books. Maria Teresa Ferrer i Mallol's excellent article "La redempció de captius a la Corona Catalano-Aragonesa (Segle XIV)" has become one of the studies that most scholars refer to when discussing captivity and especially ransoming. Many of her other works on Christian and Muslims and their lives on the frontiers of medieval Aragon have also dealt, sometimes indirectly, but always authoritatively, with the issue of captivity. The same can be said of the work of Roser Salicrú i Lluch and María Dolores López Pérez, notably the latter's *La Corona de Aragón y el Magreb en el siglo XIV*. While captives are generally not their principal focus, their extensive research and writings on diplomatic and mercantile relations between Aragon and the Muslim states of North Africa and Granada have both made my work easier and suggested new avenues of research.

A large portion of the research on captivity has revolved around the ransoming orders, the Trinitarians and Mercedarians. The older works of Faustino Gazulla still have their use, even if that use is limited. They are ably complemented by much more recent research by Giulio Cipollone, Bonifacio Porres Alonso, and James Brodman, among others. Brodman's various works, including *Ransoming Captives in Crusader Spain*, throw significant light on captives and ransoming, particularly during the thirteenth century. His work has provided those of us who have followed with invaluable road maps on numerous questions. Bruce Taylor's *Structures of Reform: The Mercedarian Order in the Spanish Golden Age* continues the work that Brodman began and charts the history of the order into the seventeenth century as well as providing a good overview of Mercedarian studies in the medieval period.

In the last five years, scholarly interest in captives has continued and even grown with the publication of at least five books on the topic, including three on captivity in the Middle Ages.[13] Anthony Lappin's work *The Medieval Cult of Saint Dominic of Silos* is an extensive treatment of the Castilian saint who is reputed to have freed hundreds of captives through miraculous intercession. What makes Lappin's work particularly useful to me is his handling of the miracles to reconstruct the captivity experience. More closely related to my work here is Yvonne Friedman's *Encounter between Enemies*. Although Friedman's focus is on the Holy Land, she does provide some useful comparisons with Iberia. Moreover, her argument has helped to contextualize the place of the captive in the non-Iberian medieval West.

13. The two nonmedieval titles are Colley's *Captives* and Davis's *Christian Slaves, Muslim Masters.*

Finally, and covering a period similar to that covered by this book, is Andrés Díaz Borrás's *El miedo al Mediterráneo*. Díaz Borrás's book, much of which was laid out in previous articles, provides an in-depth look at the organization and evolution of charity for captives in the city of Valencia. I am indebted to his work.

The majority of these pieces have focused on very specific issues and their immediate context. As such, the results have been excellent: there are very good in-depth studies on the cells in which captives were held, charity and poverty in medieval Spain, the laws of ransoming, the goings and comings of Christian merchants in Granada and North Africa, piracy and raiding, and the fund-raising efforts of the city of Valencia, for example.[14] What has been missing is a book that places the captives in their proper context within Aragonese society at the center of a complex web of social, economic, religious, and diplomatic networks. That is part of my goal here, to show that by the fourteenth century captives from the Crown of Aragon were the focus of a mobilized Christian society that allotted significant resources to secure their freedom.

The sources used in this book are varied, with the greater part coming from the rich Archive of the Crown of Aragon in Barcelona and other municipal and ecclesiastical archives in the Aragonese Confederacy. These archival sources can take many forms, but the most common ones include begging licenses, diplomatic correspondence, truce agreements, wills, contracts, and even some short letters from the captives themselves. The archival material consulted comprises both unpublished and published documents. Mediterranean scholars—and especially Iberian ones—have distinguished themselves by their efforts to

14. Sample works on these topics include, but are not limited to, Torres Balba, "Las mazmorras de la Alhambra"; López Alonso, *La pobreza en la España medieval*; Brodman, "Municipal Ransoming Law"; Salicrú i Lluch, "Catalano-Aragonese Commercial Presence in the Sultanate of Granada"; Burns, *Muslims, Christians, and Jews*; Díaz Borrás, "Notas sobre los primeros tiempos."

publish the documents relevant to their work. Thus, any giv-
en monograph on medieval Spain can have hundreds of documents in an appendix. This is in addition to the monumental
document collections that some archives have published, such
as Próspero de Bofarull y Mascaró's *Colección de documentos
inéditos del Archivo General de la Corona de Aragón,* released
in forty-one volumes.[15] The biggest drawback of the archival
sources is that they all bear the inimitable imprint of the bureaucracy that produced them and its preferred tool, the formulaic passage. When almost every begging license declares that
such and such captive is held by the Saracens in the lands of
Barbary, where he suffers innumerable torments, which he can
escape only with the help of the Christian faithful, one begins
to question their accuracy. Yet, this notarial discipline is often
enlivened by precious nuggets of unique information that falls
outside of the formulas, and we learn names, family relations,
circumstances, details of a ransom or exchange, social position,
and so on. Thus, while a single will or diplomatic letter may
not tell us much, taken as a group the archival sources consti-
tute a formidable font of information.

Perhaps the single best-known source on Iberian captives is
the collection of miracles attributed to the Santo Domingo de
Silos and housed in that Castilian monastery. Sometime in the
early to mid-thirteenth century, the Castilian cleric/poet Gonzalo de Berceo composed the *Vida de Santo Domingo,* highlighting Domingo's role as a miraculous liberator of captives
without equal. To this we must add the *Miraculos romançados,*
a collection of over seventy miracles recorded by the monks of
Silos as told to them by the grateful patrons whom the saint
had miraculously delivered from captivity.[16] Both of these col-

15. Every source that I have cited using the archival nomenclature I have
seen personally in the original. When one of these sources exists in a published
form known to me, I have noted it also. All translations in the text are mine unless otherwise noted.

16. Both can be found in Vergara, *Vida y milagros.*

lections of stories are amazingly lucid and aside from the super-natural appearance of the saint, they contain many useful and otherwise provable details. And although these are both Castil-ian sources, I have found them very useful for the sections on life in captivity—the experience of an Aragonese captive was likely to be very similar to that of a Castilian captive. I have also made extensive use of laws, histories, and narrative chroni-cles. And where these fail, equally helpful sources, such as trav-el journals, chronicles by both Christian and Muslim authors, poems and sayings, and archaeological remains, have helped to fill in details to the picture of ransoming and captivity fash-ioned in this book.

One final point concerns Muslim captives. That this book is not about them does not in any way imply that they did not exist or that they did not suffer similar tribulations as their Christian counterparts. In the warfare of late medieval Iberia and its attendant horrors, neither Christian nor Muslim could claim what we moderns might call a moral high ground. Both sides raided, both sides broke truces, both sides took captives, both sides mistreated and punished their captives, and captives from both sides died while in custody. That this book is not about Muslim in addition to Christian captives is a reflection of my interest in how the Crown of Aragon reacted to the captive problem and my determination to keep some effective limits on the research and writing process.

ABBREVIATIONS

The following abbreviations are used in the footnotes.

ACA: Arxiu de la Corona d'Aragó, Barcelona
    C: Cancillería
    Reg.: Registers
    CR: Cartas Reales
    OR: Ordenes Religiosas
    MdeH: Monacales de Hacienda
    r: recto
    v: verso

ADB: Arxiu Diocesà de Barcelona

AHCB: Arxiu Històric de la Ciutat de Barcelona
    CC: Consell de Cent
    LCO: Lletres Comunes Originals

AHPB: Arxiu de Protocols de Barcelona

AMG: Archivo del Monasterio de Guadalupe

PART ONE

CAPTIVES

CHAPTER I

RAIDING AND PIRACY

In the darkness, the strange men came ashore. Gliding through the stillness of the night, they made their way to the peaceful village as it slept—and then, chaos. Wakened from their slumber, the villagers of Gola de la Albufera opened their eyes to the presence of invaders with foreign faces and an alien language. The raiders had caught the village completely by surprise. The clashing of weapons and the sounds of shouted orders drowned out the cries of alarm and screams of panic coming from the houses and streets of the little community. In the ensuing struggle, some villagers died resisting the invaders; many others became prisoners. The attackers took their captives to their ships, departing swiftly and consigning those left behind to pick up the pieces. The town reacted quickly, putting defensive plans into action. Messengers carried the news to nearby cities and towns. Plans were made to build a defensive tower.[1] Yet how much could a tower help when the invaders could come at any time, by land or by sea? This attack was not an isolated event. Frontier settlers and those who traveled the seas had come to accept capture as

1. Rubio Vela, *Epistolari*, 1:doc. 96 (Apr. 21, 1410).

3

a common risk. The risk, moreover, was a necessary one as the Christian kingdoms of Spain sought to expand their borders at the expense of their Muslim neighbors on the Peninsula. This required a constant stream of settlers moving into perilous areas. It was one of the great ironies of frontier settlement that those settlers who came south seeking, among other things, greater freedoms did so only by exposing themselves to greater risk of captivity. The Spanish historian Claudio Sánchez Albornoz had only words of admiration for these men and women, exalting those who bore the brunt of the frontier battles and worked so hard for so many years under the constant threat of war, driven only by "hopeful expectations."[2]

PIRACY AND RAIDING

This was the reality of life on the borderlands that stood between the Christian kingdoms of Europe and the Muslim states of Granada and North Africa, where the normal situation was open war. Truces had to be negotiated to bring an end to hostilities. When truces expired or one of the combatants broke them, war returned and often manifested itself in raids like the one on Gola de la Albufera. These raids were the norm by the late Middle Ages in the Crown of Aragon.[3] The great battles that had characterized Christian-Muslim warfare between the eleventh and the thirteenth centuries had, by the fourteenth, become rare. This is not to say that large-scale combat had disappeared altogether. It had not, as can be attested by the Aragonese crusade against Granada in 1309, the Moroccan invasion of Iberia in 1340, incursions by forces from Granada during the War of the Two Peters (1356–69), and the great campaigns of Isabel and Ferdinand against Granada in the last years of the fifteenth century. These campaigns could be intense and deadly, but they

2. Sánchez Albornoz, *España*, 2:42.
3. For breaks in truces, see Ferrer i Mallol, *La frontera amb l'Islam*, 165–69.

were relatively brief. And when they were over and the armies left the field of battle, pirates and raiders took their place; their actions so widespread and common that one historian has described them as "endemic as the plague," and another has compared the omnipresent danger they presented to that posed by the weather.[4]

Piracy was an ancient vocation in the Mediterranean and one that had grown considerably as a by-product of the medieval commercial revolution, beginning in the late eleventh century.[5] Indeed, many of the merchants who stimulated the economic recovery moonlighted as pirates and privateers when the right situation presented itself—the right situation often being defined as having a bigger ship or larger crew than a potential victim.[6] Piracy was on one level a business, and the later Middle Ages were a boon time. Piracy was also state policy for many of the dozens of kingdoms, sultanates, and city-states that bordered the Mediterranean, including the Crown of Aragon. Economics and belligerent state policy came together in the person of the pirate, or more accurately the corsair/privateer.[7] By the fourteenth century, the Crown of Aragon was responsible for much of the piracy in the western Mediterranean as its ships plied the waters looking for vessels from Christian and Muslim enemies, with the king licensing the ships and re-

4. Burns, *Muslims, Christians, and Jews,* 110; Pryor, *Geography, Technology, and War,* 155.

5. The literature on Mediterranean piracy in the later Middle Ages is quite extensive. A good introduction for the Crown of Aragon is Burns's *Muslims, Christians, and Jews.* For fuller treatments of the fourteenth and fifteenth centuries, see López Pérez, *La Corona de Aragón* 577–861; Díaz Borrás, *Los orígenes de la piratería islámica.*

6. Burns, *Muslims, Christians, and Jews,* 109–11.

7. The distinction between pirates and corsairs has been long debated. One distinction historians have drawn is that corsairs attacked private ships under orders or license from their governments with the government often getting a share of the spoils. Pirates, on the other hand, were more indiscriminate in their actions, attacking targets of opportunity without the consent of their monarchs and keeping all the profits for themselves; see López Pérez, *La Corona de Aragón,* 578–79; Mollat, "Essai d'orientation pour l'etude de la guerre de course et la piraterie," 749.

ceiving a royal share that could amount to as much as 10 percent of the booty.[8]

Granada and the Muslim kingdoms of North Africa were equally aggressive. The Muslim scholar Ibn Khaldun alluded to this belligerence when he described the activity of North African pirates and corsairs: "These warriors make their descent on the coasts and islands inhabited by the Franks; they arrive when they are least expected and carry off all those who fall into their hands; they also attack the ships of the infidels, often taking them over and carrying off loads of booty and prisoners. In this manner, Bougie and the other western ports [of the Hafsid Empire] get filled with captives."[9] The fifteenth-century Egyptian writer al-Qalqasandi referred to the naval strategy of Granada in similar terms. Privateering was the main task of the kingdom's navy, with light ships roaming the Christian coastline taking captives and returning to Granada to sell them.[10] These raids left their mark in the many archives of the Crown of Aragon, often as letters circulated among the different towns and cities warning one another of pirate sightings. The weight of the attacks fell predominantly on the southern kingdom of Valencia and the Balearic Islands, with an average of three to four sightings of pirate ships a year during the last two decades of the fourteenth century. Many of the strikes, moreover, were coordinated efforts by flotillas of two or more ships, capable of attacking with more men and having space for more captives and other booty.[11] Consequently, by the fourteenth century, the coasts of and the seas adjacent to the Crown of Aragon—indeed, extending to Granada and North Africa—were serving as a laboratory for the kind of warfare that we tend to associate with the Mediterranean after the sixteenth century as the sea be-

8. López Pérez, *La Corona de Aragón*, 577–644; for the royal share, see 634.
9. Ibn Khaldun, *Histoire des Berbères*, 3:117.
10. Al-Qalqasandi, *Subh al-a'ša fîkitâbât al-inša*, 93.
11. Díaz Borrás, *Los orígenes de la piratería islámica*, 58–89, esp. table 2.

came the major avenue by which the belligerents were able to strike at one another, and "piracy expanded to fill any gaps left by the slackening of official war."[12] Piracy had become a menace to coastal inhabitants and to those who made their living from the sea.

Equally dangerous were raids across land frontiers. Aragon had ceased to have a land frontier with Muslim Granada in 1304 as Castilian Murcia interposed itself between the two kingdoms, but that did not put an end to frontier raiding.[13] When the two countries were at war, entire military columns crossed back and forth across Murcia, sometimes with and sometimes without the consent of the king of Castile. These invasions, although rare, were devastating. In 1331 an army from Granada, numbering in the thousands, attacked and sacked the town of Guardamar, taking some fifteen hundred captives, eight hundred horses, and two thousand head of cattle. And in the early 1390s, as the two kingdoms warred again, frontier raiding was so intense that municipal councils were overwhelmed repairing damage and ransoming captives.[14] Even truces did not altogether stop the raiding as adventurers, criminals, and opportunists on both sides violated truce agreements and risked the wrath of their kings for the financial windfall they could reap from captured booty and captives. The best efforts by the king of Aragon and his lieutenants to stop the attacks—both against and by his subjects—were often not enough, as royal authorities had to cope with topography, limited resources, and the fact that their own minority Muslim communities sometimes helped the raiders by turning a blind eye to their passing or even helping to hide them as they made their way into and out

12. Braudel, *Mediterranean*, 2:865; see also Ellen Friedman, *Spanish Captives*, 4.

13. The politics and dynamics of frontier life and raiding are too complex for a complete overview here. For an excellent introduction see Ferrer i Mallol, *La frontera amb l'Islam*, on which this section is based.

14. Ibid., 127–34 and 173.

of the kingdom.[15] Moreover, as Maria Teresa Ferrer i Mallol has recently pointed out, the frontier was populated by very aggressive people on both sides. Those who wanted a quiet life did not venture there. Instead, those who came were the vagabonds, the treasure seekers, the risk takers, and the lawless. This population was difficult to control and prone to taking matters into its own hands.[16] Consequently, in spite of truces and threats of dire punishments against those who broke them, illegal raids across the frontier were common and only served to beget counterattacks in a continuing cycle of raiding and counterraiding that made life on the borderlands extremely hazardous for both Muslim and Christian.

Piracy and raiding were legal as long as no truce existed between the countries of the captor and his victims. All captives taken this way were considered *de bona guerra*—legally seized as part of a "good war." The fate of those individuals was not promising, as there was little recourse for the state to get them back as long as no truce was in effect. Even when hostilities ceased, the captors had no responsibility to return their captives seized de bona guerra. For these captives, the only way out was through exchanges or exorbitant ransoms that left many excaptives begging though the streets of Barcelona, Valencia, Zaragoza, and other cities and towns of the Crown of Aragon. The situation was completely different when a person was captured illegally—while a truce was in effect—and royal ambassadors could claim the return of captives and demand the punishment of their tormentors.

Beyond these bellicose forays, there were other ways that Christians could fall into Muslim captivity. The Crown of Aragon and its Muslim neighbors had extensive diplomatic, military, and mercantile relations when they were not fighting one

15. Ibid., 47.
16. Ibid., 47–49.

another. As such, Christian merchants, travelers, mercenaries, and even religious missionaries were not an uncommon sight in Granada and the Maghrib. These interactions created additional possibilities for captivity. This chapter is about the diverse experiences of these people and the myriad ways they were captured and transported back to North Africa and Granada. Only by understanding the ubiquitous danger that captivity posed and the demographic impact it made will it be possible to make sense of the widespread response that captivity generated in the Crown of Aragon.

FALLING INTO CAPTIVITY

In the medieval conflict between Christian and Muslims, the most plentiful sources of captives had traditionally been conquered cities and strongholds.[17] Their surrender could produce thousands of captives and make the prices at slave markets drop throughout the Mediterranean.[18] When Alfonso II of Aragon (r. 1285–91) captured the island of Minorca in 1287, he held public auctions throughout his realms to sell the Islamic prisoners who fell into his hands. The Catalan chronicler Muntaner ventured that the Christian forces acquired forty thousand captives when the city capitulated, and although this figure is an exaggeration, the number of captives must have been substantial.[19] Almost a century and a half later (1423), the forces of another Aragonese Alfonso, Alfonso IV (r. 1416–58), took over three thousand captives when they raided and pillaged the Tu-

17. For an overview see Friedman, *Encounter between Enemies.*

18. As a starting point, see Ladero Quesada, "La esclavitud por guerra," especially the figures that he gives for surrendered populations that went into captivity during the last phase of the Reconquest. For the price drops and gluts of slaves that were the result of the capture of cities, see Constable, "Muslim Spain and Mediterranean Slavery," 275.

19. Muntaner, *Chrònica,* ch. 172. Charles Verlinden considered 20,000 more realistic. See *L'esclavage,* 1:254. For a longer discussion on the captives produced by the capitulation of Minorca, see 253–58.

nisian island of Kerkenna.[20] And, in the last years of the Reconquest, the Castilians took captive over ten thousand inhabitants of Málaga when the city surrendered in 1487. The victors divided them three ways: among the crown and nobles, with a third group designated to be exchanged for Christian captives.[21] In the Crusader East, capitulations followed a similar pattern. When Acre, the last Christian city in the Levant, surrendered in 1291, the Franciscan friar Ricoldo de Monte-Croce tells us that the cache of captives was so large that slavers had to send some of them to far-off places to find buyers.[22]

This model, however, does not hold true for the Crown of Aragon, or, in fact, for most of Christian Spain, after 1212 and the decisive battle of Las Navas de Tolosa, which swung the balance of military power in the Peninsula in the favor of Christian forces, never to swing back. From that point on the capitulation of Christian cities and strongholds with their large caches of captives became rare. Instead, those who were captured were mostly individuals in exposed positions due to their jobs, traveling activities, or vulnerable positions on the coast or the southern boundaries of the Crown of Aragon.

Soldiers and mercenaries were among those most at risk. In 1382 a raiding party from Granada captured two soldiers from Oriola while they were in the service of a frontier castellan. The two soldiers were the victims of a retaliatory raid, as the Muslims were looking for some collateral so that they could negotiate the release of some of their compatriots. They had merely been convenient targets in their exposed position on the frontier. The king, Peter the Ceremonious (r. 1336–87), quickly arranged for the captured Muslims to be exchanged for the two

20. Ryder, *Alfonso the Magnanimous*, 156.
21. Ladero Quesada, "La esclavitud por guerra," 71.
22. Rohricht, "Lettres de Ricolde de Monte Croce," 264. "Cristianos vero squalidos atque mente consternatos cum puelle eorum et parvulli et senes cum rumoribus at partes remotissimas orientis inter barbaras nationes captivi at sclavi minabantur gimentes."

captured soldiers.[23] In numerous other instances, the crown provided captured soldiers with begging licenses so that they could pay for their ransom. In one example that can stand for others, Juan de Epila was granted a license so that he could raise the funds necessary to free his brother, Pere. This case reflects some of the complexities of peninsular warfare, diplomacy, and alliances. The two brothers had been serving the king of Castile in a war against Granada when they were captured. The Castilians had been able to ransom Juan, but had run short on funds before they could free Pere and some of the other soldiers. It now fell to Pere's family, with some support from the king of Aragon, to get him home.[24] The *Miráculos romançados* of St. Dominic offer further evidence of the dangers for soldiers stationed on the frontier—in this case Castile—as over one-third of the captives whose profession we know were soldiers.[25] Mercenaries, even those who served Muslim rulers, were also at risk. In 1367 Peter the Ceremonious sent a letter of appeal to Abu el-Abbas Ahmed, ruler of Bougie and Constantine, asking him to release twenty-one Christian soldiers who had served as mercenaries with the sultan's enemies. Peter reminded Abu el-Abbas that he was breaking tradition, as the Muslim custom was not to enslave mercenaries after they were defeated but for the victor to take them into his service.[26]

The ubiquity of raiding and the desire by raiders and pirates to go after soft, nonmilitary targets exposed many civilians to the dangers of captivity. Capture in the course of daily business was common enough. In 1335 pirates from Málaga captured,

23. ACA, C, reg. 1273:134v–35r (June 25, 1382); see also Ferrer i Mallol, "La redempció," 245.

24. ACA, C, reg. 1895:105r–6r (Dec. 4, 1388); published in Ferrer i Mallol, "La redempció," doc. 3. For additional examples of captured soldiers see ACA, C, reg. 2207:112r (Nov. 19, 1408) and reg. 2208:9v–10r (Nov. 28, 1409).

25. Lappin, *Medieval Cult of Saint Dominic*, 342–49 (table 7). My thanks to Dr. Lappin for allowing me access to computerized versions of his tables.

26. ACA, C, reg. 1389:6r–v (June 20, 1367); also Dufourcq, "Catalogue chronologique et analytique du registre 1389," doc. 115.

tied up, and beat the butcher Matheu d'Almunia on a beach as he returned to Valencia from a fair in Murcia. Although Matheu managed to escape, his tormentors stole twenty-five *libres* in money and cloth.[27] Some years later, Peter III of Aragon ordered the prosecution of two Saracen raiders who had captured a Christian official collecting tallage. Before they could escape, Christian forces caught up with them, liberated their captive and, in turn, put the Saracens in chains.[28] A common tactic in many of these raids was for part of the pirate ship's crew to put ashore, take whatever prisoners and booty they could, and escape before defenders could rally to intercept them.[29] The raid on Gola de la Albufera, which began this chapter, provides an excellent example of this tactic in action. A similar, although much smaller raid, led to the capture of a Christian woman from Ibiza in 1409. According to the confession of one member of the raiding party that took her, four crewmen had landed on the island and captured the woman, her young grandson, and her slave. The vessel was hurrying back to Algiers when a Christian merchant ship intercepted it and gave battle. In the subsequent struggle, the Christians killed part of the Muslim crew and captured the rest, whom they took to Valencia to sell as slaves. The woman and her family were freed.[30] Others were not as lucky: they were captured, and sometimes killed, as they tended their flocks, fetched coal, enjoyed the sweet delights of an apiary, or traveled to frontier towns to settle there.[31] The common theme in all of these episodes is the exposed nature of the victims. The overwhelming number of attacks on land would have been of this kind—against targets of opportunity.

27. Sánchez Martínez, "En torno a la piratería Nazarí entre 1330–1337," doc. 11.

28. Ferrer i Mallol, *La frontera amb l'Islam*, doc. 100, dated Apr. 22, 1365.

29. Christians also used this tactic. See Ibn Battuta's description of a raid by four Christian galleys on the outskirts of Marbella. *Travels*, 3:939–40.

30. Hinojosa Montalvo, "Confesiones y ventas de cautivos," 118–20 and app. 4.

31. Bellot, *Anales de Orihuela*, 164, 192, 217.

People at sea ran even higher risks than their land-bound compatriots as the increase in piratical activity and the absence of organized naval power that could safeguard the seas made work, commerce, and travel in the Mediterranean dangerous activities. In late July 1335, Alfonso III (r. 1327–36) had to dispatch a messenger to Granada to recover two small merchant ships and thirty-five captives taken by the pirate Ibn al-'Ahsan.[32] This was an act of diplomacy often repeated by the kings of Aragon. In 1369 Peter the Ceremonious sent an angry missive to the Nasrid sultan demanding the release of Anthoni Despens, his crew, and his *leny* (small galley). The ship and the men were captured by a concerted attack by "land and sea" as the ship lay off a beach in Almeria. Peter considered the whole affair scandalous, as not only was the sultan technically responsible for the protection of Despens, his crew, and his vessel, but his own "officers" stood accused of leading the raid.[33]

Fishermen, sailors, and other men who depended on the ocean for their livelihood were also very vulnerable. In May 1335, for example, Alfonso III wrote a letter to Yusuf I of Granada to demand the release of fourteen fishermen, citizens of three different cities—Valencia, Alicante, and La Vila Joiosa—captured by pirates from that kingdom.[34] The danger to these men is also evident from the thirty-five ransoms subsidized by the city of Valencia between 1392 and 1395 and studied by Andrés Díaz-Borrás. Of the twenty-one captives whose profession Díaz-Borrás could determine, two were fishermen, another thirteen were sailors, and one was a ship's captain *(patron)*. In this small sample, sixteen of the twenty-one captives whose profes-

32. Alarcón y Santón and Garcia de Linares, *Documentos Árabes diplomáticos,* doc. 42 (July 26, 1335).

33. ACA, C, reg. 1389:79r (May 20, 1369); see also Dufourcq, "Catalogue chronologique et analytique du registre 1389," doc. 137.

34. Sánchez Martínez, "En torno a la piratería Nazarí," doc. 12. See also doc. 9.

sion is known made their living from the sea.[35] Sources from later periods, which survive in greater quantity and sometimes with more information, support these numbers. In the ten years before the battle of Lepanto, for example, 60 percent of Spanish captives in North Africa were seized off the coasts of Iberia or at sea.[36]

The threat, moreover, was not limited to Muslim pirates. Christian pirates increasingly became a part of the problem, taking Christian captives and then selling them in Muslim ports.[37] It goes without saying that this was forbidden by both canon and civil law, but permitted or not, it went on. The struggle for commercial and political supremacy in the western Mediterranean between the Crown of Aragon and the different Italian city-states, especially Genoa, pitted Christians against each other. In 1335, in a letter to Alfonso III, Yusuf I of Granada excused himself for allowing the sale of some Aragonese subjects by the Genoese in Almeria.[38] The apology was apparently less than sincere. Three years later, Alfonso's successor, Peter the Ceremonious, was again writing to Yusuf, to ask for the return of a sailor from Barcelona, Macià Descarner, whom the Genoese had captured and sold in Yusuf's domain. What was more, Yusuf himself was holding Descarner in one of his slave pens.[39]

The dual life led by many sailors and merchants, in which they easily switched from piracy to legal commerce and back, also contributed to their capture or state-sanctioned arrest. In 1372 Peter the Ceremonious had to intervene on behalf of Arnau Sola and his ship's crew, who became captives after a storm beached their vessel in Morocco. They stood accused of seizing

35. Díaz Borrás, "La organización de la caridad redentiva," 160–63; see also his *El miedo,* ch. 3.

36. Friedman, *Spanish Captives,* 4–5.

37. Pryor, *Geography, Technology, and War,* 155; López Pérez, *La Corona de Aragón,* 660–86.

38. Alarcón y Santón and Garcia de Linares, *Documentos Árabes diplomáticos,* doc. 40.

39. Sánchez Martínez, "En torno a la piratería Nazarí," doc. 14.

four subjects of the sultan of Morocco and selling them in Ibiza. Peter assured the sultan that these were not the guilty men, whose punishment the Christian king promised to carry out when—and if—authorities found them.[40] In other situations, it is difficult to decide whether Muslim authorities really considered the merchants a threat or if they accused the merchants of piracy as a pretense to seize the men and their merchandise, especially if the merchants traveled with guarantees of safe passage—which arrest, under charges of piracy, could conveniently circumvent.[41] An accusation of piracy was also advantageous when other economic matters were at stake. A mere two months after Peter negotiated for the release of Arnau Sola and his men, he again had to petition the sultan of Morocco for the liberation of another ship's crew. Muslim forces had captured the men while they were under a guarantee of safe passage, but this time the matter was a bit more complex than robbery. The local officials in the town of Honein had seized the ship and its cargo of indigo and interned the crew members, accusing them of piracy. Peter suggested that these officials were angry because on a previous journey, the ship had stopped in the town of Al-Cudia three times to unload cargoes of cloth and spices, while stopping only once at Honein. The king suspected that the officials, angry at losing custom duties, were trying to recover their loses with this ploy.[42] Occasionally, of course, it was genuine

40. Three of the four captives had already obtained their ransom for a sum of 170 dinars, which Peter also promised to return if the Christians were released. ACA, C, reg. 1389:92r; Dufourcq, "Catalogue chronologique et analytique du registre 1389,"doc. 164 (July 15, 1372).

41. See, for example, ACA, C, reg. 1389:92v, in which Peter III demanded the release of Johan Garcia, a captive in Granada, after he was captured while under the protection of a safe-passage, a *guiatge,* and accused of being a corsair. Peter took quite an interest in this case as he wrote to the sultan of Granada five months later, again demanding Garcia's release, ACA, C, reg. 1389:95r–v; Dufourcq, "Catalogue chronologique et analytique du registre 1389," docs. 165 (Aug. 12, 1372) and 170 (Jan. 15, 1373).

42. ACA, C, reg. 1389:92v–93v (Sept. 24, 1372). The sultan was already convinced that the men were not pirates and he had conveyed this to representatives of the ship's owners who had gone to negotiate for the men's freedom, but

Christian pirates who ended up in chains, as in the case of a Valencian ship that had been raiding the coast of Granada, apparently with great success. The bounty ended when Granadan forces captured it before it could make its escape.[43]

Some Christians were captured while traveling or conducting business in Muslim territories. Many of these travelers and merchants entered Muslim-held territories under guarantees of safe-conduct granted by the local authorities.[44] This, in theory, protected them and their merchandise from any kind of attack. Any free Muslim who was sane and of legal age (a *mukallaf*) could grant a safe-conduct, or *amân*, to a foreigner, which defined his legal status. For merchants, it specified where they could sell their wares, the amount of taxes owed, and the length of their stay.[45] A merchant who went into Islamic territory without an amân ran the risk of theft, capture, and even death.[46]

Truces and agreements between the kings of Aragon and their Muslim counterparts renewed and strengthened these guarantees of protection for their subjects traveling, living, or conducting business in foreign lands. The increased power of Iberian Christian monarchs vis-à-vis their Muslim counterparts that began in the thirteenth century allowed the former to demand greater rights and securities for their subjects in Islamic regions. As early as 1230, when Ferdinand III (r. 1217–52) of Castile permitted a Christian militia to serve as mercenaries to a claimant to the throne of Morocco, the Iberian king demanded that the soldiers should enjoy religious and other freedoms.[47]

---

he had not agreed to liberate them. It was this refusal that apparently prompted Peter's letter.

43. Alarcón y Santón and Garcia de Linares, *Documentos Árabes diplomáticos*, doc. 52 (Aug. 13, 1337).

44. For a specific case of the conditions and withdrawal of a safe-conduct, see Atiya, "Unpublished 14th Century *Fatwâ*,"

45. Schacht, *Introduction to Islamic Law*, 124, 131; Khalilieh, *Islamic Maritime Law*, 20.

46. Khalilieh, *Islamic Maritime Law*, 125–26; Atiya, "Unpublished 14th Century *Fatwâ*," 59–60.

47. Cenival, "L'église chretienne de Marrakesh," 74; Ibn Khaldun, *Histoire des Berbères*, 2:236.

In 1314 James II (r. 1291–1327) of Aragon required safe-conducts for Catalan merchants as a condition to truces he signed with Bougie and Tunis.[48] A few years later he demanded similar protections for his subjects before sending military aid to Tlemcen.[49] North Africa and Granada were also dependent on Christian mercantile activity for their economic well-being, and Muslim rulers sometimes went out of their way to invite Christian merchants to their realms. Abū 'Inān of Morocco in 1354 asked Peter the Ceremonious to tell his merchants to come to Morocco, where they would be treated with dignity and respect and given the protection to which they were accustomed.[50] And when the same Peter demanded the release of a merchant and his crew captured in Granada, he reminded the sultan that the merchant was there because the sultan had offered "passage and protection to all those who brought goods to his lands."[51]

Besides the safe-conducts and agreements, monarchs on both sides had another reason to ensure the safety of religious minorities in their kingdoms: communities from both sides lived as religious minorities in foreign lands. The royal treasure, as the crown called them, Muslims, or *mudejars,* constituted a substantial percentage of the population of the Crown of Aragon.[52]

48. Capmany y de Monpalau, *Memorias históricas,* doc. 88 (Jan. 7, 1314) for Bougie and doc. 89 (Feb. 21, 1314) for Tunis.

49. Masía de Ros, *La Corona de Aragón,* doc. 155 (Apr. 24, 1319).

50. Alarcón y Santón and Garcia de Linares, *Documentos Árabes diplomáticos,* doc. 100 (Dec. 18, 1354). The relationship between the Moroccan authorities and Christians living in Morocco had oscillated between total protection and open attack. The conditions imposed by Ferdinand III on el-Mamoun had led other Muslims to denounce the latter as anti-Islamic and caused Christians to be the target of violent and fatal attacks. In 1232 an assault led by el-Mamoun's nephew and opponent for the throne, Yahya ben en-Nasir, captured Marrakesh, destroyed the church, and killed most of the Christians living in the city as well as many Jews. In the 1240s and 1250s, the papacy had asked for protection for the soldiers and their families serving the caliphs after a series of attacks in diverse parts of the kingdom. See Cenival, "L'église chrétienne de Marrakech," 75–76, 80–81; for the papal letters, see Mas Latrie, *Traités de paix et de commerce,* docs. 14, 17, and 18.

51. ACA, C, reg. 1389:79r (May 20, 1369); see also Dufourcq, "Catalogue chronologique et analytique du registre 1389," doc. 137.

52. For more on Muslims in the Crown of Aragon, see Boswell, *Royal Treasure;* Meyerson, *Muslims of Valencia;* Nirenberg, *Communities of Violence.*

A considerable number of Christians lived as subjects in Granada and North Africa. Many served in the Christian militias that were an integral part of many Muslim armies. Others lived in mercantile enclaves, or *funduqs*, that the leading Mediterranean commercial powers had established in North African cities. These potential hostages frequently tempered the actions of both Christian and Muslim rulers when dealing with their religious minorities. An act of violence against Christians in Tunis, for instance, could easily bring retaliation on Muslims in Valencia. Peter the Ceremonious admitted as much in an embassy to the Egyptian sultan when he told him that many of his subjects lived abroad under foreign rule and for their sake, he desired peace, not war.[53] Some decades earlier, in 1306, James II sent an embassy to Egypt with several requests, including one for the release of certain Christian captives and the protection of Christians in Egypt and the Holy Land. In the sultan's response, he agreed to the safety of Christians in his realm, promising punishment for anyone who harmed them. He immediately followed this up with a reciprocal request that James protect the Muslims living in his realms with the same fortitude.[54] Thus, the protection accorded to Muslims in Iberia almost necessarily determined the safety of Christians in Muslim lands and vice versa.

Even with these safeguards, merchants and travelers ran the risk of capture, sometimes with the approval of the monarch who was supposed to be guaranteeing their safety, sometimes in spite of his guarantees of protection. When monarchs broke their own vows of protection, the consequences could be disastrous for people caught in the wrong country. In 1314 the *baile* (royal governor) of Valencia wrote to James II to inform him that

53. Dufourcq, "Catalogue chronologique et analytique du registre 1389," doc. 257 (June 17, 1379).

54. Alarcón y Santón and Garcia de Linares, *Documentos Árabes diplomáticos*, doc. 148 (Feb. 16, 1306).

the king of Bougie had broken his peace treaty with Aragon by seizing a ship and killing its crew. The Muslims had also captured a Valencian merchant and confiscated his merchandise. The baile was now asking permission to apprehend a merchant from Bougie and hold him in retaliation.[55] Merchants were also at risk when the situation was reversed. In 1316, in another dispute with Bougie, the royal consul and a group of merchants living in the North African kingdom wrote a letter to James II urging him to release a group of captured Muslims. If James did not acquiesce, the Muslims would seize Catalan merchants currently in Bougie.[56] In a similar episode, Yusuf I of Granada threatened Peter the Ceremonious, saying that he would have no choice but to take Christian hostages if Peter did not make reparations for the damage caused by Christian pirates.[57] In 1365, in yet another episode, authorities in Tlemcen retaliated for the capture of some Muslims by Mallorcan pirates by taking some of the local Christians hostage. An angry Peter sent a letter to the governor of Mallorca demanding the immediate release of the Muslims. The bold Christian buccaneers had gone into a port in Tlemcen and seized the Muslim captives there during a truce. Foot-dragging by the governor of Mallorca in returning the illegally seized men had induced the sultan to answer in kind against Christians in his realm.[58] In 1379 Peter again had a similar problem, which forced him to dispatch an embassy to the court of the Egyptian sultan. The sultan had seized several Aragonese subjects and their ships in response to acts of piracy committed by Peter's subjects. The Christian king complained that the Muslims had been taken in spite of his will, while the sultan had explicitly ordered the capture

55. Masía de Ros, *La Corona de Aragón*, doc. 138.

56. Ibid., doc. 146 (Feb. 22, 1316).

57. Alarcón y Santón and Garcia de Linares, *Documentos Árabes diplomáticos*, doc. 52 (Aug. 13, 1337).

58. ACA, C, reg. 1389:52v–53r (Nov. 20, 1365); cf. Dufourcq, "Catalogue chronologique et analytique du registre 1389," doc. 67.

of the Christian captives. He demanded their immediate release.[59]

In some cases the provenance of the captives was not even that important. In 1420 Alfonso the Magnanimous of Aragon complained to officials in Fez about the capture of some of his subjects. Their capture was in retaliation for the taking of a ship full of Muslims off the coast of Murcia by the local authorities. As Alfonso patiently made clear in his letter to Fez, Murcia was not part of his kingdom, belonging as it did to Castile. He also explained that he had made what efforts he could to see the ship and its Muslim passengers set free.[60] This may have been a case of mistaken identity. But more likely, it was a deliberate effort by the authorities in Fez to force Alfonso to apply pressure against the Castilians by threatening Aragonese subjects. The tactic appears to have worked, as not only Alfonso but also his queen, Maria, demanded that Castile release the Muslim captives.[61]

In these affairs, the merchants and others living or traveling overseas became pawns in the political intrigue practiced by their sovereigns. They were instruments of diplomacy: effective instruments, judging by the frequency of their use by Mediterranean rulers. Threats and actions against foreign merchants and other foreign citizens were a way to force the hands of rulers hundreds, or even thousands, of miles distant in an age when the ability to project power beyond one's own borders was otherwise severely limited. Moreover, like the human shields so beloved of modern petty dictators, captives and potential hostages often served to equalize the power relations be-

59. Dufourcq, "Catalogue chronologique et analytique du registre 1389," doc. 257 (June 17, 1379). For more examples, see Masía de Ros, *Jaume II*, 255; ACA, C, reg. 2386:70v–71r (Nov. 26, 1414).

60. ACA, C, reg. 2568:147r (Mar. 30, 1420); cf. Salicrú i Lluch, *Documents per a la història de Granada*, doc. 61.

61. ACA, C, reg. 2569:77v (May 23, 1420); reg. 3108:194r–v (May 31, 1420); cf. Salicrú i Lluch, *Documents per a la història de Granada*, docs. 66–67.

tween polities that were not equal in power. As such, they were
an intricate part of the diplomatic reality of the medieval Mediterranean.

Friars and other religious, including members of the ransoming orders, comprised another group exposed to the dangers
of captivity. Since at least the early thirteenth century the
dream of converting Muslims to Christianity had been a staple
in certain Christian circles, most notably the Franciscans. St.
Francis himself, in an episode immortalized by Giotto among
others, in the midst of the Fifth Crusade gained an audience
with the sultan of Egypt, al-Kāmil, for the purpose of preaching
to him. He also included chapters in both the *Regula Bullata*
and *Regula non Bullata* on what to do in the case of friars who
wanted to preach to the Muslims. As Benjamin Kedar has noted, the inclusion of these chapters in the rules "present the friars' desire to work among the Saracens as legitimate, and efforts
at Saracen conversion as laudable."[62] A desire for martyrdom
animated many of these attempts to preach Christianity in
Muslim regions. An exercise that sought to "engage the forces
of heaven at some mystical level,"[63] the primary goal of these
missions was to find death in the name of God by preaching
Christianity and blaspheming against Islam and its prophet. In
many cases, the preachers were successful. However, other
times their efforts did not yield the desired results. Some were
heard politely, as was the case with Francis; others were simply
deported—this was the likely fate of the Franciscan tertiary
Raymond Llull, who is reputed to have been martyred in Bougie
in 1315 but more likely died a peaceful death after being expelled from the North African city. And others were made captives. Three of the twelve captives released by the sultan of
Egypt in response to an embassy sent to him in 1306 by James II

62. Kedar, *Crusade and Mission,* 119–26, here 124. See also Burns, "Christian Islamic Confrontation in the West," 1395–97.
63. Burns, "Christian Islamic Confrontation in the West," 1395.

were friars.[64] Eight years later, the king of Aragon again had to intercede on behalf of captured friars. The sultan agreed to release them but not before warning James that these men were nothing but "[d]elinquents who have organized themselves to cause disruption in this country [Egypt] and only as a gesture to the petition of His Majesty, the King, who had sent his emissaries for this objective, and had interceded on behalf of said captives, do we free the ringleaders among them, namely Friar Guillem, Friar Delmat, and their companions."[65] In 1378 Peter the Ceremonious had to appeal to the sultan of Granada for the release of two Franciscans being held in that kingdom. And a few years later, Peter's successor, John I (r. 1387–95), had to ask the Mercedarians to contribute the substantial sum of 200 florins so that the Franciscans could liberate two of their brethren held in the "power of the Saracens."[66]

The members of the ransoming orders, although often given assurances that they would be protected as they conducted their transactions, were not immune to the dangers of captivity and even death.[67] The most famous Mercedarian captive was undoubtedly St. Peter Pascual, the bishop of Jaén, who was captured in 1296 and beheaded in Granada three years later. During his captivity, he penned his *Sobre la seta Mahometana*, a work aimed at keeping his fellow captives and other Christians from converting to Islam.[68] The same year that Peter Pascual

64. Alarcón y Santón and Garcia de Linares, *Documentos Árabes diplomáticos*, doc. 148 (Feb. 16, 1306).
65. Ibid., doc. 149 (Mar. 17, 1315). For James's letter to the sultan, see Masía de Ros, *La Corona de Aragón*, doc. 37.
66. ACA, C, reg. 1887:135v–36r (June 17, 1395), published in Sáinz de la Maza Lasoli, "Los Mercedarios ," doc. 43.
67. For a brief discussion, see Brodman, *Ransoming Captives*, 110–11. For promises of protection, see Alarcón y Santón and Garcia de Linares, *Documentos Árabes diplomáticos*, doc. 69 (Sept. 9, 1354). A brief study in 1978 placed the number of Mercedarians who died or were killed in the course of ransoming between the foundation of the order in 1198 and 1490 at sixty-eight: Dossat, "Les ordres de rachat, les Mercédaires," 384.
68. There is some question as to whether Peter Pascual actually wrote the

was captured, James II had to intervene with the king of Granada to gain the release of a party of Mercedarians captured in Málaga.[69] There are also ransom contracts from the later fourteenth century, negotiated to bring about the liberation of captured ransomers, suggesting the dangers to which the ransoming brethren exposed themselves.[70] Much has also been made of the Mercedarian practice of substitution, whereby ransomers would exchange themselves for captives when their money ran out during an expedition. However, as James Brodman has argued, there is very little evidence that the Mercedarians practiced this custom in the medieval period. Moreover, Brodman suggests that it would have been impractical for ransomers to jeopardize an entire ransoming expedition and all the planning and money involved for the sake of freeing one or two more captives.[71] Consequently, ransomers seem to have fallen into captivity for the same reasons as other Christians: breakdown in their protection, retaliation for the capture of Muslims by Christians, unauthorized travel in Muslim regions, and proselytizing.

TRANSPORT

Those captives who were taken as part of a raid or an act of piracy had to survive not only the initial, often violent, confrontation but also the days that followed when they were transported back into Muslim territory. In the case of those captured on land, this often entailed a flight by the raiders and their prizes as Christian militias, soldiers, and trackers chased them, trying to recover both captives and booty. Pirates faced similar problems from the Christian marine patrols. Muslim pirate

---

works attributed to him. For a brief discussion and additional bibliographic information, see Burns, *Crusader Kingdom*, 2:app. 2.

69. Dossat, "Les ordres de rachat, les Mercédaires," 383.

70. Mitja, "L'orde de la Merce," doc. 7 (June 3, 1393); ACA, C, reg. 1910:165v–66r.

71. Brodman, *Ransoming Captives*, 111–13.

ships, often small, coastal craft or fishing vessels, could be at a severe disadvantage if pirate-hunting galleys were able to stage a concerted chase. Before addressing questions of transport by sea more fully, however, let us now turn our attention to the transport of captives overland.

The initial flight must have been a harried affair. The raiders had to get themselves and their booty back to friendly territory before local militias caught up with them and brought an end to the expedition. Consequently, raiding parties (on both sides) traveled light and were usually composed solely of horsemen, making them much more difficult to catch or even contain. One awestruck Christian commentator remarked that two hundred Muslim raiders could cause more destruction and cover more territory than six hundred Christians.[72] The *Anales de Orihuela*, which offers a history of that frontier town, includes similar comments, noting that it was exhausting work for the Christians to guard the frontier, with weapons always at the ready. The expanse of the terrain was an even bigger problem, since raiding parties could be in and out with their booty before soldiers had time to arrive.[73]

To counteract the stealth and speed of raiding parties, some Christian frontier towns employed trackers *(fieles de rastros)* to recover captured cattle and captives. These men relentlessly followed the trail left behind by raiding expeditions up to the boundaries of municipal jurisdiction. At that point they would pass the trail on to another set of trackers to continue the pursuit. If the raiders had conducted an illegal attack while a truce was in effect, they would find no sanctuary once they reached Muslim-controlled lands. The pursuit would continue, with Muslim troops taking over.[74] Failure to escape could mean death for the raiders, either at the hands of the Christians who chased

72. Ramos y Loscertales, *El cautiverio*, 110–11.
73. Bellot, *Anales de Orihuela*, 185–86.
74. Carriazo, "Relaciones fronterizas ," 33–38; also Torres Fontes, "Notas sobre los fieles de rastro y alfaqueques murcianos."

them or at the hands of the Muslim authorities who punished them for breaking a truce.[75]

After evading initial pursuits, the raiders may have tried to lie low during the daylight hours, traveling at night in hopes of avoiding Christian patrols. The guidelines established for Christian raiders *(cavalgadores)* by Alfonso X in *Las Siete Partidas* suggest that they should "move quickly . . . and move more at night than during the day." Moreover, they should choose men who knew the local geography to guide them and avoid enemy patrols.[76] Both sides likely followed this sensible advice. More so when we consider that Christian converts, known as renegades, often guided and even led these raiding expeditions, adding a certain homogeneity to the tactics employed by both sides as well as negating any advantages that Christian forces may have had due to their greater knowledge of the terrain.[77] Raiding parties may also have sought and received help from sympathetic local Muslim communities.

Pursuit was not necessarily a positive development for the captives either. Raiders sometimes killed their prisoners when they were cornered or to lighten their load and make their escape more feasible. In 1314 James II sent a letter to Ismail I of Granada complaining about one of these raids, which had gone terribly wrong for the captives. On July 15 of that year, a group of Muslim raiders had entered through Murcia, stolen a large number of cows, and taken several captives. Local residents organized a pursuit, with a number of them going after the men and cattle. At some point during the chase, either as a way to stave off the pursuit or simply to hasten their escape, the raiders killed seven of the captives. It was presumably a successful tactic since the purpose of James's letter was to ask the Granadan monarch to identify and punish those responsible for the

75. Bellot, *Anales de Orihuela,* 164.
76. Alfonso X, *Las Siete Partidas,* II:23:27; see also Martínez Martínez, La cabalgalda," 55.
77. Torres Fontes, "La frontera de Granada," 195–96.

death of the Christians.[78] A similar attack in the region around Oriola led to the death of one of three captives; his captors beheaded him as the Christian pursuit closed in.[79]

Numerous sources mention raiders binding or chaining their captives for transport. The assailants who attacked Gola de la Albufera bound the residents before transporting them to North Africa.[80] The captive depicted in one of the *Cantigas de Santa Maria* also had his hands bound, although his feet were not shackled.[81] The captors of the Castilian Johan de Marthos took special care to tie his hands and legs. They bound him so tightly that his nails bled. He remained in this condition for three days and nights. When he managed to loosen his bonds, they discovered it, beat him, and tied him even more tightly. The bonds were not yet tight enough, however, for Johan, apparently an early incarnation of Houdini, still managed to escape.[82] Johan's captors bound him for the first time during the first night, suggesting that raiders used the chains and ropes as a precaution when they stopped to rest but disdained them while traveling, at least with small groups of captives. This would make sense, since a bound captive or, as the above-mentioned cantiga suggests, one with leg irons, would not be able to walk very quickly or ride, thus hindering the escape attempts of his captors.

Besides the humiliation of enchainment, the captives became the center of ridicule in other ways during this period of transport. When a Muslim raiding column ventured into Castilian territory and captured Martin Dominguez after a bloody engagement, they made him pull the severed heads of four other Christians killed during the fight. He dragged them all the way to Ronda.[83] Female captives, as usual, faced the danger of

78. Ferrer i Mallol, *La frontera amb l'Islam*, doc. 42 (July 24, 1314).
79. Bellot, *Anales de Orihuela*, 164.
80. Rubio Vela, *Epistolari*, 1:doc. 96 (Apr. 21, 1410).
81. Alfonso X, *Las Cantigas de Santa María*, no. 83.
82. Vergara, *Vida y milagros*, 210–11.
83. Ibid., 169.

rape. Their risk was especially high during the initial capture and transportation.[84] Lacking any form of effective male protection, female captives existed in a liminal state with very limited means of defending themselves. The raiders, moreover, separated from the company of their own women for what were often extended periods, found in the captured women a convenient way of satisfying their lust. The Muslim commander and protagonist of a frontier *Romance* who ordered the abduction of a Christian woman whom he wanted as his bride certainly knew about these dangers. He sent a trusted lieutenant to ensure that his beloved would reach him with her honor preserved (*porque venga mas honrrada*).[85] The captivity of women resonated loudly in peninsular society. The early town fueros allowed sons to stand as hostages in place of their fathers while the latter arranged for a ransom. The same laws punished with death by burning the father who placed his daughter in a similar situation.[86] In an embassy to the papal curia, Peter the Ceremonious raised the specter of Muslim raiders ravaging Christian maidens in an effort to convince the pope, Benedict XII, to support a crusade against Morocco.[87] In a similar fashion, myths and stories such as the romances "express[ed] well-founded anxieties of medieval Spaniards for the safety and chastity of Christian women often taken in the raiding expeditions that characterized peninsular warfare."[88]

Pirates and their ships provided a different set of conditions for transporting captives. The evidence that we have for late medieval North African and Granadan pirate ships is lim-

---

84. Salicrú i Lluch, "Cartes de captius cristians," suggests that most of the abuses committed against captives occurred during their capture and transportation (553–54).

85. Rodríguez Moñino, *Cancionero de romances*, 249, "Moricos los mis Moricos . . . ."

86. Brodman, "Municipal Ransoming Law," 324.

87. Canellas, "Aragón y la empresa del estrecho," doc. 9 (1340).

88. Dillard, *Daughters of the Reconquest*, 134.

ited and fragmentary at best. What survives suggests that the ships were usually small, coastal vessels falling under the designation of lenys and *galiots* (small galleys) and even *fustas* (powered by oars).[89] Cervantes's captive in *Don Quixote* feared running into small merchant galleys armed for piracy during his escape. The captive was, however, quite confident that his own small ship with fewer than twenty crewmen could easily overcome an unarmed merchant ship.[90] The Egyptian writer Al-Qalqasandi referred to the pirate vessels as light craft, and other sources confirm this assessment. A coast-watching galiot outfitted in Barcelona in 1455 specifically to deal with pirates had a crew of about forty men, of whom twenty-four were oarsmen.[91] If we assume that a ship of this size was capable of dealing with the most typical type of enemy pirate vessel it was likely to encounter, then presumably authorities expected the ships and manpower available in a typical pirate raid to be smaller than this.[92] The cruising radius of Granadan ships—usually limited in range to the Balearics—also points to their smaller size.[93] By way of confirmation, the pirate ship that seized the woman from Ibiza and her family described earlier had a crew of twenty-one men and lost its battle with a merchant vessel.

For purposes of speed and maneuverability, galley-type ships,

89. For a good overview of Mediterranean ship types during this period, see Mott, *Sea Power*, 186–209; also Pryor, *Geography, Technology, and War*, 67–68; Díaz Borrás, *Los orígenes de la piratería islámica*, 83–84 and table 2. It is difficult to make a general statement concerning the types of ships involved in piracy, although it does appear that a majority of them were smaller vessels. This did not preclude the use of war galleys or large merchantmen in piratical acts when targets of opportunity presented themselves. See Pryor, *Geography, Technology, and War*, 154; cf. López Pérez, *La Corona de Aragón*, 748–49; Torres Delgado, "El Mediterraneo Nazarí," 230–31.

90. Cervantes, *Don Quixote*, ch. 41.

91. Unali, *Mariners, pirates i corsaris*, 51.

92. Barcelona also outfitted larger, more heavily armed vessels to deal with pirates. For instance, a coast-watching ship outfitted in 1449 had a total crew of 232 men, including 152 rowers and 34 archers (see ibid.). Some of these bigger ships, however, may have been destined to patrol against the large ships that Genoese and Venetian pirates used, and not necessarily against the typically small Muslim vessels.

93. Torres Delgado, "El Mediterráneo Nazarí," 230–31.

with both sails and oars, were more suitable for the exigencies of piracy and raiding.[94] A galley could, in times of need, reach speeds between seven and ten knots for short spurts by using its oars. A vessel that depended solely on sails had a top speed of less than three knots.[95] The biggest problem with the oar-sail hybrids from the point of view of taking captives was their limited cargo-carrying capacity owing to the large number of oarsmen they required—usually about two-thirds of the crew. Charles E. Dufourcq has provided a useful description of the lenys and other small galley-type ships. He suggests that they were between twelve and twenty-five meters in length and one and a half meters in width. Their normal complement was between twenty and thirty rowers.[96] Sailors had to share this space with the ship's equipment—rowing benches, oars, rigs, ropes, sails, and so on—and cargo. Captives would have made an already cramped ship much more so. Any voyage would be an uncomfortable affair with the prisoners and crew tightly packed on board.

On board ship, as on land, the pirates shackled or bound their prisoners. The Aragonese soldier and chronicler Muntaner noted that Christian sailors "untied" Christian captives whom they rescued from Muslim ships after a naval battle.[97] Christian mariners made similar provisions for prisoners, suggesting that chains or restraints were standard procedure in the western Mediterranean. Catalan maritime law, codified in the *Consolat del mar (Consulate of the Sea)*, required special guards on privateering expeditions to watch Saracen captives and to chain them and unchain them. If the prisoners escaped, the guards

---

94. Unali, *Mariners, pirates i corsaris*, 23; Guilmartin, in *Gunpowder and Galleys*, 81, points out that in the sixteenth century the Spanish were forced to use oared galleys to counter the threat posed by French and English privateers, who regularly used oared vessels due to their mobility. In dealing with oared ships, the large armed galleons, which depended solely on wind power, simply could not keep up with their more nimble opponents.

95. Guilmartin, *Gunpowder and Galleys*, 62; Pryor, *Geography, Technology, and War*, 36.

96. Dufourcq, *La vie quotidienne dans les ports méditerranéens*, 60.

97. Muntaner, *Crónica*, ch. 19.

were responsible for the loss.[98] The ship's quartermaster had to provide the rivets "needed to fasten the fetters of the prisoners" as well as the chisels necessary "for putting on the fetters" and "ropes to tie up the prisoners."[99]

Geography and weather also played roles in the seaborne transport of captives. Those captives who went to Granada after capture did not experience the same difficulties as captives taken to North Africa, Morocco, or Egypt. The northern Mediterranean coast is generally welcoming to small ships. A rapidly dropping sea bottom lessened the possibilities of running aground or having reefs, rocks, and shoals gut a ship. The ubiquitous beaches, inlets, and protected coves meant that Muslim pirates could find safety from pursuing Christian ships with relative ease.[100] This was a mixed blessing for captives. Although it lessened the chances that Christian ships could rescue them, a suddenly appearing, secluded anchorage could mean the difference between survival and being thrown overboard in order for a pirate ship to lessen its load and make a more effective escape. Finding a secured place to stop also became a necessity in inclement weather. The captive in *Don Quixote* recalled finding a small cove just in time as strong winds threatened to drive his ship aground.[101]

Those captives who went to North Africa had a more dangerous voyage. Unlike its northern counterpart, the southern shore of the Mediterranean has been an inhospitable locale for ships since antiquity.[102] Reefs, cliffs, and offshore islands complemented by strong currents made any voyage along the Tunisian littoral a dangerous affair.[103] The ports of Bougie and Bone,

98. Jados, *Consulate of the Sea,* ordinance 333.

99. Ibid., ordinance 331.

100. Guilmartin, *Gunpowder and Galleys,* 63–64; Pryor, *Geography, Technology, and War,* 21–24.

101. Cervantes, *Don Quixote,* ch. 41. In this case, the bad weather accosted them on the African coast.

102. Semple, *Geography of the Mediterranean Region,* 140–41.

103. U.S. Naval Oceanographic Office, *Sailing Directions,* 87–150.

two of the principal destinations for Christian captives, possess some of these dangers.[104] The Gulf of Bougie has a strong, inbound current and lacks any safe anchorage. Moreover, it was, and is, dangerous in bad weather. The approaches to Bone have perilous shoals, and gales create heavy seas at the entrance to the harbor.[105] Captives who traveled through the Straits of Gibraltar to Morocco experienced all the complications that the Straits as a geographical entity exhibited: changes in winds and currents, frequent fog, reefs and sandbanks along the shores.[106]

The Christian coast-watching ships posed an even bigger problem for the pirate crew and its captives. The approach of a Christian galley signaled the beginning of a chase that could have fatal repercussions for the captives on board. Any kind of combat would have placed the captives, crammed on the deck as they were, in harm's way. Neither Christians nor Muslims were above using captives as human shields to discourage attacks.[107] Although most condemned it, some Islamic jurists allowed for captives to be thrown overboard if a vessel were in danger of sinking due to the weight of its cargo. One jurist, Al-Lakhmî, specified that this could be done only with skillful swimmers among the captured and only when the ship was in sight of the shore. In other words, the captive was to have a sporting chance of surviving and, if he swam to a friendly coast, of escaping. Of course, the challenge here for the pirates would have been identifying the skillful swimmers from among the captives in the heat of a chase—sometimes legal opinions may have had little impact in the real world. The Tunisian jurist al-Shammâkhî did not make such nuances. He believed it permis-

104. For the importance of Bougie and Bone as destinations for captives, see López Pérez, *La Corona de Aragón*, 720.

105. U.S. Naval Oceanographic Office, *Sailing Directions*, 120–24, 131–35.

106. Braudel, *Mediterranean*, 117; U.S. Naval Oceanographic Office, *Sailing Directions*, 1–18; Lewis, "Northern European Sea Power," 140–41.

107. Khalilieh, *Islamic Maritime Law*, 120.

sible to jettison any non-Muslim captive if doing so would save Muslim sailors and soldiers.[108] Pirate ships pursued by what were often bigger and more heavily armed vessels would have certainly entertained these possibilities, even if they were means of last resort. Pursuit also meant that a pirate ship was more likely to take risks, increasing the dangers posed by natural elements such as dangerous seas, storms, and underwater obstacles. A dash toward a rocky coastline was likely to discourage pursuing ships, but the pirate craft also increased the risk of ripping out its hull.

NUMBERS

Before finishing this chapter, we must ask: What demographic impact did raiding and piracy have on the people of Aragon? How many captives were there? It is a simple question that defies an easy answer. Few sources exist to guide our way, and the number of captives in any one place was subject to a number of variables that make any estimate difficult. What follows remains speculative at best.

Perhaps the best source we have is a remarkable letter from October 1327, written by the captives held in Tlemcen to their monarch, Alfonso III. The writers say that there were 280 captives from the Crown of Aragon in the North African city.[109] An earlier document corroborates this number. In 1319 James II had sent an embassy to Tlemcen proposing a truce for ten years in exchange for the release of 300 captives.[110] A ten-year truce would have been inordinately long—most were between three and five years—and the 300 captives discussed in the negotiations probably represented the bulk if not all of the captive population in Tlemcen. Other numbers have emerged that could be

108. Ibid., 96–97, 116–17.
109. ACA, CR, Alfonso III, box 24:3669, published in Masía de Ros, *La Corona de Aragón*, doc. 173.
110. Masía de Ros, *La Corona de Aragón*, doc. 155 (Apr. 24, 1319).

useful in these calculations, but they seem exaggerated. Among these are James II's estimate in a letter to Pope Clement V that there were 50,000 renegades living in Granada, many of whom must have been onetime captives. This number is so high as to be almost useless in any estimate. Mercedarian historians have claimed 7,000 captives ransomed over the course of the fourteenth century. Although this figure seems more reasonable, it still averages seventy redemptions a year, every year. When we take into account the limited effectiveness of the Mercedarians, especially in the second half of the century, and the smallish number of captives that they usually redeemed, the figure seems a bit high. Moreover, it does not tell us how many captives the Mercedarians were forced to leave behind every year. A recent study using some of the figures above has suggested an average of about 1,000 captives in the larger North African cities and considerably more in Granada.[111] However, it is difficult to see how the author makes the jump from around 300 captives—the number given by the letter writers and embassy above—to 1,000 captives in any given city, unless the difference is being made up by captives from Castile, France, and the Italian states. Considering only subjects of the Crown of Aragon, I would suggest about 300 captives in places like Tunis, Bougie, Bone, Morocco, and Tlemcen, with perhaps another 500 scattered through North Africa in any given year—some 2,000 for all of North Africa. Granada likely had a larger captive population than any of the North African kingdoms based on its proximity, but not many more—perhaps in the neighborhood of 1,500. This gives us a total population of some 3,500 Aragonese captives in both regions in any given year.

We are not done yet. The Crown of Aragon signed truces with the Muslim states on a regular basis. These truce agreements often called for the mutual release of captives—sometimes some of the captives, sometimes all of them. Moreover,

111. Díaz Borrás, *El miedo*, 29–34.

the truces made the subsequent capture of additional captives illegal. Even when pirates and raiders broke truce agreements, there is no doubt that a cessation of hostilities drove down the captive population. Consequently, we must reduce the above figure substantially since at almost any given time there would have been Muslim kingdoms with a much smaller number of captives than estimated above. Surviving truce agreements, embassy instructions, and other documentation suggest that Aragon was at peace with one or another of the Muslim kingdoms only about 40 percent of the time in the years between 1351 and 1400.[112] The rest of the time, the situation was either open war, truce agreements that had expired and allowed for captive taking, or periods of negotiation, which also did not limit incursions (see table 1). Therefore, allowing for truces and taking into account that captives were still taken even while truces were in effect, a reduction of about one-third from the above figure of 3,500 seems reasonable. This leaves us with an approximate figure of about 2,300 men, women, and children from Aragon in captivity in any given year during the later Middle Ages. With a medieval population of some 1 million people, this would have represented about .23 percent of its citizens. This may seem insignificant, but for a country the size of the United States, with a current population of 300 million people, it would mean about 690,000 captives a year. Captivity was not a minor problem but a significant political, economic, moral, and military predicament.

One final point on the demographics of captivity: the captives from Aragon were overwhelmingly male. The nature of the frontier played a decisive role in determining the gender of the captured. Land frontiers, such as the one between Castile and Granada, did not offer much protection to women because raiding parties came to where the women lived. Many captives

112. Of the two hundred possibilities (fifty years multiplied by four polities) that we find in table 1, only eighty-one of them show a completely peaceful year with any one country.

Table 1. Relations between Aragon and Its Muslim Neighbors

Year	Granada	Tunis	Tlemcen	Morocco
1351	P	C	P	P
1352	P	C	P	P
1353	P	C	P	P
1354	P	C	P	P
1355	P	C	P	P
1356	P	C	P	P
1357	P	C	P	P
1358	P	C	P	P
1359	P-W	C	P	P
1360	W-P	P	P	P
1361	P	P	P	P
1362	N	P	P	N
1363	W	P	P	W
1364	N	P	P	N
1365	N	P	P	P
1366	N	P	P	P
1367	N	P	P	P
1368	N	P	P	P
1369	N	P	P	P
1370	P	N	P	P
1371	P	N	P	P
1372	P	?	P	P-W
1373	P	W	P	W
1374	P	W	?	W
1375	P	W	?	W-N
1376	P-N	W	?	N-W
1377	N-P	W	?	W
1378	P	W	?	W
1379	P	W	?	W
1380	P	W	W	W
1381	P-N	W	P	W
1382	N-P	W	P	W
1383	P	W	P	W
1384	P	W	P	W
1385	P	W	P	W
1386	P	W	P	W
1387	?	W	P	W
1388	?	W	P	W
1389	?	W	W	W
1390	W	W	W	W
1391	N	W	W	W
1392	N	W	W	W
1393	W	W	W	W
1394	W	W	W	W
1395	W	W	W	W
1396	W	W	W	W
1397	W	N	W	W
1398	W	N	W	W
1399	W	N	N	N
1400	W	N	N	N

Sources: López-Pérez, "Las relaciones diplomáticas," 169; López-Pérez, "Sobre la guerra y la paz"; Udina Martorell, "Relaciones entre Túnez y la Corona de Aragón"; Arribas Palau, "Los benimerines en los pactos"; López-Pérez, *La Corona de Aragón y el Magreb*, 107–12, 123–30, 146–66; Ferrer i Mallol, *La frontera amb l'Islam*, 139–222.
Key: P = peace; W = war; N = no truce, but negotiations taking place; C = civil war and kingdom incapable of conducting foreign policy; ? = unknown. Cells with more than one letter indicate that the situation fluctuated throughout the year.

taken across land frontiers became prisoners during raids on villages or cities where there were plenty of women present for raiders to capture. Castilian male captives are still likely to have outnumbered the female captives, but the latter formed a substantial portion of the Castilian captive population. The situation was different with maritime frontiers like the one that existed between the realms of the king of Aragon and the Muslim kingdoms. In maritime frontiers pirates usually captured their victims at their place of work.[113] It was sailors, fishermen, merchants, and others whose occupation took them to the sea and over it who formed the bulk of the human booty seized by pirates. These were all male-dominated vocations. Muslim captives taken by Aragonese corsairs were also predominantly men since both sides used similar methods of acquisition.[114] The chance of being captured for Castilians was closely linked to where they lived. For the subjects of the Crown of Aragon, it depended much more upon their occupation.[115]

The constant raiding and piracy galvanized the Crown of Aragon and its citizens into action to deal with the problem of captivity. However, we must also consider the reports, real or fictitious, that continuously reached the kingdom detailing the atrocities that were being committed against captives as they languished in their imprisonment as important motivating factors that animated the population of the kingdom to save their Christian brothers and sisters from such a fate. To understand why Aragon reacted to the problem of captivity the way that it did, we must also understand the captivity experience and how it was perceived back home.

113. Pirates sometimes landed and attacked isolated villages or small groups of people. This was the case of Gola de la Albufera, the example with which this chapter opened. This, however, took more daring and was less common than attacking a ship at sea.
114. Hinojosa Montalvo, "La esclavitud en Alicante," 376–79, 385–86, and apps. 1–2.
115. See also Davis, *Christian Slaves, Muslim Masters*, 36.

CHAPTER 2

LIFE IN CAPTIVITY

For those captives who survived the initial capture and the hurried flight that followed, a hard life awaited. At best, they became hostages waiting for embassies and ransomers to come and rescue them. At worst, they were slaves, strangers in a foreign land, torn from family and friends, toiling daily in the harshest labor, underfed, at times mistreated, sometimes brutally. For the majority it was a life they would never escape in spite of the best efforts of their families and others in the Crown of Aragon. This chapter will study the conditions experienced by captives in their daily lives. What was it like to live in captivity? What kind of work did captives do? Where did they live? What did they eat? As the details emerge, we must keep in mind that the conditions of captivity were well known back home and the harsh life of the captives, at times exaggerated for effect, became a significant aspect of the propaganda used by those who worked on their behalf. The suffering of the captives and the fear that they might convert to Islam became important motivating forces in the efforts to set them free.

Any discussion on life in captivity must begin by addressing the captive's legal status and a definition of his condition. Was the captive a slave? This question is partly demanded by the sources themselves, which do not use the words *captive (cautivo, captivi, catiu)* and *slave (esclavo, servus, esclau)* interchangeably. The two terms meant different things, even if the difference was a subtle one. In recent years, many who have written about captivity have compared captives to slaves, with some authors closely linking the two conditions.[1] To a point they are correct to make this connection. The natal alienation that resulted in a loss of freedom and rights, the subjugation to the master's will and dependence on the master for basic survival, the forced labor and services captives were forced to render, and the loss of honor associated with captivity meant that the captive and the slave shared many similar experiences.[2] In spite of these similarities, however, there were two significant differences between the two. The first is highlighted in both Muslim and Christian legal codes. The Mālikī legal school, which was dominant in Granada and the Maghrib in the Middle Ages, permitted prisoners of war to be executed, enslaved, or ransomed.[3] This view allowed for a distinction between the prisoner who is made a slave and the prisoner who is set aside for ransom or exchange, allowing for both types of bondage and accepting the possibility of ransom and liberation.[4] Consequently, Christian captives could expect that Muslim authorities would acquiesce to their

1. See, for example, Davis, *Christian Slaves, Muslim Masters,* in which Davis makes little distinction between the two; Colley's recent *Captives* follows a similar path, as she uses slavery and captivity almost interchangeably, again equating the two terms; Yvonne Friedman's *Encounter between Enemies* is somewhat ambiguous as to the differences between the captive and the slave, if any.

2. In these categories, I have been influenced by the work of Patterson in *Slavery and Social Death,* 1–14; Davis, *The Problem of Slavery,* 31–35; Lovejoy, *Transformations in Slavery,* 1–9.

3. Khadduri and Liebesny, *Origin and Development of Islamic Law,* 356; also Ruxton, *Mâliki Law,* II:3:2:4.

4. Charouiti Hasnaoui, "Esclavos y cautivos según la ley Islámica," 3–8.

freedom if a ransom or exchange were involved. The captives could also expect that their own compatriots would make every effort to free them, as the law of the Christian states of the Iberian Peninsula made explicit the captive's right to be freed.[5] For José María Ramos y Loscertales, one of the earliest scholars to write about captivity in the Crown of Aragon, this was critical, as he saw the possibility of being ransomed as the defining characteristic that separated the captive from the slave.[6] Moreover, the access to freedom available to the captive was different from the manumission that slaves sometimes received. Manumission was a personal exchange between a master and a slave. Ransoming, on the other hand, functioned on a much broader level. It was the right of a captive to be ransomed and the responsibility of his family and society to initiate it. As the *Siete Partidas* clearly stated, "men should liberate those who are held in captivity."[7] That most captives were probably never ransomed is irrelevant, as almost all who went into captivity did so knowing that those left behind had a responsibility to get them out. Thus, it was not so much the possibility but the expectation of liberation that becomes the first marker of difference between the captive and the slave. In this context captives shared characteristics with slaves, as they lived as slaves while in captivity, but also with prisoners of war, who could anticipate that their side would attempt to set them free.

There was an additional difference between the captive and the slave, and again the *Siete Partidas* is helpful here, as it defined captives as "those . . . who come under the control of men embracing another belief."[8] Islamic law complemented the *Par-*

5. Alfonso X, *Las Siete Partidas*, II:29:2; Brodman, "Municipal Ransoming Law," 318–19.

6. Ramos y Loscertales, *El cautiverio*, 135.

7. Alfonso X, *Las Siete Partidas*, II:29:2–3.

8. Ibid., II:29:1. The *Partidas* shares some of the ambiguity found in the secondary scholarship, as in a later section it makes captives a subset of slaves: "There are three kinds of slaves, the first is those taken captive in war who are enemies of the faith . . ." (IV:21:1).

tidas by allowing for the enslavement only of non-Muslims.[9] A recent work by Andrés Díaz Borrás has highlighted this point admirably, noting that "the slave was a social concept while the captive was an ideological one."[10] In the world of medieval Iberia, therefore, captives were those individuals who, although they suffered many of the limitations and degradations of slavery, had a reasonable expectation of freedom and who owed their bondage to the religious wars between Christianity and Islam.

These academic and legalistic differences probably mattered little to the average captive, who upon capture entered a state of difficult, frightful, and humiliating servitude. The first stop for arriving captives was likely to be a customs house, where the local ruler received his share of the booty, human and otherwise, taken during the raids.[11] The ruler's share—typically one-fifth of the captured booty—could mount quickly, so much so that the sultan of Granada had large pens, or *corrals*, constructed to house his captives. The authorities may have interrogated some captives for military information and questioned others about the legality of their seizure.[12] If the capture was legal—de bona guerra—then captors could proceed with the sale. The purchasers may have received documents of ownership that legitimized their claim over their new property and eliminated most of the rights that the captives enjoyed as free men or women.[13] Events could move very quickly from here, adding to the captives' sense of confusion and isolation. The world turned upside down for them. The Muslims, whom until recently the captives had regarded, at best, as subjugated second-class citi-

9. Schacht, *Introduction to Islamic Law*, 127.

10. Díaz Borrás, *El miedo*, 19–29; for the quotation see 19.

11. García Antón, "Cautiverios, canjes y rescates," 551.

12. On interrogations, see Vergara, *Vida y milagros*, 201; on questions of legality, see Hinojosa Montalvo, "Confesiones y ventas de cautivos," 114–21.

13. Hinojosa Montalvo, "Confesiones y ventas de cautivos," app. 3 (Aug. 2, 1409). This is the Christian equivalent of one of these documents awarded in Valencia.

zens or slaves and, at worst, as "fifth column" traitors and enemies of Christendom, now became their masters.[14] This change
climaxed at the slave markets, where the captors turned their
daring into profit. Sales took place in almost any public place,
with plazas and marketplaces among the most common locations.[15] The *Miraculos romançados* describe captives being pa-
raded through the streets as their captors tried to sell them.
The hustle and bustle of the streets and markets, the glares of
strange faces, and the sounds of foreign tongues signaled the
beginning of the captives' alienation from society: their social
death, a concept elucidated by Orlando Patterson to explain the
social position of slaves. Patterson has argued that the captive
suffered this social death because society conceived him as an
individual who did not belong, who had lost all claims of birth,
and who "ceased to belong in his own right to any legitimate
social order." The fact that captives were foreigners served to
isolate them further from the Muslim communities in which
they now found themselves.[16] A different religion and language
marked the Christian captives as strangers. They were not of
the community that now had control over their lives. They had
become commodities of which owners could dispose in any way
they thought fit.

14. For the legal fiction of Muslims as slaves, see Boswell, *Royal Treasure*,
30–37; for Muslims as subjugated minority, see Lourie, "Anatomy of Ambivalence," 51–68; Nirenberg, *Communities of Violence*, 21–26; for Muslims as
slaves, see Meyerson, "Slavery and Solidarity"; Verlinden, *L'esclavage*, vol. 1,
chs. 4–6; for the fear of a Muslim "fifth column," see Nirenberg, *Communities
of Violence*, 33–34; Meyerson, *Muslims of Valencia*, 63–64.
     15. García Antón, "Cautiverios, canjes y rescates," 551.
     16. Patterson, *Slavery and Social Death*, 5, 44; see also Lovejoy, *Transfor-
mations in Slavery*, 2–3; see also Bradley, "*Servus Onerosus*," 137, where he
highlights the importance of linguistic isolation for new slaves arriving in imperial Rome without knowing Latin. Dockes has emphasized the similarity
between slavery and death by noting that "the slave is one who should have
been killed and who survives by the grace of the master; he is one of the living
dead. . . . To be reprieved, to be living dead is the fate of the prisoner of war who
would traditionally have been killed by his captor. If the captor allows his prisoner to live, the latter recognizes the former as his master, and in fact cannot
but so recognize him"; *Medieval Slavery and Liberation*, 4–5.

After purchase, the captives would be taken to their new homes. Here conditions could vary tremendously. The unluckiest ones were quartered in what had once been subterranean grain silos where the predecessors of the current owners had stored their harvests after each reaping. Now, these holes in the ground, shaped like upside-down funnels, became homes and prisons for the captives. Cramped—some barely twenty feet across—damp and crowded, the silos, commonly known as *mazmorras*, housed twenty to thirty captives each. Small cubicles made of earth and stones that served as pillows gave the captives their only private space. A shallow trench ran the perimeter of the enclosure, providing the occupants with water and simultaneously removing their waste. A modest opening in the ceiling served as entrance and exit with the aid of a rope ladder that guards pulled up at night. During the wet months, rainwater seeped in and joined with the moisture that penetrated through the walls and floor. The air, made putrid by the filth and foul smells, competed with the dim illumination, the infestations of rodents, and the ever-present humidity to torment the captives' every moment. This was the fate of many of the captives who wound up in large cities such as Granada. The sultan used for his mazmorra or corral a large open area surrounded by a wall where fourteen funnel-shaped caves burrowed into the living rock.[17] These were infernal places, yet for many became the only homes they would return to every night for years.[18]

Not all Christian captives lived in these underground facilities. Many of them, especially the women who worked as domestic servants, experienced more humane living conditions in the houses of their masters. Other owners kept their slaves in caves, towers, small rooms, and houses, in short, in almost

17. Münzer, *Viaje por España y Portugal*, 93.
18. See the multiple descriptions of the mazmorras provided in the Vergara, *Vida y milagros.* Cossío has collected and summarized them in "Cautivos de Moros," 74–81, and the archaeological findings of Torres Balba have verified much of the textual representations: "Las mazmorras de la Alhambra," 205–17.

any place that could prevent their escape.[19] Málaga, like Granada and other large cities with significant captive populations,
held its captives either in the local fortress, the Alcazaba, or in
a corral next to it.[20] In smaller villages, different owners kept
their captives communally in a single mazmorra. In the village of Montefrio, for example, thirty captives resided in one
of these holes next to the local castle. Their masters brought
them in and out daily, depending on the workload.[21] In the sixteenth century, many captives in North Africa resided in large
state prisons called baños (baths) in addition to those who lived
in the corrals.[22] Cervantes's captive awaited his redemption in
one of these, and there he spent his idle time sitting on the
prison roof overlooking a courtyard.[23] The range in living conditions typically depended on the number of captives a particular master controlled. Since it was in the best interest of masters to safeguard their investments, captives often fared better
when their numbers were small and worse when they fell under
the jurisdiction of the sultan or other great lord who held many
captives.[24] The need to maintain control also forced the holders
of large numbers of captives to use a harsher form of discipline,
of which the mazmorras were but one aspect.[25]

No matter where captives lived, they all shared the experience of being bound in chains and manacles that kept them

19. See Ferrer i Mallol, "La redempció," 238 and n3. For a specific example
see her doc. 1 (Feb. 26, 1377), "los quals soferen en lo dit corral gran misèria e
grans afanys," and ACA, C, reg. 1871:167r (Mar. 11, 1389), "tenez cautivo el ffiel
vasallo e natural nuestro Miguel del Abat en el corral de Granada."

20. Guillén Robles, Málaga musulmana, 521.

21. Carriazo y Arroquia, Don Miguel Lucas de Iranzo, 103.

22. Bunes Ibarra, La imagen de los musulmanes, 155–56; Friedman, "Christian Captives," 624–25; Friedman, Spanish Captives, 59–62; Davis, Christian
Slaves, Muslim Masters, ch. 4.

23. Cervantes, Don Quixote, ch. 40.

24. For comparison, see Friedman, Spanish Captives, 59.

25. Salicrú i Lluch, "Cartes de captius cristians," 553. Ferrer i Mallol has
suggested that as a way to maintain discipline among the captives, the captors
sometimes used harsh punishments in order to make "examples": "La redempció," 239.

from escaping and symbolized their captive status. Muslims as well as Christians subjected their slaves to this humiliation, and the irons came on early. The raiders and pirates who took the captives from their homes and ships chained them to reduce their chance of escape (see chapter 1). From that moment on, the shackles rarely came off. They became part of the captives' attire, of their person. They wore them when they went to work in the fields or when they traveled. They wore them when they ate their meager rations and when they raised their hands to pray.[26] They wore them as they slept in their earthen beds, although their chances of escaping through the roof were mostly limited to miracles.[27]

The chains were more than a restraint. They were symbols of bondage. Their meaning, according to Patterson, was ritualistic.[28] Many former captives, upon achieving their freedom, donated their chains as ex-votos to religious houses, thus fulfilling vows they had made in captivity.[29] The captives also used them to appeal to Christian charity. In a letter to Ferdinand I of Aragon some Sicilian captives, begging for the king's help,

26. Franciscans visiting Christian captives in Cairo in the first quarter of the fourteenth century reported that captives were held in shackles and chains while the friars heard their confessions and gave them communion. These captives were probably natives of Iberia, even though they were quite far from home. The friars had gone to Egypt at the order of their master general bearing letters of recommendation from James II of Aragon, Ferdinand IV of Castile, and Frederick III of Sicily, James's brother: Golubovich, *Biblioteca bibliografica,* 3.68–72.

27. Among the many examples see Vergara, *Vida y milagros;* Münzer, *Viaje por España y Portugal,* 151; Bernáldez, *Historia de los reyes católicos,* 1:249–50. For the use of chains by Christian slaveholders, see Ramos y Loscertales, *El cautiverio,* 140–41. He cites an ordinance in Mallorca that required a ten-pound chain for every Saracen on the island between the ages of eighteen and fifty.

28. Patterson, *Slavery and Social Death,* 52; Friedman has made a similar argument for the use of chains in the Levant; see *Encounter between Enemies,* 119.

29. Many of the captives in the *Vida de Santo Domingo* and the *Miraculos romançados* offered their chains to the monastery of Santo Domingo de Silos, with whose aid they had supposedly escaped. Similar caches of chains and shackles are found in other religious institutions in Iberia, with the Cathedral of Toledo being the best-known example. See Lappin, *Medieval Cult of Saint Dominic,* 363–72.

pointedly complained of the irons put on them.[30] Those working on their behalf appealed to Christian compassion for those "who spent nights sleeping on the ground, some with shackles and other restraints, and spent their days weighed down by irons and chains."[31]

Life for the captives often centered around exhausting work, especially for those engaged in agriculture or in public works. If medieval Arabic proverbs are any indication, captives had to work very hard, because, as one commentator put it, the master who "causes [the slave] fatigue is dearer to him than another, because [the slave's] natural disposition is to bear humiliation."[32] Work began at the break of dawn and usually lasted until sunset in the harshest heat that the North African and Granadan countryside had to offer.[33] The captives in the *Vida de Santo Domingo* plowed, dug, laid bricks, cut wood, and fixed walls, among other tasks.[34] The men held in the village of Montefrio went to work the fields daily.[35] The captives in the city of Ronda would have sympathized with the ancient Greek fig-

30. "Simo morti de fame, et de frido et carricate de ferri." ACA, C, CR, Ferran I, box. 6:657, (Dec. 23, 1415), published in Salicrú i Lluch, "Cartes de captius cristians," letter 4. Aragonese captives writing to Alfonso III voiced a similar complaint in 1327, ACA, C, CR, Alfonso III, box 24:3669, published in Masía de Ros, *La Corona de Aragón*, doc. 173.

31. "La noche durmiendo sobre la tierra dura . . . e algunos de ellos con esposas e otras crueles presones, e de dia van cargados de hierros e de cadenas," ACA, OR, MdeH 2676: 453v. This is an eighteenth-century copy of a document dated 1422. The entire document (453v–55v) is a plea to Christians to give alms to the Mercedarians, and it gives nine reasons designed to appeal to the altruism of the audience. Kings also mentioned chains among the list of hardships borne by captives in the licenses granted to them to beg for alms, "qui eos talibus fame sitique compendibus et cathenis ac aliis cruciatibus depresserunt," ACA C, reg. 1895:105r–6r, published also in Ferrer i Mallol, "La redempció," doc. 3 (Dec. 4, 1388).

32. For Muslims proverbs, see Al-Maydani commenting on the proverb "Dear to a slave is he who overworks him," cited in Sersen, "Stereotypes and Attitudes," 99.

33. Muslim captives working in the Castile and Aragon worked similar hours: "sunset and sunrise find me a slave to the wishes of the devout of the idols and the cross," quoted and translated from Ben Driss, "Los cautivos entre Granada y Castilla," 307.

34. Vergara, *Vida y milagros.*

35. Carriazo y Arroquia, *Don Miguel Lucas de Iranzo*, 103.

ure of Sisyphus, condemned for all eternity to roll a boulder up a hill only to watch it fall to the bottom each time he reached the peak. These captives had the task of bringing water up a four-hundred-step mine shaft from the river below, only to have to start their task again once they attained the summit, for the inhabitants of Ronda depended on their labor for the daily water supply.[36] In Egypt, the Muslim traveler Ibn Jubayr recalled seeing prisoners from Rum (Byzantine or Eastern Christians), "whose number was beyond computation," working on a citadel. Jubayr justified the use of the captives in these tasks by pointing out that they spared Muslims such toil, "no work of this nature falling on any of them [Muslims]."[37] A Franciscan friar ministering to captives in Egypt recounted that they worked digging the moats of castles and porting away the dirt in baskets.[38] In Granada, Christian captives had raised the Torre de los Picos in the Alhambra.[39] Others worked on drainage projects, waterworks, and transport.[40]

Skill and ability in certain crafts could excuse some captives from the harshest labor, but this could prove both a benefit and a burden. The benefit usually came in the form of better treatment and living conditions as well as gradual, if limited, acceptance into their master's circle. A craftsman who could cast cannons and direct artillery during a siege was a valued addition to any princely household and treated accordingly.[41] By way of comparison, in Christian Valencia, a skilled Muslim captive who could do specialized jobs might buy his freedom back much more quickly than the unskilled men and women who labored in simpler tasks.[42] It is a possibility that a similar pattern

36. Medina, *Libro de grandezas y cosas memorables de España*, ch. 136; Torres Balba, "La acrópolis musulmana de Ronda," 479–80.
37. Ibn Jubayr, *Travels*, 43, 51–53.
38. Baird, *Salimbene de Adam*, 314.
39. Arié, *El reino Nasrí de Granada*, 321–22.
40. Ferrer i Mallol, "La redempció," 238–39.
41. Brunschvig, *Deux recits de voyage*, 216.
42. Sixto Iglesias, "Emigrantes musulmanes y cautivos," 358.

developed in Muslim regions, but a slim one when we consider the following evidence to the contrary.

For craftsmen, the burden of their professions arose from the lack of skilled workers and the reluctance of masters to release competent laborers once they had found them.[43] In an often-cited letter that suggests the importance of captive artisans to local economies, the sultan of Tlemcen responded to an appeal to release Christian captives made by James II with the following words: "In respect to your request to free all the captives in our realms, there is no possibility that this will occur, just as there would be no possibility if we would ask you to free all the Muslim captives in your kingdom, since you should know that in our [kingdom] all the jobs are entrusted to captives, the majority of whom are artisans in different trades. If you were asking for the release of five or six . . . we would fulfill your petition and satisfy your wishes, but the liberty of all of them is very difficult [to grant] because our towns would be depopulated and the effective functioning of the different industries would be paralyzed."[44]

Shipbuilding, an area in which Christian craftsmen were highly valued, would likely be one of the paralyzed sectors. In an ironic twist of fate, Christian carpenters, coopers, caulkers, and others associated with ship construction sometimes found themselves building ships for their Muslim captors; ships that could, in turn, go out and catch more captives.[45] Occasionally, even captives who had been freed were kept working by their

43. Muslims were not the only ones who refused to release captives based on the need for their technical skills. In 1263 the Knights Hospitallers had refused an offer from the Mamluk sultan Baybars to exchange prisoners because most of the captives in Hospitaller hands were highly valued craftsmen with whom the order was reluctant to part; see Forey, "Military Orders and the Ransoming of Captives," 276.

44. Alarcón y Santón and Garcia de Linares *Documentos Árabes diplomáticos,* doc. 91 (undated, but most likely early 1320s).

45. ACA, C, reg. 1389:131v (June 13, 1377); 132r–v (July 15, 1377); 136v–37r (Aug. 2, 1377); cf. Dufourcq, "Catalogue chronologique et analytique du registre 1389," docs. 236, 238, and 242.

masters because their skills were so crucial. This was the case when Muhammad V of Granada released the Mallorcan carpenter Bartolomé Aparicio but forbade his departure until he finished working on some oared vessels that the sultan had commissioned in Málaga.[46]

Other captives fell into the category of domestic laborers. Some of them were responsible for making bleach *(lexia)*, drawing water from wells, or tending ovens for heating bath water.[47] Women worked as household help or nurses of children.[48] Some even found themselves serving in royal households. In 1392 John I sent a series of letters to the sultan of Tlemcen asking for the return of a Christian woman who was serving as handmaiden to one of the sultan's daughters.[49]

In some cases the duties of female captives extended into the bedroom of their masters or into the harems.[50] The mother of the Tunisian sultan Utman was one of these captive women who ended up in a harem. Born a Christian in Valencia, she was bought by Utman's father after she fell into captivity and then she became his concubine. Impregnated by her new master, she became the mother of the future king.[51] Her story was not unique. At least five sultans of Granada were the sons of

46. ACA, C, reg. 1389:132r–v (July 15, 1377); 136v–37r (Aug. 2, 1377); cf. Dufourcq, "Catalogue chronologique et analytique du registre 1389," docs. 238 and 242. The carpenter's wife had already acquired a Muslim captive to exchange for her husband. However, the deal that "liberated" her husband also freed the captive she had procured and she was forced to turn him over to the governor of Mallorca for his repatriation while her husband remained in Granada, technically free, working on the sultan's ships.

47. Vergara, *Vida y milagros*, 169, 202–3, 161.

48. Goitein, *Mediterranean Society*, 2:134–35.

49. ACA, C, reg. 1880:28v (May 3, 1392); 118v (Aug. 30, 1392); 123v (Sept. 6, 1392).

50. For female captives in harems, see Giménez Soler, "La Corona de Aragón y Granada," 19:101–34; 20:186–224; 21:295–324; 22:333–65; 23:450–76; 24:485–96; 26:49–91; 27:146–80; 28:200–25; 29:271–98; 30:342–75, here 22:352–53. It is also certainly possible that some of the men imprisoned with them raped female captives. But there is little evidence for this beyond the fact that slaveholders housed their captives together for long periods regardless of sex. For captives locked up together, see Vergara, *Vida y milagros*, 147–48 and 181–82.

51. Brunschvig, *Deux recits de voyage*, 207.

captured Christian women who had become part of the harem.[52] Islamic law considered the child of a Muslim father and a slave mother a free Muslim and a legitimate heir to his sire as long as the father recognized the infant as his own. This recognition had significant implications for the mother. Although she could not care for or educate her Muslim children—a responsibility that fell to the father's female relatives—she assumed a special status: *umm walad*.[53] This new standing prevented the master from selling her, though it did allow him to rent her out or marry her off to someone else. Most important, her master's death automatically manumitted her.[54] Sometimes the manumission came earlier. Some women, especially those who had little chance of returning to their families, converted to Islam and gained their freedom this way, remaining with their child as Muslims.[55]

The sexual use of female captives entailed more than a physical assault upon their bodies.[56] Like the chains, sexual exploitation was a symbolic aspect of their conquest and captivity. It confirmed their powerlessness and lack of control over their own bodies.[57] Unlike the chains, however, the ravishing might taint a woman for life, as sexual crimes in medieval Christen-

52. Al-'Abbadi, *El reino de Granada*, 161.

53. One of the stories in the *Vida de Santo Domingo* describes the captivity of Caterina de Linares of Jaén whose Muslim master had regular sexual relations with her and with whom she had two sons over the course of four years. When she was finally able to escape, she could take only the younger child with her. The story says that Santo Domingo, her miraculous redeemer, told her to take the younger son with her but does not mention the older one. Perhaps the firstborn had already been taken by the father's family, making his escape impossible: Vergara, *Vida y milagros*, 214–15.

54. Marmon, "Domestic Slavery," 4; Lewis, *Islam*, 2:238–39. Similar laws existed on the Christian side. Aragonese legislation from 1283 demanded that if a Christian master slept with his female captive and had a child with her, both mother and child were to be baptized and freed. It was the second requirement that probably gave masters pause since the law equated lust with economic loss. See Meyerson, "Slavery and Solidarity," 302n52.

55. Echevarría, *Fortress of Faith*, 187.

56. For more on Islamic sexual slavery, see Davis, *Slavery and Human Progress*, 42; Murray, *Slavery in the Arab World*, ch. 4, "Sex and Slavery in the Arab World."

57. Card, "Rape as a Weapon of War," 9; Bakare-Yusuf, " Economy of Violence," 178.

dom had "the peculiar quality of contaminating the victim as much as the aggressor."[58] In the Iberian Peninsula, inaccessibility, a privilege that did not exist in captivity, was the foundation upon which a woman's honor and reputation rested. Once the barrier of inaccessibility was breached, the possibility of a female captive portraying herself as a virtuous woman or a valuable marriage prize was seriously damaged.[59] Read from a different point of view, the rape of female captives was a way to destroy social cohesion that depended on the integrity of a woman's honor and chastity.[60]

Christian authorities readily recognized this danger and used the fear of rape and miscegenation to mobilize the Christian communities to give help to captives.[61] Mercedarian friars often ransomed women before men to keep the women from converting. They complained that the Muslims charged exorbitant prices for their release because they were easier to convert.[62] This would fit in with the above suggestion that pregnant women or those who had given birth to a Muslim child became apostates more readily than those who managed to avoid maternity. The anxiety over women was shared by Christian monarchs. In 1386 the king of Aragon, Peter III, expressed fear that Muslim captors would deflower Christian virgins.[63] And in Castile, the will of Henry II bequeathed money for the liberation of one hundred captives, all of whom were to be beautiful women under forty years of age.[64]

58. García Herrero, *Las mujeres de Zaragoza*, 1:67.

59. Dillard, *Daughters of the Reconquest*, 191–92.

60. Attacking women is a way to destroy cultural and social stability in times of war because families and communities depend on the women: Seifert, "The Second Front," 39.

61. Islam and Judaism also considered captive women to be in grave danger of rape. Jewish law prescribed ransoming for women before men and some Muslims thought it better for a loved female relative to die than to be disgraced by Franks. See Friedman, "Women in Captivity," 81–84.

62. Molina, *Historia general*, 1:148.

63. ACA, C, reg. 948:144r–45r (Dec. 15, 1386); cited by Ferrer i Mallol, "La redempció," 241n23.

64. Rosell y López, *Crónica de los Reyes*, 2:40.

Concern for the female captives was obviously at play here, but in the highly masculine societies of medieval Iberia the failure to protect women from Muslim aggressors also represented a failure of Spanish men. "The act that is played out upon [the woman] is a message passed between men—vivid proof of victory for one and loss and defeat for the other."[65] Along these lines, but with the roles reversed, David Nirenberg has suggested that the rape of Muslim women by Christian men "reiterated those very acts of conquest and degradation that formed much of the basis for Iberian Christian ideas of masculinity and honor."[66] The medieval Christian belief that considered all women to be the brides of Christ further added to the humiliation brought on by the rape of Christian women and, "through such synecdoche, miscegenation becomes the cuckolding of Christ."[67] The rape of female captives thus played a double role. From the women's point of view, it marked them with the indelible signs of rape and branded them as the property of their Muslim masters. For the men who experienced capture and captivity at their side or who allowed it to happen, the rapes symbolized their defeat and were a direct attack on their manliness and faith. It was a clear sign of their impotence to act in defense of their women, their country, and their God.[68]

Captives were also subject to beatings and punishments in spite of stipulations in the Koran and the hadiths that called for the humanitarian treatment of slaves.[69] As in the case of living conditions, the physical treatment of captives depended on the master and his need to maintain discipline. Masters administered a variety of punishments. The *Vida de Santo Domin-*

65. Brownmiller, *Against Our Will*, 38; see also Card, "Rape as a Weapon of War," 7; Seifert, "The Second Front," 39–40.
66. Nirenberg, *Communities of Violence*, 141.
67. Nirenberg, "Religious and Sexual Boundaries," 144–45.
68. For more on the symbolism implied in rapes, see Richters, "Sexual Violence in Wartime," 116–18.
69. Brunschvig, "'Abd," 25; Charouiti Hasnaoui, "Esclavos y cautivos según la ley Islámica," 8–9.

go and the *Miraculos romançados* mention beatings and floggings in many of the miracle stories. They probably embellish actual conditions with literary license. Archival sources, however, also describe some of the harsh punishments inflicted on captives. A group of enslaved Aragonese subjects writing to Alfonso III in 1327 complained bitterly of the bad treatment they received at the hands of their captors, specifically bodily torments *(turmens corporals)*. The captives described even harsher tortures for the daring ones who attempted to escape and were recaptured. Failed escapees had their noses or ears cut off and suffered in heavy chains.[70] They were not describing an isolated incident. In 1361, in a very well documented case, Peter the Ceremonious accused Abu-Hamu, sultan of Tlemcen, of severing the noses of some Aragonese captives.[71] And in 1409 Martin I (r. 1395–1410) granted a begging license to a captive whose treatment in captivity had left him a cripple. The king gave him the right to beg so that he could sustain himself.[72] Later in the fifteenth century, Christian slave owners began the odious practice of branding their captives, and it did not take long for this new method of control and subjugation to reach North Africa, notably Morocco and Fez.[73] Brandings, even more than other

70. ACA, CR, Alfonso III, box 24:3669; published in Masía de Ros, *La Corona de Aragón*, doc. 173.

71. These captives had been part of an Aragonese fleet of four galleys that Peter had sent to aid Abu-Hamu in a regional conflict. The galleys ran into a squadron of Castilian galleys (Aragon and Castile were at war), and ended up surrendering. Most of the crew managed to escape and make their way to Tlemcen. In Tlemcen, some joined Abu-Hamu's Christian militia. Some of the crew, however, refused to join and asked to return to their homes. The sultan apparently refused and threw them into prison as if they had been legally seized captives. It was while in prison that the nose-cutting incident took place. The primary source for this incident is register 1389 of the ACA. Most of the documents have been at least partially transcribed and translated in Dufourcq's "Catalogue chronologique et analytique du registre 1389." The first two documents concerning the abduction of the men are ACA, C, reg. 1389:29r–v and 30r, nos. 20 and 21 in Dufourcq's work. They are dated Nov. 5, 1361 and Feb. 24, 1362, respectively. For more, see Ramos y Loscertales, *El cautiverio*, 176–78.

72. ACA, C, reg. 2208:9v–10r (Nov. 28, 1409); see also Ferrer i Mallol, "La redempció," 239n12.

73. Origo, "The Domestic Enemy," 340–41; Ramos y Loscertales, *El cautiverio*, 143.

physical punishments, "became indelible signs of a servile status, and suggested a deformity of character which deserved contempt."[74] The bodily markings served a function akin to that of the chains: to mark the servile status of the individual and place him outside of society.[75]

The floggings, other beatings, and torture occurred for a variety of reasons, including the need to maintain discipline. Medieval Islamic literature on purchasing slaves advised masters not to give their slaves free rein, lest they become bold. On the other hand, a master who trained his slaves would make them obedient.[76] Masters also abused their charges when they wanted to induce a quick ransom. They reasoned, correctly in many cases, that captives could only take so much punishment before they would agree to inflated ransom demands. "Agreements" reached in this manner and secured by a hostage when the goods or capital were not immediately available often left the captive and his family impoverished. Escape attempts also brought down heavy punishments and not just in the form of severed noses. The captives held in the Muslim village of Montefrio in Granada formulated one of the more daring breakouts. Their plan was not only to free themselves but also to take over the village in an uprising that would coincide with an outside attack by the constable of Castile, Don Miguel Lucas de Iranzo. The plan, however, fell apart when one of the conspirators, an eleven-year-old boy, told his master of the contemplated plot. As in many other locations, the thirty captives held in Montefrio lived in a communal mazmorra where the only access to the surface was a rope ladder. When the Muslims discovered the plot, they quickly surrounded the mazmorra and ordered the captives out. Fearing the reprisal that they certainly knew was coming, the men inside the hole refused. A down-

74. Davis, *The Problem of Slavery*, 48–49; see also Stella, "*Herrado en el rostro con una S y un clavo*," 147–53.

75. Patterson, *Slavery and Social Death*, 51–62, esp. 58–59.

76. Lewis, *Islam*, 2:244–45.

pour of flaming embers and burning leaves cascaded through the hole as the guards sought either to burn or, more likely, smoke out the insurgents. Forced to choose between asphyxiation and whatever punishments awaited them outside, the captives emerged. Still caught in a dangerous situation—Iranzo's force was outside the settlement—the guards savagely beat the captives, both as a punishment and in a frenzied effort to discover the details of the plan that threatened their village. The threat was not as imminent as the villagers believed. Iranzo had brought only enough supplies for a five-day sojourn, and waning provisions forced him to retire the day the insurrection was discovered. A relief force from Granada ensured that Montefrio would remain safely in Muslim hands. The young boy who exposed the conspirators wisely converted to Islam, perhaps fearing more the earthly retributions of his enraged cellmates than the divine punishments of his God.[77]

The specter of hunger also haunted the daily existence of many captives. Sources speak repeatedly of captives receiving small rations, often limited to bread and water. The purpose behind these limitations was not typically to starve the captives to death. Some captors did not eat much better than their charges. Some may have believed that they were feeding their charges the right food even if the quantities were insufficient. No less a voice than Averroës (Ibn Rushd) had suggested that the best foods that one could eat were those prepared from wheat.[78] Why, then, should captives need fruit or meat? Others may have thought that the meager diets ensured the well-being of their captives. They would have been well supported by the great fourteenth-century Tunisian scholar Ibn Khaldun, who had some noteworthy ideas on food and hunger. He argued that "hunger has a fa-

77. Carriazo y Arroquia, *Don Miguel Lucas de Iranzo*, 103–9. The Catholic monarchs finally freed the captives when they took Montefrio in 1486. There were still twenty-six captives in the mazmorra at the time: Bernáldez, *Historia de los reyes católicos*, 1:223.

78. Cruz Hernández, *El Islam de Al-Andalus*, 202.

vorable influence on the health and well-being of the body and intellect." On the other hand, too much food could lead to "stupidity, carelessness and a general intemperance."[79] Not exactly ideal traits for captives/slaves. Whatever the reason, it is evident that captives did not have enough to eat, especially those engaged in heavy labor. Almost every episode in the *Vida de Santo Domingo* and the *Miraculos romançados* denounces the meager rations that the captives ate. In one memorable case, a master placed a restraining bit in his captive's mouth to prevent the man from eating grain as he milled it.[80] Another captive recalled eating only one and a half pounds of bread a day.[81] The Franciscan Salimbene de Adam reported that Christian captives in Egypt ate only three small pieces of bread, in spite of being engaged in the backbreaking task of digging moats around castles.[82] The diet was so deficient in some cases that Christian princes writing to their Muslim counterparts on behalf of captives based the appeals for their release on the captives' weakness caused by hunger.[83] Even the begging licenses granted by Aragonese kings to captives or their families mention the hunger and thirst suffered by those in captivity.[84] Sources that describe the condition of captives after their release also suggest that they were not well fed. The German traveler Jerónimo Münzer saw a group of these captives after the Christian conquest of Málaga in 1487. He describes them as so overcome with hunger that the king had to order chicken soup and other foods to feed and comfort them.[85]

Against this harsh picture we must keep in mind that many of the descriptions come from polemical or propagandistic works whose strict accuracy is questionable—even the begging

79. Ibn Khaldun, *Muqaddimah*, I:1:5.
80. Vergara, *Vida y milagros*, 138.
81. Ibid., 161–62.
82. Baird, *Salimbene de Adam*, 314.
83. ACA, C, reg. 2397:126v–27r (Feb. 22, 1414).
84. ACA, C, reg. 2180:59r–59v (June 8, 1406); reg. 2180:59v–6or (June 8, 1406); reg. 2207:116r (Dec. 3, 1408).
85. Münzer, *Viaje por España y Portugal*, 149.

licenses are formulaic and unlikely to reflect the specific conditions of the supplicants who received them. One must also contend with the argument that masters would not endanger their
economic investment by starving their captives and that many
Muslims would have been benevolent to their charges as dic-
tated by their law or simple human kindness. Most likely, the
truth is somewhere in the middle. The typical master, on both
economic and humanitarian grounds, would not willingly starve
his charge. However, there are too many sources complaining
about the food deprivations to ignore them. Furthermore, more
reliable and extensive captivity narratives from the sixteenth
and seventeenth centuries also point to the lack of food.[86] Consequently, I would argue that the average captive was probably
underfed, some severely so, to the point that although they were
able to execute their tasks, they could not do so without risking
the harsh side effects of malnutrition, such as susceptibility to
disease and serious weight loss. The German Münzer observed
that of seven thousand captives in Granada before the city was
besieged, only fifteen hundred survived the Christian conquest;
most of the dead fell victim to starvation.[87] Although Münzer's
exact figures may be questionable, they do suggest that a large
proportion of the captive population succumbed to starvation.
Those who survived did so by eating dead horses, donkeys, and
mules, further exposing their weakened bodies to the infectious
pathogens of rotting meat.

The bread-loaded diet that many sources describe was also
far from nutritious, even by the standards to which the captives
would have been accustomed in their home countries. Captives
from wealthy households and well-off religious institutions had
the biggest gap to overcome between the diets they enjoyed as
free individuals and their rations in captivity. Estimates for caloric intake for the residents of a religious house of even mod-

86. Friedman, "Christian Captives," 619–20, 622.
87. Münzer, *Viaje por España y Portugal*, 93.

est means in the fourteenth century range from 4,700 to almost 6,900 calories a day; an impressive amount—apparently the image of the overweight churchman has its basis in reality. The daily portions, which included bread, cheese, legumes, and two bottles of wine (1,500 ml) or beer, were augmented with meat or fish three times a week and on religious feast days. Meals in wealthy households were as bountiful.[88]

Sailors also ate better aboard ships than in captivity. The *Consulate of the Sea* required shipmasters to provide meat three times a week and soup the other four days. Bread was a daily staple supplemented by cheese, onions, and sardines. Mariners also received wine thrice weekly and double rations on holidays.[89] Although the diet for seamen was probably sufficient in caloric content, it displayed the same disregard for fruits and vegetables and their associated nutritional content that plagued most premodern sailors. The diets of the Spanish poor were often similarly affected by an absence of greens. Their meals consisted mostly of bread, wine, and meat. At about 2,400 calories, and notably deficient in essential vitamins and minerals, the medieval poor were nutritionally underfed even if their bellies were full.[90] Thus, although the difference in precaptivity and captivity diet for poorer captives was not as drastic as that for richer prisoners, the poor often went into captivity already suffering nutritional problems. When combined with heavy labor, the poor diet probably proved fatal to many captives, especially the poorer ones, who were less capable of fending off the implications of malnutrition. It was this deadly combination of work and diet that was behind the widespread casualties suffered by the captives in Granada during the city's final siege and the pitiful conditions of freed captives described by some of the chroniclers.

Besides malnutrition, captives are likely to have suffered

88. Claramunt, "Dos aspectes de l'alimentació medieval," 168–71; see also Dyer, *Standards of Living*, 55–70.
89. Jados, *Consulate of the Sea*, ch. 145.
90. Claramunt, "Dos aspectes de l'alimentació medieval," 172.

other nutrition-related problems. A 75 kg (about 165 lb) adult male captive who engages in heavy physical activity requires about 4,500 calories per day to meet his energy requirements and maintain his body weight. Female captives, usually occupied in more moderate tasks in the household, would have had smaller caloric requirements. A 55 kg (120 lb) woman would need some 2,180 calories.[91] If captives ate less or, at best, on a par with the medieval poor, they were consuming about 2,400 calories a day in the best-case scenario. Thus, by this conservative standard, male captives were getting only about 60 percent of their needed calories, while women were getting enough. The example cited earlier from the *Miraculos romançados* in which the captive noted that he only ate 1.5 pounds of bread daily suggests that at least some captives were not receiving even these 2,400 calories. A pound of grain yields about 1,200 calories and is barely adequate to maintain life. The 1.5 pounds that this particular captive was receiving would be enough for an older person engaged in light activities. A young man engaged in heavier work would require about 2.5 pounds (about 3,000 calories), and captives engaged in the heaviest activities probably needed between 3.5 and 4 pounds of bread daily if they were not eating any other food.[92] Even if captives had received this much bread, it would have only filled their caloric needs while still leaving them far short of achieving anything resembling a balanced diet.

Insufficient calories also had a direct impact on the body's use of protein. The human body uses proteins for a variety of

91. I have calculated the amount of calories needed by eighteen- to thirty-year-old adults from figures put forth by the World Health Organization. Younger and lighter captives had smaller caloric needs. Male captives between ten and eighteen engaged in similar activities as the older captives needed about 3,980 calories per day, while females required about 2,160 calories. Captives over thirty needed fewer calories than those between eighteen and thirty, but not significantly so. See Schutz and Jéquier, "Energy Needs," 107–9; see also Passmore et al., *Handbook of Human Nutritional Requirements*, 8–11 and tables 2–3.

92. Dyer, *Standards of Living*, 153; Blum, *End of the Old Order*, 183–89.

purposes: growth, tissue synthesis, repair of broken or worn-out tissue, formation of enzymes and hormones, and to provide energy.[93] This last occurs when the body is calorie deficient and is unable to meet its energy requirements with more basic nutrients—namely fats and carbohydrates. Proteins that under better conditions would have gone to help a captive recover from injury or disease or to fulfill normal wear-and-tear replacement of tissue were instead diverted to meet daily energy needs that other nutrients were not providing. The bread-only diet certainly made matters much worse, since cereals are notably lacking in certain essential proteins such as lysine.[94]

This moderate starvation and protein deficiency had adverse effects of the captives' health and physical condition. Mercedarians often had to intern sick captives in the order's hospitals when they returned to Spain.[95] Münzer lamented that the "specter of death" was on the captives; an Italian who witnessed the capitulation of Granada recalled that captives were "disfigured under their clothes"; and another chronicler complained that they were "gaunt and pallid due to the great hunger."[96] The most obvious sign of this "specter" was loss of body weight. Weight loss is a defense mechanism that the body triggers to adapt to lack of food and results from the body feeding off its stores of fat and lean tissues. The reduction in lean tis-

93. Passmore et al., *Handbook of Human Nutritional Requirements*, 15–16.

94. Ibid., 16–18.

95. Millán Rubio, *La Orden de Nuestra Señora de la Merced*, 100.

96. Münzer, *Viajes por España y Portugal*, 151; Marineo Sículo, *Vida y hechos de los reyes católicos*, 136–37; Bernáldez, *Historia de los reyes católicos*, 1:250. Both Münzer's and Bernáldez's accounts are from the siege of Málaga, and the hunger of the captives is probably reflective of the siege conditions they had been under. However, a similar description of hungry captives is provided by Bernáldez concerning the captives liberated in Ronda in May 1485. Ronda was also besieged, but it was not a protracted affair, about two weeks, and the city surrendered because its water supply was cut off, not due to waning food provisions. In short, although sieges tended to aggravate the captives' conditions, and, in turn, the shock of their Christian liberators, it also seems likely that captives were already going hungry and getting sick even without the severe starvation that set in when a siege reached an advanced stage.

sue has the added benefit of reducing metabolic rate which, in turn, lowers the energy requirements of the individual. In time, weight loss reaches a plateau and stabilizes as energy needs equilibrate with food intake.[97] The captive could survive in this state of accommodation indefinitely as long as new factors—less food, more work, disease—did not intervene on the fragile equation. This accommodation came at a price. The loss of insulating fat limited the body's response to environmental cold, and the decrease in muscle mass brought on a decline in physical power.[98] Muscles in starving bodies also produce less heat, making the person even more vulnerable to cold temperatures.[99]

Any reduction in productivity could have far-reaching effects on the captives' future. Sources suggest, not surprisingly, that no one wanted sick or weakened captives. Owners were very willing to ransom them off as quickly as possible. Ransomers, for their part, preferred to use their limited funds on captives who were likely to survive the trip home. Such was the case with a Mercedarian ransoming expedition that went to Tunis in the early fourteenth century, as told by one of the order's historians. A disagreement arose over a sick captive, with some of the friars wanting to leave the man behind and one of the ransomers opposed to doing so. Eventually, the sick captive was ransomed, but only after his defender threatened to stay behind in his place if the other friars did not go along with the ransom.[100] The words of Diego Zurita, a Castilian official in charge of receiving freed captives, address the Muslim perspective. He complained that

97. Hoffer, "Starvation," 927–29.

98. Ibid., 937; Jordan, *Great Famine*, 142. Muslim captives in the Christian kingdoms also complained of weight loss and diminished strength, as evidenced by a poem attributed to 'Abd al-Karim al Qaysi al Basti, who was himself a captive. He complained that "[his] body had grown feeble and the condition of his extremities had changed. [He] would have died of weakness and anguish if not for [his] laments and tears." Quoted and translated from Ben Driss, "Los cautivos entre Granada y Castilla," 307.

99. Hoffer, "Starvation," 934.

100. Molina, *Historia general*, 1:242.

some of the recently arrived captives were overworked and sick
and that it would be some time before they were in a condition
to travel.[101] It was not by coincidence that the captives whom
Zurita received were part of a tribute that the king of Granada,
Muhammad IX, had to render to Castile as a condition of a truce
agreement and that they probably represented the least valuable
of the captives that the Nasrid king had in his corrals.[102] Muhammad was apparently supposed to deliver healthy individuals since the letter that accompanied the captives stated that
they were "healthy in body." As we have observed from Zurita's
testimony, this was not always the case. The phrase "healthy
in body" is the only descriptor applied to the captives, and its
prominent inclusion may indicate that the Castilians, perhaps
previously cheated in these exchanges, specifically demanded
healthy captives as part of their agreements.

Had a modern doctor examined the group of sick captives
received by Zurita and others, he or she would have found problems that went beyond those described above. Dysentery, other abdominal ailments, and a weakened immune system were
likely present, all side effects of the poor diet. Problems in the
digestive system when combined with immunodeficiency could
prove deadly to captives who already were not getting enough
calories to meet their needs since the body's caloric requirements typically double under these conditions.[103] Captives were
also likely to suffer from anemia, complications with their re-
spiratory system, tuberculosis, and impaired healing.[104] To make
matters worse, the close quarters and stagnant environment of
the mazmorras provided an excellent setting for the propagation
of any disease that found its way in. Moving from one disease
environment to another, from Mallorca to Tunis, for example,

101. "Algunos de ellos avian llegado a esta çibdat trabajados, e estavan en-
fermos e por esta cabsa no sabia sy tan en breve podrian ir a la merced del dicho
señor Rey," cited by Torres Delgado, "Liberación de cautivos," 646.

102. Ibid., 649.   103. Bang, " Role of Disease," 71.

104. Hoffer, "Starvation," 936.

could also increase susceptibility to disease.[105] In short, the malnourished captives became much more vulnerable to diseases
and other health problems.[106] It is very difficult to measure in
quantitative terms the effects that this increased morbidity had
on captive populations, but the fate of the captives of Granada
observed by Münzer hints at the tragic possibilities.

Medical attention may have alleviated this somber picture,
but the sources are very limited and, at times, contradictory on
this subject. We can assume that out of compassion and economic incentive, masters tried to get their captives help when
they became outwardly sick. Ellen Friedman has noted that
Muslim authorities supported the efforts of Trinitarian friars
when these began running a hospital in Algiers in the seventeenth century. The Algerians clearly saw the economic benefits of trying to maintain their captives' health, a point that was
probably not lost on their fourteenth- and fifteenth-century predecessors.[107] Surprisingly, the number of patients in the Trinitarian hospitals was always very low, a fact that Friedman at-
tributes to captives receiving treatment in the master's home.[108]
The masters' decision to treat their captives at home instead
of sending them to the hospital suggests a tradition of home
treatment and it is likely that this was already the norm in the
fourteenth and fifteenth centuries.[109] At times there were also
Christian physicians, either among the captive population or
the local merchant funduqs, with whom the captives had contact, but I have not uncovered any sources that describe the role
they played, if any, with sick captives.[110] Local Christians or ren-

105. Lovejoy, *Transformations in Slavery*, 7.
106. For a brief look at the interaction between nutrition and disease, see
Livi Bacci, *Population and Demography*, 32–39.
107. Friedman, "Trinitarian Hospitals," 560–61.
108. Ibid., 556.
109. Díaz Plaja, *La vida cotidiana*, 327.
110. A power of attorney enacted by a French captive ordering that all her
goods be sold in order to raise the money for her ransom was put on paper by a

egades may have also aided sick captives, but their help could only have been limited, since for renegades, at least, helping the captives would have brought unwanted speculation about their true loyalties.[111] For their part, Christian observers had mixed reports on the efforts made by Muslims to alleviate the suffering of their captives. The Mercedarian historian Tirso de Molina noted the efforts made by the Crown of Granada to provide medical attention to a captive Mercedarian whom a crowd had beaten.[112] An appeal to Christians to give alms for ransoming captives expressed a different opinion. It accused Muslims of forcing captives to work when they were sick to the point of exhaustion. The writer also charged that masters failed to give the captives any medical help or the medicines or other necessities required by the sick.[113]

Due to their inadequate diets, captives probably lost a substantial amount of their insulating body fat deposits. The loss of this natural insulation made the captives more susceptible to temperature drops. In spite of the sweltering heat that we usually associate with North Africa and the adjacent Sahara, the Maghrib can be quite cold, especially during winter nights. One sixteenth-century observer noted that the whole Barbary Coast and the nearby mountains tended to be cold.[114] He also noted that winter began in December and lasted until February, with January having the distinction of being the coldest month.[115] In Granada, a typical winter outfit included a leather coat or a felt

certain Antoine Garsia, who is identified as "chirurgien de Bougie." If "chirurgien de Bougie" is a title, then Antoine was likely a surgeon serving the local Christian merchant community. Document in Baratier, *Documents de l'histoire de la Provence,* 132–33 (Oct. 2, 1395).

111. For an example, see Guillén Robles, *Málaga musulmana,* 331; Ladero Quesada, "La esclavitud por guerra," 69–70.

112. Molina, *Historia general,* 1:159.

113. ACA, OR, MdeH 2676: 453v.

114. Africano, *Descripción de África,* 35.

115. Ibid., 38. Africano's descriptions are confirmed by modern temperature records, which put the average minimum temperature in January around the freezing level: Buckle, *Weather and Climate in Africa,* table 3.4.

jacket.[116] By consequence, the loss of their protective fatty tissue left the captives more exposed to the frigid winter nights, a point that is made in some of the sources. The begging licenses counted cold *(frigus* and *algor)* among the torments that captives faced.[117] And in one of the rare occasions where we have access to the captives' own voices, a group of Sicilians held in Tunis complained to the king of Aragon about the cold they had to endure.[118]

The captives' unsuitable clothing also made the winter chill more pronounced. Numerous Christian sources object to the captives' nudity—*nuditatem* [*sic*].[119] Although it is highly unlikely that captives went about totally naked, it does suggest that captives were probably underdressed—suitable for the hot work of the summer months, but not the winter. If we assume that most captives retained whatever clothes they had on when they were captured, then we only need imagine the typical dress of a sailor or fisherman to have some idea of the attire that captives spent the cold months in. Even those who went into captivity with suitable garments were likely wearing rags after two or three years due to the natural deterioration of their outfits. Their liberators often noted the captives' poor and flimsy dress and sometimes provided them with new clothing. The court of John II of Castile welcomed a group of freed captives with new vestments.[120] And two different chroniclers noted that when he freed the Christian captives held in Málaga, Ferdinand of Aragon ordered that new clothes be given to them.[121] Archival sources also make note of the captives' poor dress. A royal privilege

116. Cruz Hernández, *El Islam de Al-Andalus,* 214.
117. ACA, C, reg. 2206:11v–12r (June 6, 1408); reg. 2206:49v–50r (Sept. 18, 1408); reg. 2588:2v (May 2, 1418); reg. 3150:74r–v.
118. ACA, C, CR, Ferran I, box 6:657 (Dec. 23, 1415).
119. ACA, C, reg. 2180:59r–59v, 2180:59v–60r (both documents are dated June 8, 1406); Bernáldez, *Historia de los reyes católicos,* 1:206.
120. Rosell y López, *Crónica de los reyes,* 2:334.
121. Bernaldez, *Historia de los reyes católicos,* 1:249–50; Pulgar, *Crónica de los reyes católico,* 2:333.

granted to the Mercedarians by Henry II of Castile in 1373 forbade royal officials from taking the *lienzo* (coarse linen cloth)
that the Mercedarians carried with them during their ransoming
expeditions to make crude clothing for captives.[122] And in 1485
Queen Isabel gave 3,000 *maravedís* to a female captive to help
her buy new clothes.[123] In short, the loss of their natural insulation combined with unsuitable clothing likely made the winter
the most difficult time of the year for captives.

Captives lived pitiful lives. Hard and difficult work usually awaited them at first light. Meager rations and inadequate
clothing took away their health, and for those unlucky ones
who had harsh or sadistic masters, beatings and other punishments became a common part of their routines. Even for those
who experienced kindness and humanity from their masters,
the fact remained that they were not free. Under the best conditions, the captive was still under the power of others, separated
from relatives and friends, torn from familiar surroundings, and
subject to a future that was almost completely beyond his control. The sixteenth-century Benedictine friar Diego de Haedo
succinctly captured their experience when he commented that
"if there is hunger in the world, if there is thirst, nudity, cold,
and heat, if there are beatings, floggings, injuries, affronts, prisons, chains, needs, anguish, regrets, torments, martyrdoms, and
pains, you will find them all in a captive."[124] These conditions
reinforced their servile status and served to remind them that
they had lost power over their persons. However, it was also
these harsh conditions that provoked the compassion and pity
of their compatriots, prompting many to donate alms for their
rescue. For some, the only hope that maintained them was the
belief that their fellow Christians would take pity and help to

122. Millán Rubio, *La Orden de Nuestra Señora de la Merced,* 447n238.
123. De la Torre and De la Torre, *Cuentas de Gonzalo de Baeza,* 1:53.
124. Haedo, *Topografía e historia general de Argel,* 2:26.

ransom them. Others, for whom this toil became unbearable, converted to Islam and gave up almost all possibility of ever returning to Christendom. They became *renegados*, and they will claim much of our attention in the next chapter, as we look at religious life in captivity.

CHAPTER 3

CAPTIVES AND RENEGADES

In May 1395 John I, king of Aragon, ordered the Mercedarians in his kingdom to dispatch a mission to Bone in North Africa as "quickly as possible." The king had "heard from many" about many Christians in captivity there, suffering terrible conditions and in danger of losing their faith.[1] Just two years later, John's brother and successor, Martin the Humane, wrote a similarly concerned letter to his young nephew Henry III, king of Castile. In the letter, Martin tells Henry how he had recently learned that several Castilian subjects languished in captivity, under "such oppression and despair" that they were in danger of "death or apostasy." Martin continues by asking Henry "out of reverence for God" to negotiate with the king of Granada for their freedom.[2] These two letters are instructive in beginning any discussion on the religious life of captives because they highlight a deep concern by Christians, even at the highest levels, over the conversion of Christian captives to Islam. Concerns over apostasy were, by the thirteenth century, an increasingly important aspect of Christian/Muslim relations, and captives became the focus of

1. Sáinz de la Maza Lasoli, "Los Mercedarios," doc. 42 (May 18, 1395).
2. ACA, C, reg. 2171:85v–86r (Dec. 17, 1397).

much of this worry. This chapter begins by exploring the anxiety over the religious conversion of captives and then contrasts these fears with the realities that captives actually faced as they sought to worship and maintain their faith while under the control of their Muslim captors. These fears were not mere chimeras since a significant number of captives did in fact convert to Islam for numerous reasons. These converted Christians, derisively known as renegades, posed serious dangers for Christian Spain, a topic that the last part of the chapter looks at more closely. Like the incessant raiding and the physical tribulations suffered by captives and discussed in the previous chapters, the anxiety over religious conversion and its real and imagined effects was a key reason why the Crown of Aragon responded to captivity the way it did over the course of the fourteenth and fifteenth centuries. The fear of captives who might convert to Islam became a powerful tool in the hands of those who worked to set them free, and the panic and destruction caused by renegades reminded the citizens of the realm of the price to be paid if the problem went unresolved.

APOSTASY AND CAPTIVITY

In the year 1311, James II wrote a letter to Rome in which he claimed that of Muslim Granada's two hundred thousand inhabitants, perhaps five hundred were of Arab ancestry. The rest, he argued, were Christian apostates or their descendants.[3] A few years earlier, James's countryman, the Franciscan Raymond Llull, had voiced a similar concern for those Christians who lived under Muslim domination, "whereas they have no more belief in the Holy Catholic Faith, but renounce it, and take the faith of those among whom they live in opposition to the will of God."[4] Similarly, in 1409 James's great-grandson, the aforemen-

3. Giménez Soler, "La Corona de Aragón y Granada" 22:352–53; Ferrer i Mallol, *Els sarraïns*, 78–79.
4. Llull, *Blanquerna*, 85:1. (This work is cited by chapter and section.)

tioned Martin, prohibited Christians from living inside the Muslim quarter in Valencia out of fear that they would be inclined toward the "superstition of the Saracens."[5] These are but three examples of the chorus of voices in the Crown of Aragon that expressed distress over the conversion of Christians to Islam.[6]

The nervousness that permeated the bureaucratic and literary sources was also present in legal codes. Apprehension over preserving the faith, not only of captives but of all Christians, had forged a series of laws and penalties that sought to inflict punishment on the bodies of those who ignored the eternal damnation to which they exposed their souls. The *Furs* (legal code) of Valencia called for the burning of Christians who abandoned their faith.[7] The inquisitor-general of Aragon in the fourteenth century, Nicolas Eimeric, confirmed the punishment in his *Directorium Inquisitorum*. In his view, anyone who apostatized and converted to Judaism or Islam was to be handed over to the secular authorities for burning.[8] The *Siete Partidas*, in neighboring Castile, demanded the forfeiture of the apostates' property, which reverted to their children or heirs.[9] Moreover, as with the Furs, the converts faced execution if they ever returned to Castilian territory.[10] The threat of capital punishment, moreover, went beyond mere rhetoric. Christian secular authorities put captured apostates, and in some cases those Muslims who had influenced their conversion, to death.[11] Even when apostates evaded the law and made their way to Muslim regions, they usually lost whatever immovable property they owned.[12] In short, as Robert Burns has noted, apostasy was among the vilest crimes that one could

5. Roca Traver, "Un siglo de vida mudejar," 125–26.

6. Dufourcq, *L'Espagne Catalane*, 582.

7. Burns, "Renegades, Adventurers, and Sharp Businessmen," 345.

8. Eimeric, *El manual de los inquisidores*, 85.

9. For a brief introduction to this issue in Castile, see López de Coca Castañer, "Institutions on the Castilian-Granadan Frontier," 135–36.

10. Alfonso X, *Las Siete Partidas*, VII:25:4.

11. See, for example, Ferrer i Mallol, *Els sarraïns*, doc. 28 (Aug. 11, 1322); Torres Fontes, "La frontera de Granada," 4:191–211, doc. 3 (Oct. 6, 1406)

12. Ferrer i Mallol, *Els sarraïns*, 80.

commit in the Middle Ages, with other offenses such as man-slaughter, usury, and gross immorality "[yielding] pride of place to the . . . charge of being a 'renegade.'"[13]

These anxieties played out against a backdrop of Christian crusading and missionizing failures. The thirteenth century witnessed the high point of medieval missionary activity, which the Mendicants had infused with their energy and religious zeal. Spurred on by the words of luminaries such as Joachim of Fiore (d. 1202), Francis of Assisi (d. 1226), and Jacques de Vitry (d. 1240), Christian preachers regularly made their way to Islamic communities, intent on converting Muslims to Christianity. In regions where Muslims had political and military control, such as North Africa, Granada, and the Levant, these actions were short-lived as preachers were quickly punished and either expelled or executed when they launched into attacks against Islam or Muhammad, and the missions became "more conducive to filling heaven with Christian martyrs than the earth with Muslim converts."[14] But even in Muslim communities in Spain where Christian authorities forced the local population to hear Christian preachers, the inroads made by missionaries were slight.[15] Consequently, by the end of the thirteenth century, the "dream of conversion flickered, fitfully dimmed, and died."[16]

More worrisome and demoralizing was the fear that Christians were converting to Islam in greater numbers than Muslims to Christianity.[17] After decades of trying to make Muslims followers of Christ, there was an uneasy feeling that not only had the effort failed, but the pendulum of conversion had

13. Burns, "Renegades, Adventurers, and Sharp Businessmen," 347. For the specific renegade that Burns is discussing, see Roca Traver, "Un siglo de vida mudejar," doc. 27 (Apr. 1321).

14. Kedar, *Crusade and Mission,* 155.

15. For a brief overview of this approach to the conversion of non-Christians and its results, see Mark Johnston, "Ramon Llull and the Compulsory Evangelization of Jews and Muslims," 5–13; Chazan, *Barcelona and Beyond,* 84.

16. Burns, "Christian Islamic Confrontation in the West," 1434.

17. Dufourcq, *L'Espagne Catalane,* 582.

swung in the opposite direction. As a result, the tangible missionizing optimism of the thirteenth century gave way to the
grim realities that followed in the fourteenth, embodied in the
failed missions to convert the Muslims; the crumbling crusader
kingdoms, which would completely collapse by 1291; the Great
Famine; the Babylonian Captivity; and finally, the Black Death.
These recurring episodes of loss, defeat, and turmoil brought
about a siege mentality in which Europeans saw themselves as-
sailed from all sides, with forces beyond their control threatening their way of life. It is notable that as early as the 1270s,
Humbert of Romans, the master-general of the Dominicans and
one of the leading proponents of Christian missions to Islam,
aligned the twin failures of the crusading movement and the
missionizing effort to convert the Muslims with the realization
that Christians were converting to Islam.[18] He was not alone
in his despair. Voicing widely held views prompted by the fall
of Acre, the Cortes of Aragon declared in 1292 that Christendom faced its greatest peril ever.[19] The anguish was echoed by
the Dominican friar Ricoldo de Monte Croce, who wondered after the fall of Acre if God had wanted the whole world to become Saracen.[20] Even the Catalan Ramond Llull, another ardent
proponent of preaching to Muslims, expressed his doubts "by
mentioning a string of discouraging reports concerning Christian failure in converting Muslims and Tartars." Moreover, he
was quick to point out that one of the "three Tartar Emperors"
had converted to Islam along with his entire army, choosing to
become Muslim rather than Christian.[21]

If Tartar emperors were vulnerable to conversion pressures,

18. Brett, *Humbert of Romans*, 178; Kedar, *Crusade and Mission*, 155;
Throop, *Criticism of the Crusade*, 144–45, 149–50.

19. Cited in Schein, *Fideles Crucis*, 139.

20. Rohricht, "Lettres," 293; Sylvia Schein, in her analysis of the letters of
Ricoldo, suggests that he was having a crisis of faith and that he was "one of the
best exponents of what many others must have felt after the fall of Acre—total
bewilderment"; *Fideles Crucis*, 125–27.

21. Quoted in Beattie, "'Pro Exaltatione Sanctae Fidei Catholicae,'" 115 n6.

what chance did captives stand? Very little, if the literature produced by those who worked on their behalf is any indication. Ransomers, religious authorities, local governments, families, and the crown were among the many groups that feared the spiritual danger in which captives toiled, and they used this fear to encourage Aragonese society to get behind the efforts to free them. Papal bulls encouraging donors to give alms for ransoms certainly gave voice to this fear.[22] In a similar manner, the begging licenses and other documents produced by the crown played on the probability that Christian captives would convert if they did not receive aid quickly (see chapter 6). In popular literature, this fear surfaced in works such as the *Romances fronterizos* and Ramond Llull's *Blanquerna,* which expressed concern for those Christians who lived under Muslim domination "whereas they have no more belief in the Holy Catholic Faith, but renounce it, and take the faith of those among whom they live in opposition to the will of God."[23] All of these efforts capitalized on these anxieties to encourage quick action because every day that a captive spent in shackles threatened to carry him closer to the brink of apostasy.

WORSHIPPING IN CAPTIVITY

Concerns over the possible conversion of captives helped to energize the movements to free them and also led to efforts to ensure that captives had as much access to priests and religious services as was possible. Providing religious care for captives could be done only with the acquiescence and support of the Muslims holding them. The religious tolerance of medieval Islam helped, as Muslim rulers recognized the rights of Christians to worship and maintain their cult. This was especially true in

22. See, for example, bulls issued by Boniface IX in 1397 and 1400, *Bullarium Franciscanum,* 7:74 and 218.
23. For the *Romances,* see MacKay, "The Ballad and the Frontier," 26; the quotation is from *Blanquerna,* 85:1.

the North African kingdoms and in Granada, where Christian soldiers served in the sultans' militias and Christian merchants were a vibrant part of the local economies. In Granada, for example, the Genoese enjoyed great economic and political success.[24] They were not alone as Catalans, Mallorcans, Valencians, and Castilians also staked their claims to the Nasrid economy. In addition to merchants, Nasrid sultans employed Christian militias well into the fifteenth century, and there was also a small but active Mozarabic Christian community.[25] A similar situation developed in North Africa, where Iberian Christian mercenaries had been serving in local armies since the eleventh century, and numerous merchant funduqs, one for each Christian state, began appearing in many Maghrebi cities as early as the twelfth century.[26]

These individuals were able to serve in and visit the Muslim polities because their religious freedoms were typically guaranteed. As early as 1233, Pope Gregory IX had warned the king of Morocco that he would forbid Christians from serving in his kingdom if the Muslim ruler interfered with the work of the local bishop and his friars.[27] A few years later, Innocent IV sent a letter to the kings of Tunis, Bougie, and Ceuta asking for the protection of Christian friars in their kingdoms.[28] Farther east, Egypt also tolerated its Christian minorities. Abundant sources confirm the freedom of Christians under the Mamlûk sultans.[29] Indeed, the Franciscans, whom the Muslims often saw as troublemakers, enjoyed a series of rights and privileges in Mamlûk Jerusalem from the thirteenth century onward.[30] The integral

24. For Genoese merchants, see Heers, "Le royaume de Granade."

25. Simonet, *Historia de los mozárabes*, 791–94.

26. Dufourcq, *L'Espagne Catalane*, 69–70; Alemany, "Milicias Cristianas," 133–35.

27. Mas Latrie, *Traités de paix et de commerce*, doc. 10 (May 27, 1233).

28. Ibid., doc. 14 (Oct, 25, 1246).

29. See, for example, Alarcón y Santón and Garcia de Linares, *Documentos Árabes diplomáticos*, docs. 148 and 150 (Feb. 16, 1306 and Feb. 23, 1323); Golubovich, *Biblioteca bibliografica*, 3:68–72.

30. Little, "Christians in Mamlûk Jerusalem," 214. Little concludes that

role played by Christian soldiers in the defense of some of the Maghrebi kingdoms and by Christian merchants in the Muslim economies gave Christian authorities leverage when they made demands about religious services.

These Christians required and received religious services. The bishopric of Granada had titular bishops since at least the thirteenth century, some of whom visited the kingdom and attended to their pastoral duties. It is also probable that some of the Mozarabic churches survived under the Nasrids.[31] The seventeenth-century chronicler Francisco Bermúdez de Pedraza even suggests that captives administered the church of Saint Cecilio [sic] when there was no available clergy. The Muslims allowed it as a boon to the Christian merchants and soldiers working in the kingdom.[32] Moreover, the close proximity of the Christian realms to Granada and the shifting alliances that characterized the relationship between them ensured a certain degree of autonomy and freedom for Christians living in the kingdom.[33] Christians in Morocco similarly enjoyed a church and its attendant clergy in the thirteenth century, and later Christian merchants had become accustomed to "respect, protection, and other considerations" when conducting business in the kingdom.[34]

That Muslim authorities allowed Christian merchants, soldiers, and their own Mozarabic population the right to worship does not necessarily imply that they extended this privilege to captives. Justino Antolínez de Burgos, in his *Historia eclesiástica de Granada*, written in the early years of the seventeenth century, claimed that Muslims punished those captives who

"the Mamlûks and the Muslim bureaucracy gave Christian institutions, residents, and pilgrims considerable latitude to conduct their affairs as they saw fit, as long as they acted in accordance with law and custom so that religious, social, and political equilibrium could be maintained in the city" (218).

31. Bermúdez de Pedraza, *Historia eclesiástica de Granada*, 3:29; Simonet, *Historia de los mozárabes*, 791–94; Al-'Abbadi, *El reino de Granada*, 162–63.

32. Bermúdez de Pedraza, *Historia eclesiástica de Granada*, 3:15.

33. Arié, *El reino Nasrí de Granada*, 143–45.

34. Cenival, "L'eglise chrétienne"; Alarcón y Santón and Garcia de Linares, *Documentos Árabes diplomáticos*, doc. 100 (Dec. 18, 1354).

sought to pray or otherwise show their devotion by beating to death any they found "on their knees worshipping any image or cross." Moreover, they "ripped out the tongues of those who sought to comfort Christians to stay strong in their faith."[35] The miracles associated with Santo Domingo, chronicles, diplomatic correspondence, and other archival sources offer enough scattered references of Muslims forcing their captives to convert or keeping them from devotion that one could certainly construct a case for Islamic religious intolerance toward captives. However, with many of these sources it was in the best interest of the writers to present captives as living through the worst possible conditions, either to fulfill personal agendas or to try somehow to accelerate their release. Moreover, other equally credible sources suggest that many captives enjoyed some independence when it came to their right to worship. The image that emerges is one in which the majority of Muslim masters, due to a series of economic, religious, and legal reasons, did not go out of their way to convert their charges and in some cases may have facilitated access to Christian religious services. That is not to say that forced conversions and punishments that infringed on the captives' right to worship never occurred. They did, but that seems to have been the exception and not the rule.

Christians who fell into captivity appear to have enjoyed some access to religious services, even if this access was limited and sporadic. The long history of conflict between Christians and Muslims in the Middle Ages had created ample opportunities for Christians to become imprisoned by Islamic forces and vice versa. This extensive experience had fashioned a rather elastic system under which captives received the sacraments, had access to priests, said confessions, and performed many other religious obligations outside of the traditional religious channels, all under the constraints of captivity.

35. Antolínez de Burgos, *Historia eclesiástica de Granada,* 126.

Captured priests and friars helped to ensure that other captives received pastoral care. The most famous of these was undoubtedly Pedro Pascual, the Mercedarian bishop of Jaén.[36] During his captivity from 1297 to 1300, he "exercised his office of teacher and pastor of the captives in Granada, seeking to teach and indoctrinate them, because upon his arrival in the corral of the prison ... he found in it much ignorance of the principal mysteries of the faith, and great danger of apostasy."[37] While in prison he wrote a series of books, including the *Biblia Pequeña*, which he intended to use as a teaching tool with the captives. The *Biblia* encompassed a series of questions and answers "to teach [the captives] what they ought to believe and how to answer the Muslims and Jews," who Pedro believed were trying to convert them.[38] In 1300 his Muslim captors accused him of blasphemy against the Prophet—likely true, considering his writings—and martyred him.[39] Others took his place. The proselytizing spirit that infused the Mendicant orders and other preachers after the thirteenth century, and which drove many of these men to Islamic lands to try to convert the Muslims, ensured that many wound up in prison. The ever-changing diplomatic relationship between Muslim and Christian kingdoms as well as retaliatory arrests or raids also brought a fair number of friars and priests to the slave pens.[40] Among those captives released from Egypt in 1306 were three friars. Another group freed from a Mamlûk prison in 1315 included at least two friars.[41] In subsequent years, letters of appeal from Christian chanceries were often on behalf of captured clerics and friars. In 1378 Peter the Ceremonious had to intervene on behalf of two Franciscans

36. For a brief biographical note, see Burns, *Crusader Kingdom*, 2:309.
37. Ximena Jurado, *Catálogo de los obispos*, 288–89.
38. Ibid., 289.
39. Simonet, *Historia de los mozárabes*, 786–87.
40. Little, "Christians in Mamlûk Jerusalem," 213–14.
41. Alarcón y Santón and Garcia de Linares, *Documentos Árabes diplomáticos*, doc. 148 (Feb. 16, 1306) and doc. 149 (Mar. 23, 1315).

captured in Tunis.[42] A few years later, Peter's successor, John I, asked the Mercedarians to turn over 200 florins to the Franciscans so that they could ransom two of their brothers held in captivity—unfortunately, the document does not say where.[43] And in 1397 two more Franciscans were martyred in Granada for blasphemy.[44] Priests joined friars in captivity, according to documents from the reigns of Ferdinand I and his son, Alfonso IV, among others.[45]

Members of the ransoming orders also provided religious services to the captives since they had free access to them. The conversations that they had with them, which helped the ransomers to identify those who were closest to converting and thus in greatest need of ransom, could also be used to give a few encouraging words, offer blessings, hear confessions, and assign penance. Indeed, by the sixteenth century, ransomers were under strict instructions to visit captives immediately upon their arrival and administer the sacraments.[46] Religious delegations from Christendom, such as the group of five friars that visited captives in Egypt in the early fourteenth century and was allowed to perform masses and hear confessions from captives, also saw to their spiritual needs from time to time.[47] These delegations may have been a semiregular occurrence for the Franciscans, as Salimbene de Adam, a chronicler of the order, also recalled one of his companions traveling to Egypt to comfort captives.[48] The priests attached to the local Christian communities in Islamic lands could perform similar services. The Mer-

42. ACA, C, reg. 1261:44v (Mar. 3, 1378).

43. ACA, C, reg. 1887:135v–36r (June 17, 1395), published in Sáinz de la Maza Lasoli, "Los Mercedarios," doc. 43.

44. Ramos y Loscertales, El cautiverio, doc. 25 (May 19, 1397).

45. ACA, C, reg. 2384:36r–37v (June 11, 1413); ACA, C, reg. 2596:43v–44r (Apr. 11, 1431), the latter published in Salicrú i Lluch, Documents per a la història de Granada, doc. 241.

46. Friedman, "Exercise of Religion by Spanish Captives," 25–26.

47. Golubovich, Biblioteca bibliografica, 3:68–72.

48. Salimbene de Adam, Chronicle, 314–15.

cedarians, for example, maintained a brother in Granada with the title of "chaplain of the Christian merchants" who organized the religious activities of captives.[49]

Finally, in those situations in which religious personnel were not available, the captives themselves could tend to their spiritual needs. As early as the beginning of the thirteenth century, Pope Innocent III had allowed captives to be elevated to the rank of deacon to administer religious services to their fellows.[50] The importance of finding support from other captives when it came to questions of faith should not be discounted. Innocent III obviously recognized this, and Inquisitional records from the sixteenth century suggest that he was right, as ex-captives testified that their fellow captives were the first, and sometimes only, line of defense for those men and women whose faith was wavering.[51] Consequently, captured Christians came to count on other captives as a source of strength as they comforted themselves through mutual encouragement and sympathetic advice. We only need to look at the Muslims of Valencia studied by Mark Meyerson to see the impact that a coreligious community could have in keeping captives in their native faith. Meyerson, partly following the work of Orlando Patterson, argues that the presence of Valencia's Mudejar population played a critical role in ensuring that Muslim captives did not defect to Christianity. His point is worth quoting in detail: "Granadan and Maghriban Muslim captives would have seen much that was familiar on Valencia's socioreligious landscape, since the Mudejars still constituted a society, which, in terms of ritual life and social practice, was recognizably Islamic, a society bound to western Islamdom by ties of kinship, culture and commerce. Awareness of, and contact with, the free Muslim population would have lessened the impact on the cap-

49. According to Friedman, this occurred as early as 1222 : "Exercise of Religion by Spanish Captives," 23.
50. Delaville le Roulx, *Cartulaire*, doc. 1374 (Jan. 18, 1212).
51. Bennassar, "Frontières religieuses entre Islam et Chrétienté," 71–72.

tives of being deracinated and thrust into a new and, in significant respects, hostile environment; it would have lightened the psychological burden of 'natal alienation' from lineage, community, and culture that they bore."[52]

The identity of captives, including their religious identity, was continuously under siege. They were constantly being "desocialized and depersonalized."[53] It was here that a local coreligious community could play a significant role in ensuring that captives did not convert by providing a social and religious context that allowed the captive to cling to parts of his identity. In fact, not only would the community lessen the sense of alienation, but through its "ritual life and social practices" the community would reaffirm the sense of identity in the captive. Christian captives in North Africa and Granada did not enjoy the luxury of a significant group of local coreligionists. Although free Christian merchants and mercenaries, among others, lived in these regions, these were by and large transient groups, which could not provide the same cohesion as a native contingent such as the Mudejars in Valencia. Consequently, captives were often left to rely on each other for spiritual support.

When these bonds of support were broken by defections through apostasy, the ability of all captives in that particular group to withstand the pressures of conversion could be compromised, as each individual apostate could have encouraged others to follow in his wake. In this dynamic, the work of Richard Bulliet is instructive. In his study of early converts to Islam in Iran, Bulliet determined that the conversion rate followed a familiar pattern, with the most venturesome individuals— the innovators—converting first, and the most conservative— the laggards—being the last to switch religions.[54] Applying the same model to groups of captives, it would not be farfetched to

52. Meyerson, "Slavery and Solidarity," 308; see also Meyerson, *Muslims of Valencia*, 255–59; and Patterson, *Slavery and Social Death*, ch. 2.

53. Patterson, *Slavery and Social Death*, 38.

54. "If one individual adopted a new technique [in this case, the "new tech-

suggest that these innovators posed a real threat. Their conversion and any tangible rewards gained thereby—freedom, better treatment, business opportunities, and greater access to Muslim women, among other benefits—opened the way and illuminated possibilities for those who were more ambivalent about their spiritual intentions. As more individuals converted in any one particular cohort, the bonds and networks of support that they had created among themselves slowly eroded, thereby speeding up the conversion of even more Christians. Therefore, as with most innovations, the daringness of the first group allowed their more conservative peers to convert, making the innovators the essential, and from the Christian point of view, the most dangerous, element in the conversion chain.[55]

The flow of religious personnel and spiritual support ensured that captives on the verge of apostasy often had another Christian around to drag them back from the precipice. It also meant that sacraments and confessions were not totally abandoned in captivity. Even masses were possible with some help from the Muslim masters. Yet in spite of this, there is no doubt that captives converted to Islam for a variety of reasons.

---

nique" is conversion to Islam], he might have five contacts with other potential adopters of whom perhaps three would see the superiority of the new technique and adopt it themselves. Then these three would each 'infect' with the new idea three out of five of their potential adopter contacts and so on." See Bulliet, *Conversion to Islam*, 29.

55. This is a simplified model of the diffusion of innovation theory proposed by Rogers in his *Diffusion of Innovations*. Rogers identifies five adopter categories: innovators, early adopters, early majority, late majority, and laggards. The role of the innovators was to be "gatekeepers [for] the flow of new ideas into the system." The innovators, however, were usually individuals who do not command an optimal amount of respect in a community, and this is where the early adopters come in. They do have the respect of their peers, and when they adopt an innovation, it is often a signal that the floodgates have opened and that the rest of the community will follow (see 261–66). For this argument, I am lumping the innovators and early adopters into the same group, since they play the roles of bringing the idea to the rest of the community and showing them that adopting the new innovation is a good thing.

RENEGADES AND THE ROAD
TO RELIGIOUS CONVERSION

The anxieties over captives' conversion that galvanized Aragonese society to put its collective efforts behind initiatives to free captives and to ensure that they had as much access as possible to religious services were based partly on real coercions faced by Christians in captivity. The lack of freedom and protections inherent in the sociolegal status of captives made them easy targets for masters who wanted to convert them by argument, force, or guile. The number of sources that list captives who were beaten, threatened, cajoled, enticed, or otherwise convinced to convert suggests that apostasy, although not the rule, appears to have occurred. In a recent study on captives held by the Barbary Corsairs, Robert Davis has suggested that about 4 percent of those captives renounced their faith.[56] There is no reason to think that captives in the fourteenth and fifteenth centuries converted at a much higher rate. In fact, they may have had less reason to apostatize as their living conditions, wretched though they were, were still better than those experienced by people who fell into captivity after the sixteenth century and were sent to the hellish oar banks on galleys. It would be fair to say that many captives never seriously entertained conversion. Those who did were faced by a series of contradictory reasons for and against their conversion. Before we examine those factors that prompted captives to convert, we should take a closer look at those that discouraged their abjuration.

Islam is not a proselytizing religion in the same sense as Christianity. In the Middle Ages, it lacked an organized priesthood or any tradition of preaching to Christians in order to bring them into the fold. Forced conversions were also forbidden, as the Koran declared that there "should be no compulsion in reli-

56. Davis, *Christian Slaves, Muslim Masters,* 22.

gion."[57] The missionary spirit, instead, rested on the individual believer who became the one responsible for converting nonbelievers and on more general socioeconomic forces.[58] This lack of organized mission ensured that individual experiences varied from one captive to another depending upon their masters' religious convictions. Many masters simply ignored the possibility of converting captives because of their own economic interest. For masters who wanted to ransom their captives back to Christendom and make a profit, renegades were, from an economic point of view, damaged goods.[59] The friars from the ransoming orders were ill disposed to turn over their limited funds to ransom someone who had abandoned the faith. *Alfaqueques, exeas,* and other ransomers also kept their distance from apostates, at times demanding the return of ransoms from Muslim slave owners when rescued captives turned out to be renegades.[60] After the sixteenth century, when the ransom of captives became even more important to the economy of the Barbary states, some North African rulers either actively discouraged conversions or banned them outright. Officials went so far as to punish those captives who openly expressed their wishes to convert to Islam, so fearful were they of losing the ransoms and the custom fees imposed on departing captives.[61]

Captives who converted also posed problems for Muslim officials when the time came to arrange exchanges. Islamic legal opinion expressed in the *fatwâs* opposed both the ransom and the exchange of converts.[62] These legal restraints resulted in negative consequences for Muslim captives, since Christian captives lost their value as an exchangeable commodity upon

57. Koran, 2:256.
58. Arnold, *Preaching of Islam,* 408–9.
59. López de Coca Castañer, "Institutions on the Castilian Granadan Frontier," 135; Salicrú i Lluch, "Cartes de captius cristians," 556.
60. Lagardère, *Histoire et société,* no. 1:291.
61. Friedman, *Spanish Captives,* 88–90; Friedman, "Christian Captives," 629–30.
62. Hasnaoui, "La ley islámica," 554.

accepting Islam. Especially in the frontier towns, which often arranged their own exchanges at the local level, converts greatly complicated the process of prisoner exchange. Due to the limited number of captives involved in such transactions—often two or three captives per side—any captive lost to conversion could adversely affect negotiations for both sides. Thus, when a Christian captive from Castilian Jaén converted to Islam in 1479, the mayor and city council of Muslim Colomera wrote to his native city asking "his mother and other relatives to come to Colomera so that they can convince the young man to return with them [to Jaén]." A Christian delegation, which included his father, went to persuade the young man to return to his faith, but to the dismay of all involved, he refused.[63]

Finally, it is worth noting that the decision to convert to Islam was a momentous one for captives.[64] For those who did not use conversion as a means to escape, it was a life-changing event that altered their identity and shattered the bonds that linked them to their former Christian lives.[65] In one swift stroke, the renegades gave up all that had been part of their former existence. They were no longer Christians; they gave up their religion, national identity, homes, spouses, children, parents, siblings; their former lives were further away than any frontier or ocean could separate. The rupture of personal ties, moreover, was only part of the price that renegades paid. In Christendom, as in Islam, the penalty for apostasy was death.[66] Should renegades ever return to their former homes, their lives were forfeit.

63. Carriazo, "Relaciones fronterizas," 30–31.
64. For some brief discussions on the renegades and the penalties they faced, see Bunes Ibarra, *La imagen de los musulmanes*, 184–99; Burns, "Renegades, Adventurers, and Sharp Businessmen"; Ferrer i Mallol, *Els sarraïns*, 77–82.
65. For a modern model, see Rambo, *Understanding Religious Conversion*, 53–54. Rambo notes that "conversion is painful for many because it uproots converts from their past and throws them into a new future. However exciting the new options may be, the convert may not want to give up past relationships and modes of living that are still in many ways part of his or her core identity."
66. For the Muslim punishments against apostasy, see Burns, "Renegades, Adventurers, and Sharp Businessmen," 345n8.

Nor was there any guarantee that converting to Islam would improve one's situation, as conversion was not the equivalent of manumission. Muslim tradition considered releasing a non-Muslim slave who had converted a pious act, but there was no legal requirement to do so.

Balancing these arguments against conversion was a host of pressures that captives faced and which daily pushed them to apostatize. Those captives who served in a domestic setting, which put them on the fringe of family life, felt some of these pressures. The close relationship that some domestic captives developed with their masters opened their eyes to a variety of opportunities to which they could have access as Muslims. Captives held in the royal mazmorras or by other great slaveholders were under a different set of constraints, but these settings also encouraged conversions. The physical punishments, atrocious living conditions, heavy workloads, and other harsh treatments drove many captives away from Christianity, as they hoped to receive better treatment and perhaps even manumission by converting to Islam.

Some captives converted because they felt a spiritual calling to change religions. These were the ecstatic converts who accepted Islam not because it gave them economic prosperity or freed them from the horrors of the slave pens, but because they were convinced that the path to salvation lay with the Prophet and not with Christ.[67] Many of them began to appear before the Inquisition in the sixteenth century, refusing to return to Christianity even as the black-hooded torturers of the Holy Office made their errors evident to them. Ecstatic converts may have found conversion to be relatively easy, as some Christian teachings coincided with the message entrusted to Muhammad.[68] In the late thirteenth century, the Dominican William of Tripo-

67. Bulliet, *Conversion to Islam*, 35.
68. Bennassar, "L'Europe devant l'Inquisition," 40; and Bennassar, *Los cristianos de Alá*, 494–95.

li had already highlighted the similarities between Christianity and Islam in his attempt to convert Muslims through reason. William strongly believed that the many points of connection between the two religions could serve as the "basis for the successful conversion of the Saracens."[69] What the Dominican friar was referring to is what religious scholars call "congruence"— similarities between two religions that ease the transition from one to the other—which is one of the determining factors needed for conversion to occur.[70] The points of connection between Christianity and Islam, however, flowed in both directions and just as easily served as the basis for the successful conversion of Christians. Congruence convinced some Christians that Islam, with its many parallels with Christianity, was not a completely different religion. They saw Islam as an attractive option in an age when the church was becoming increasingly divided.[71] Islam may also have gained converts because it was a more approachable religion on an intellectual level.[72]

Complementing these areas of attraction was the Christian belief that Islam was an easy religion in terms of what it required from its followers, especially by comparison to Christianity.[73] The perceived permissiveness of Islam is one that Christian theologians had also identified in the waning years of the thirteenth century and which they warned was a leading cause of conversion to Islam. Humbert of Romans and Ricoldo de Monte Croce counted themselves in this group.[74] The possibility of attaining the Muslim version of paradise while doing less work was appealing to the potential convert. Thus, one of Hum-

69. Throop, *Criticism of the Crusade*, 120–21.

70, Rambo, *Understanding Religious Conversion*, 37–38.

71. Echevarría, *Fortress of Faith*, 187. Sixteenth-century renegades also gave the compatibilities between the two religions as a reason for their conversion: Bennassar, *Los cristianos de Alá*, 494.

72. Hodgson, *Venture of Islam*, 2:535.

73. Echevarría, *Fortress of Faith*, 187.

74. Brett, *Humbert of Romans*, 178; Echevarría, *Fortress of Faith*, 187–88; Kedar, *Crusade and Mission*, 155 n60.

bert of Romans's biographers has summarized his views on Islam as a religion that "[p]ictures paradise as a place of sensuous pleasure. Mohammed encouraged lust and sanctioned polygamy, while frowning on the Christian virtues of asceticism and continence. He did not advocate self-sacrifice and mortification nor did he teach that the unjust would be punished with eternal damnation. One may accordingly conclude that the life of a Muslim is easy while the path of the Christian is difficult to follow. As a result, those reared in the culture of Islam find the religion of Christ too demanding, while all too often foolish Christians abandon truth to follow the doctrines of pleasure found in the teachings of Mohammed."[75] For the average Christian captive, the prospect of multiple wives, the end of hunger, cold, harsh work, and other mortifications, as well as the promise of an afterlife filled with "bashful, dark-eyed virgins, as chaste as the sheltered eggs of ostriches" and gardens watered by "rivers of purest water and rivers of milk for ever fresh; rivers of wine delectable to those that drink it, and rivers of clearest honey," where "they could eat therein of every fruit and receive forgiveness from their Lord," may have been difficult to resist.[76]

Regardless of these divine rewards, most renegades were not ecstatic converts. They converted for a multitude of worldly purposes, and it is clear that some incentives affected men and women differently. Leaving aside conversions undertaken to facilitate escapes, which we will return to in the epilogue, some male captives converted for the promise of economic opportunities, although these types of conversion were probably rare for captives and more common among free Christians. But for a lucky few, conversion could open the door to financial prosperity. The Florentine noble Leonardo Frescobaldi recalled that dur-

75. Brett, *Humbert of Romans*, 178; see also Munro, "Western Attitude toward Islam," 342. For medieval and early modern European concepts of the Islamic paradise, see Smith, "Old French Travel Accounts."

76. Descriptions of paradise are common in the Koran. The quotations are from surah 37:37–50 and 47:15.

ing his visit to Cairo in 1384 he had met a Venetian renegade who, as grand interpreter to the sultan, had become an affluent person. After encouraging him to return to Christianity, Frescobaldi realized that "it was a hard thing for him to leave the two wives he had [one of whom was also a renegade], and the children and the riches and the position. We had to be content with what we could get and took leave of him."[77] The Irish pilgrim Symon Semeonis encountered similar renegades made rich in the service of Muslim rulers.[78] And a captive in Tunis reneged with his freedom already assured due to the "beauty of a Moorish woman and the promises of her parents."[79] The conversion of the Franciscan Anselm de Turmeda, although himself not a captive, illuminates how Christians acquired some of their wealth upon conversion: "The sultan assigned me a daily stipend of 4 dinars . . . and gave me the daughter of Hâyy Muhammad al-Saffâr in marriage. When I took her home the day of our wedding, she gave me 100 gold dinars and a magnificent new outfit. We joined and had a son whom I named Muhammad. . . . Five months after my conversion to Islam, the sultan did me the honor of naming me director-general of the marine customs office."[80] Some of the poorer Christian captives may have seen these opportunities as reasons enough to convert, however farfetched they may have been in reality. The alternative was to stay a captive and possibly be freed one day and return to Christendom and penury.

Conversion as a road to increased economic prosperity was so gender specific, however, that it has prompted some scholars to note how much more resistant women were to conversion because these opportunities were not available to them.[81]

77. Bellorini and Hoade, *Visit to the Holy Places*, 53.
78. *Itinerarium Symonis Semeonis ab Hybernia ad Terram Sanctam*, 97–99, 103.
79. Molina, *Historia general*, 1:243.
80. Epalza, *Fray Anselm Turmeda*, 228–30.
81. Shatzmiller, "Marriage, Family, and the Faith," 237–38; Coope, "Religious and Cultural Conversion to Islam," 59–60.

Instead, female captives were subject to other pressures. Just as some male captives converted because they fell in love with Muslim women, some Christian women fell in love with Muslim men. Among these was a Castilian woman from Huelma, who converted after her capture and married a Muslim man. A visit from an alfaqueque failed to persuade her to return to Christianity. Eventually, she left her husband and ran off with another Muslim man, prompting the Muslim officials to wonder why the Christians were so interested in getting a woman of her questionable moral fiber back.[82] The relationship between marriage and conversion was a common one in Muslim societies, as Islam allowed interfaith marriage, which often led to the conversion of the non-Muslim spouse. The connection was a deep one, as laws having to do with conversion were often found in the same chapter as marriage laws in Muslim law books.[83] The interfaith marriages, however, could exist in only one combination: Muslim husband and Christian wife.[84] Children born of a union with a Muslim man also served to pressure the Christian woman to convert. Although of conflicting opinion, the different Muslim legal schools gave the father more power over the child than they gave to the mother, some even requiring that the female relatives of the father raise the child if the mother was not a Muslim (see also chapter 2).[85]

Captive children and adolescents comprised a third group that was subject to particular conversion pressures, since their religious identity was not completely developed. A series of studies on conversion suggest that it is most frequent during the teenage years when the adolescent is still trying to figure out who he or she is; they see "conversion [as] a remedy for [an] identity crisis."[86] This is not just a modern trend, as a study

82. Carriazo, "Relaciones fronterizas," 31.
83. Shatzmiller, "Marriage, Family, and the Faith," 257.
84. Ibid., 242–43.
85. Ibid., 247–48; Marmon, "Domestic Slavery," 4.
86. See Ullman, *Transformed Self,* ch. 4. For a review of the studies suggesting a link between age and conversion, see 109–10; for the quotation see 114.

of sixteenth-century renegades arrived at a similar conclusion, noting that about 50 percent of all apostates were little more than infants when they fell into captivity.[87] Christianity and Islam both explicitly recognized this vulnerability. Hence the Islamic insistence on obtaining children to fill the ranks of the slave armies—the Mamlûks and Janissaries—as children were easier to convert than adults, and the soldiers had to be Muslims. Similarly, there was a Christian preoccupation with ransoming children as quickly as possible because they were prone to convert.[88] The ease with which children and young adults converted prompted the inquisitor-general of Aragon to recommend that although the authorities should consider them apostates, they should treat them with less harshness than adult converts.[89] The case of Jean Esclavon, a twenty-one-year-old man brought before the Inquisition on charges of apostasy, although a very late example (1587), is representative of the difficult and confusing situation in which children and adolescent captives found themselves. Jean had converted to Islam after his capture, at age seven, because he did not know what to believe. "When the Turks spoke to him about their faith, he believed them and wanted to be saved with them; but on other occasions, the Christian captives in Algiers conversed with him about our holy faith, [then] the Holy Spirit would illuminate him and he believed that which they told him."[90] This case not only highlights the puzzlement of young captives, it also confirms the role played by other captives in ensuring that those who were considering apostasy did not act upon it.

Although captives converted for all the reasons listed above —ecstatic conversion, economic gain, love, children, and youthful vulnerability—the overriding reason for conversion appears

87. Bennassar, "L'Europe devant l'Inquisition," 35.
88. Arnold, *Preaching of Islam*, 150–51; Pipes, *Slave Soldiers and Islam*; Molina, *Historia general*, 1:148.
89. Eimeric, *El manual de los inquisidores*, 87.
90. Bennassar, "Frontières religieuses entre Islam et Chrétienté," 71.

to have been a desire to escape or to improve the terrible conditions in which they lived and toiled. Some captives abjured their faith when the pressures of their daily existence became too much to bear and the hope of being ransomed dimmed into darkness. These are the captives that Christian authorities often highlighted in their begging licenses and diplomatic correspondence as being on the verge of apostasy and in dire need of help from the faithful. Others converted under duress as their masters physically abused them or threatened them with violence. In spite of objections put forth by the Koran and by legal scholars to conversion by force, there is no doubt that conversion by force occurred. For instance, the mere threat of being thrown into the slave pen in Granada convinced Johan Sanchez that conversion was his only way to escape such a fate.[91] For some captives the punishments and threats were much more direct. James II of Aragon, for example, received a letter from a captive who recounted the story of how Muslims from Bougie tried to force him and other captives to abandon Christianity. The king appeared before the gathered captives and ordered them to convert to Islam; when the captives refused, he executed five of them.[92] For some, the punishments were delivered individually. Thus, a captive given a begging license by Ferdinand I had been ordered to convert or perish.[93] Amputation of an arm or other physical mutilation was another way of torturing the captive, to see if his will would break.[94] These tortures and punishments were useful tactics for those masters who actively sought to convert their captives using coercion. The captives made excellent subjects for those who sought to expand Islam by force, since the masters had total control over their lives and their futures.

The relationship between religious conversion and control

91. ACA, C, reg. 2381:69r–69v (July 16, 1414).
92. ACA, C, CR, Jaime II, 135:418 (undated).
93. ACA, C, reg. 2446:14v (Oct. 5, 1413).
94. See, for example, ACA, C, reg. 2208:9v–10r (Nov. 28, 1409); reg. 2208:81v–82r (Apr. 16, 1410); reg. 2593:67r–v (Feb. 28, 1424).

over a person's life is critical. Studies on forced religious conversions have identified seven measures that are common in coercive situations, and most of these were present in the captives' daily lives.[95] In using these coercive methods, the masters slowly eroded the captives' reality. Following the work of Elaine Scarry on torture and pain, I would suggest that sadistic masters were "unmaking" the captives' world and inflicting pain, both physical and psychological, that was "world destroying." It made that world—composed of the captives' life prior to their capture: their families, associates, nationalism, daily rhythms and, most important in this context, religious identity—cease to exist. Once that world had been unmade, the captive could not betray it—how can one betray something that does not exist? The moment religious, familial, and national betrayal stopped being an issue; that is, when the bonds to one's former life broke, conversion by coercion became a very real possibility.[96]

Those Christians who converted to Islam were known as renegades, despised and feared throughout Christian Iberia. Some of them became the bane of frontier municipalities, participating in, guiding, and even leading raids against their former coreligionists. Other acted as spies.[97] Moreover, many of them also carried the zeal of the recent religious convert, desiring to prove the sincerity of their conversions. This sincerity was often expressed through brutal attacks on their former

95. See Lofland and Skonovd, "Conversion Motifs," 381–82, for an overview. The seven measures are: (1) total control of the prisoner's round of life; (2) uncertainty of the charges against one and one's entire future; (3) isolation from the outside world; (4) torture in the form of mental and physical punishment; (5) physical debilitation achieved by a special diet; (6) personal humiliation and loss of dignity and status; (7) certainty of the captive's guilt. In the case of captives, the first six measures were present to varying degrees.

96. For a full expansion of the idea of torture, pain, and the making and unmaking of the world, see Scarry, *Body in Pain*. In using her ideas for this work, I have found chapter 1, "The Structure of Torture: The Conversion of Real Pain into the Fiction of Power," most useful.

97. See, for example, the case of the three Christian renegades jailed because it was feared that they were spies for Granada: Hinojosa Montalvo, *Textos para la historia de Alicante*, 412.

coreligionists.[98] As a result, renegades were considered even more dangerous than other Muslims. For one, they knew the landscape of the Christian kingdoms very well. As one chronicler put it in his charges against one recently killed renegade, "he had done many evils entering the lands of the Christians, since he knew the terrain from when he was a Christian."[99] In a very notable and daring raid, a renegade by the name of Fusta piloted four North African galleys against the small village of Torreblanca in Valencia in 1397.[100] Armed with local knowledge, the renegade placed the other Muslims in a position to deliver a devastating attack against the village, which ended up with many of the villagers taken captive and some of the raiders stealing the consecrated Host from the local church.

The fear and hatred of the renegades was most palpable when they were captured. Then frontier justice could be swift and terrible. Apostates were typically killed on sight and their heads and ears taken as trophies to present to local town councils, which often paid bounties for dead renegades.[101] The death of these hated enemies was a cause for celebration. When four Muslims were captured and killed in southwestern Valencia, "[t]heir heads were brought to Orihuela, and among them was recognized the head of Palomares and of another renegade, the latter a servant of the bishop. There was much rejoicing in seeing dead they who had caused so much harm and concern, and the council rewarded those who had killed them with 100 florins and letters of commendation."[102] In a similar case, when the renegade Alfonso Savando was cornered and beaten to death by a local militia that was chasing him, the town council of

98. Friedman, *Spanish Captives*, 73; Bunes Ibarra, *La imagen de los musulmanes*, 191–92.

99. Bernáldez, *Historia de los reyes católicos*, 1:151–52.

100. Ivars Cardona, *Dos creuades*, xli. For a more recent study see Díaz Borrás, *Los orígenes de la piratería islámica*, 142–94.

101. Torres Fontes, "La frontera de Granada," 195–96.

102. Bellot, *Annales de Orihuela*, 301.

Mula sent letters to its neighbors announcing the good news.[103]

These celebratory responses went beyond any sensible anger a typical Christian would have toward a person defecting to another religion. These renegades posed a genuine threat. In a practical and a military sense renegades were dangerous because of their language skills, their knowledge of mountain passes, locations of garrisons, hidden coves, and other key points in the Christian frontier defenses. To use a well-known anthropological model, the renegade posed a threat because he knew how to return to the Christian body he had left behind, get through the defenses that guarded its boundaries, and wreak havoc once inside.[104] This analogy is particularly iconic for Christianity, which used the body to represent the bounded system that was Christendom. Any individual who had the ability to function on the borders of this body and to enter it and leave it at will posed a very real threat, and measures had to be taken to limit or eliminate the menace.[105]

Along with the continual raiding and the appalling conditions under which captives lived, the religious vulnerability of captives and the danger posed by the renegades contributed to the development and strengthening of a ransoming society in the Crown of Aragon. It was under the combined pressure of all these threats that Aragonese society reacted and slowly fashioned the ransoming networks, institutions, and political and military measures that did significant good in alleviating, even if never completely solving, the problems of captivity.

---

103. Torres Fontes, "La frontera de Granada," doc. 3 (Oct. 6, 1406).

104. "The group is likened to the human body; the orifices are to be carefully guarded to prevent unlawful intrusions," in Douglas, *Natural Symbols*, viii. See also Douglas, *Purity and Danger*, 115–16, 122–24.

105. For a similar archetypal figure working on the boundaries of Christianity and Islam and the dangers she posed, see Nirenberg's reading of the prostitute in medieval Aragon: *Communities of Violence*, 127–65.

PART TWO

SAVIORS

CHAPTER 4

LIBERATING THE CAPTIVES

Family-Initiated Responses

When a Christian fell into captivity, a complex network composed of ransomers, crown and ecclesiastical officials, merchants, and sea captains was set in motion to set the captive free. Due to the myriad reasons explored in the first part of this book, the Crown of Aragon had developed one of the most elaborate ransoming systems in Christian Europe by the fourteenth century. To examine more closely how it functioned we will have to wander from the royal court to merchant houses, from the parish churches to the houses of the ransoming orders, and from the homes of ordinary Christians to the mazmorras where the captives sometimes became active participants on their own behalf. The next three chapters will explore the responses generated by the problem of captivity and show the full range of alternatives available to Aragonese captives. In this chapter, we will look at the options available to families, friends, and associates when they answered the calls for help of their loved ones and tried to initiate a ransom. Chapter 5 examines the institutional and communal responses to captivity, with a special emphasis on the role played by the crown, municipal authorities, and the ransoming orders. The last chapter in this section analyzes how families, communities, and institutions raised the large sums of money needed to secure the ransom of the captives.

"I WAS IN PRISON AND YOU CAME TO VISIT ME"

Religious and legal provisions from the earliest days of Christianity to the world of medieval Iberia gave the captive certain rights that ensured that his kin and community would make every effort to free him. The captive—or, more accurately, the prisoner—was a central figure in the world of Christian charity, reflecting the Jewish and Roman traditions that Christianity inherited. Alluding to the long years of servitude experienced by the ancient Hebrews, the Old Testament exhorted believers to have compassion for those who had fallen into slavery.[1] Moreover, "the commandment to 'ransom captives' ranked among the highest in Jewish religious law."[2] The Romans also had a long history of ransoming captured soldiers, sometimes with the help of the state.[3] Cicero, for example, in his essay on moral duties, *De Officiis*, suggested that the liberal man, who put the welfare of the state before his own personal benefit, ransomed captives from slavery.[4]

The New Testament took up the theme in the Gospel of Matthew in the parable of the Last Judgment. A Christian could expect that visiting and succoring prisoners would help bring about his or her own salvation. There was no difference between charity toward the needy and charity toward Christ himself,

1. See, for example, Deuteronomy 15:15: "And thou shalt remember that thou wast a bondman in the land of Egypt and the Lord thy God redeemed thee." Also Isaiah 58:6: "Is this not the fast that I choose: to loose the bonds of injustice, to undo the thongs of the yoke, to let the oppressed go free, and to break every yoke?" For a brief discussion see Osiek, "Ransom of Captives," 365–67.

2. Baron, *Social and Religious History of the Jews*, 1:259.

3. Levy, "*Captivus Redemptus*," 160–63.

4. Cicero, *De Officiis*, 2:63; see also 2:55. Also Dyck, *Commentary on Cicero*, 451.

and feeding the hungry, clothing the naked or, indeed, visiting the prisoner was the equivalent of feeding Christ, giving him clothes, or comforting him as he languished in prison.[5] The early church fathers promoted this view. Many of them ransomed prisoners at some point in their ecclesiastical careers. The roll call of fathers who devoted their energies to captives reads like a "Who's Who" of early Christianity: Ambrose of Milan, Augustine of Hippo, Caesarius of Arles, Cyprian of Carthage, Pope Gregory I, Pope Leo I, and Patrick of Ireland were among those who took the plight of captives into their own hands.[6] Ambrose, in a clear reference to Cicero, believed that ransoming captives was "the highest kind of liberality."[7] Cyprian had considered it an honor to his congregation that they could help ransom Christian captives.[8] And Patrick severely chastised the Irish chieftain Coroticus for reducing Christians to slavery and selling them "as to a brothel."[9] These churchmen were the first to deal with many of the issues that are the focus of this work, such as raising money, the conversion of captives, slave raiding, and the reintegration into society of former captives. The problem of captives and ransoming achieved such importance that by the time Emperor Justinian finished his codification of Ro-

5. For the development of the ransoming theme in early Christianity, see Osiek, "Ransom of Captives."

6. There is very little secondary literature on captives in the early Christian period. An excellent article by Klingshirn, "Charity and Power," concentrates on the ransoming activities of Caesarius of Arles. For the activities of other church fathers and early bishops, see the relevant primary sources. For Ambrose, see his De Officiis Ministrorum, 2:15, 21, 28, in Migne's Patrologiae Cursus Completus, vol. 16; for Augustine, see his Letter 10* in Eno, Saint Augustine, and letter 111 in Parsons, Saint Augustine, among others. See also Possideus's "Life of St. Augustine," in Hoare's Western Fathers, ch. 24, and Augustine's own Concerning the City of God, 1:14–28. For Cyprian, see letter 62 in Donna, Saint Cyprian, 199–202; for Gregory I, see letters 6:35, 7:13, and 8:38 in Schaff and Wace, Nicene and Post Nicene Fathers, 12:200, 216, and 228; for Leo the Great, see letters 159 and 166 in Schaff and Wace, Nicene and Post Nicene Fathers, 12:102–4, 108; for Patrick, see his "Epistola ad Coroticum" in Hood, St. Patrick, 35–38 and 55–59.

7. Ambrose, De Officiis, 2:15.

8. Cyprian, Letters, 49:3.

9. Patrick, "Epistola ad Coroticum," in Hood, St. Patrick, 37, 57–58.

man law between 529 and 533, imperial authorities allowed the sale or melting down of sacred vessels solely for the purpose of ransoming.[10]

Medieval Spanish legal theory placed similar emphasis on the responsibility to ransom captives. Town *fueros* and legal texts starting in the early twelfth century defined and clarified the rights and obligations owed to and by captives.[11] Numerous fueros, such as that of Cuenca, decreed that any Christian soldier captured during a battle had the right to be exchanged for captive Muslims if any were available. Then, and only then, could commanders distribute the remaining Muslim captives as part of the booty.[12] The earliest town fueros in the peninsula had also made ransoming the responsibility of the parents, which meant that only they were eligible to purchase or receive a Muslim slave whom they could exchange for their son or daughter. The obvious impracticality of this rule (what if parents were unable, unwilling, or dead?) led to changes that extended the eligibility to other family members and friends.[13] The fueros in the Cuenca-Teruel tradition even allowed sons to stand in as hostages for their captured fathers, while the father returned home to arrange the ransom.[14] The *Siete Partidas*, compiled in the late thirteenth century, maintained the onus of responsibility for ransoming on the immediate family while adding punitive clauses against neglectful relatives. It was the obligation of children to ransom their parents and of relatives to ransom one another. If not, the captive could, once released,

10. *Codex Justinianus*, 1:2:21, in *Corpus Iuris Civilis*. Ambrose of Milan was the first to provide scriptural justification for the sale of sacred vessels in his *De Officiis*, 2:28, based on the instructions given by Christ to his disciples in Matthew 10, specifically verse 9: "Provide neither gold, nor silver, nor brass in your purses."

11. For a good overview, see Brodman, "Municipal Ransoming Law"; see also Ramos y Loscertales, *El cautiverio*, 135; Powers, *Society Organized for War*, 179–81.

12. Powers, *Code of Cuenca*, 30:32–33.

13. Brodman, "Municipal Ransoming Law," 322.

14. Ibid., 324.

legally write out of his will all those who did not help him.[15] The *Partidas* even suggest that if a captive died in captivity, the king should seize his property and sell it at auction, with the funds earmarked for future ransoms, preventing those family members who had allowed the captive to die such a death to benefit from it.[16] A contemporary compilation in the Crown of Aragon, Vidal de Canellas's *In Excelsis Dei Thesauris,* had an analogous provision that disinherited sons who failed to ransom their fathers.[17]

The large number of captives and their different social and occupational backgrounds ensured that numerous institutions evolved to help their families ransom them. By the turn of the fourteenth century, families had several options at their disposal to help them liberate their loved ones and fulfill the requirements of the law. Merchants, with their ubiquitous contacts throughout the Mediterranean and well-organized networks of moneylenders, factors, and ships, offered an attractive alternative to those families who could afford them. The ransoming orders could also be asked to help. However, since these focused their efforts on liberating large numbers of captives at a time and had more rigidly scheduled ransoming missions, the help they could offer a family seeking to free a specific captive was limited. Finally, families could turn to their king or local authorities for aid, and although getting government officials to help may not have been the easiest task in the world, it was certainly worth trying, as letters from the crown or a municipal official often had successful results.

---

15. Alfonso X, *Las Siete Partidas,* II:29:3. See also Justinian's *Novella* 115:5 in the *Corpus Iuris Civilis* for the origins of this statute in Roman law. For a discussion of the impact that Justinian's legal texts had on medieval law and how they applied specifically to Spain, see Van Kleffens, *Hispanic Law,* 171–84.

16. Alfonso X, *Las Siete Partidas,* II:29:3.

17. Canellas, *Traducción aragonesa de la obra "In Excelsis Dei Thesauris,"* 6: 24:3.

THE ROLE OF THE FAMILY

When captured, the best hope that most captives had was that their family would be able to mobilize the necessary resources to set them free. The first critical step was to somehow let their loved ones know that they had been taken. Little evidence has survived to illuminate this communication process, but we can assume that messages were taken to and from captives by merchants, adventurers, mercenaries, released captives, ransomers, or any other individual who went back and forth between the captives' homes and their place of captivity.[18] We can also assume that many captives were never able to communicate their predicament to their families, leaving their kin to wonder about their fate for the rest of their lives. Once a captive had been located, the work of family members began in earnest by setting the ransoming process in motion.[19] Some took matters into their own hands and marched off to Granada or North Africa to attempt to find and ransom their relatives themselves. Many of these attempts did not end well.[20] This should not surprise us. By the fourteenth century, ransoming captives was a job increasingly handled by professionals with experience. And it was these professionals whom wiser or less daring families hired or petitioned to bring back their loved ones.

Merchants and their agents in foreign ports often acted as facilitators in the ransoming process, and some families applied to them in their time of need. Merchants played two distinctive roles in the ransoming process. Some merchants assisted captives by lending the ransom money in accordance with the wishes of the families or the captives themselves.[21] Others

18. One fascinating example is provided by Azmet d'Arandigna, a Muslim who made a living locating missing captives, ransoming them, and bringing them back to their homes. See Díaz Borrás, *El miedo,* 70.

19. For a very brief discussion of this topic, see Ramos y Loscertales, *El cautiverio,* 154.

20. Díaz Borrás, *El miedo,* 69.

21. There is a substantial bibliography on the merchants as ransomers. See,

played a more active role and brokered ransoms and exchanges, going directly to North Africa or Granada and engaging the captives' owners in the negotiations for their release. Even the crown and the ransoming orders employed their services from time to time. In 1376, for example, Peter the Ceremonious sent the Catalan merchant Pere de Manresa to Granada to negotiate the release of captives held in that kingdom.[22] And in 1397, before launching a crusade against North Africa, Martin the Humane instructed a Mallorcan merchant to ransom as many captives as he could from Tunis because he feared for their safety during the invasion.[23] The orders, whose ransomers sometimes ended up as captives themselves, employed the services of the merchants to free brothers who had fallen into captivity.[24]

Maria Teresa Ferrer i Mallol and María Dolores López Pérez have argued that some of these merchants were semiprofessional ransomers who engaged in these types of transactions with regularity.[25] López Pérez's meticulous research in Barcelona's notarial archive allows us to follow the work of two of these merchants from Barcelona, Bernat Descoll and Guillem de Fonollet. Their ransom contracts, although few in number, are sufficiently rich and diverse that when treated as a group they provide a coherent image of the merchant-ransomers. These men engaged in the trade of other goods, handling ransoming on an ad hoc basis and developing a reputation as successful ransom negotiators. With established mercantile connections in Muslim cities, they employed representatives or factors who oversaw their business affairs in these places and were point men in the ran-

---

for example, Ferrer i Mallol, "La redempció," 267–68; López Pérez, *La Corona de Aragón*, 806–12; Malausséna, "Promissio redemptionis."

22. ACA, C, reg. 1389:119v (June 17, 1376).

23. ACA, C, reg. 2167:67v–68r (Dec. 13, 1397); the incident is discussed in Ferrer i Mallol, "La redempció," 268.

24. AHPB, Bernat Nadal, *Manual*, Jan. 23, 1393–July 4, 1393, fol. 82v (June 3, 1393), published in Mitjà, "L'orde de la Mercè," doc. 7.

25. Ferrer i Mallol, "La redempció," 267; López Pérez, *La Corona de Aragón*, 811.

som negotiations.[26] Guillem de Fonollet had a factor in Bone who negotiated the ransoms of the Sicilian sailor Jacob Pisany and of Guillem Arpau, also from Sicily.[27] The four contracts linked to Bernat Descoll are even more descriptive.[28] Descoll's contracts imply that he was only the most visible member of a ransoming web whose strands extended into other sections of the ransoming networks. In two of the four contracts involving Descoll, it was another merchant, Francesc Desperer, who initially contracted him. Desperer also advanced him the money for the ransoms.[29] The silence of these agreements regarding family members suggests that Desperer was probably the initial contact for the families, acting partly as an agent to handle further negotiations but also as a moneylender who provided the cash that the captive (or his family) then owed him. Desperer presumably would hire someone such as Descoll whose organization and contacts were better suited to handle the actual ransom. The person who acted as agent on the family's behalf and the person who fronted the money were, however, not necessarily the same person, as we shall see below.

A typical contract engaged the merchant to ransom a captive from North Africa or Granada. The party acting on behalf of the captive made an advance payment, ordinarily about half the price of the ransom, and the agreement also included stipulations as to how the rest of the money would be paid. In 1394, for instance, Berenguer and Gabriel Barata concluded a contract with Pere Serra, a merchant from Barcelona, for the liberation of Anthoni Mayens. Serra had advanced the ransom money, 75

26. López Pérez, *La Corona de Aragón*, 806–12.

27. AHPB, Joan Nadal, *Manual*, Apr. 3, 1408–Sept. 20, 1408, fol. 35v (Apr. 1408) and fol. 36r (Apr. 25, 1408).

28. The four surviving contracts are AHPB, Bernat Nadal, *Manual*, Nov. 13, 1395–Apr. 12, 1396, fols. 13r–v (Dec. 4, 1395); fols. 61r–v (Feb. 24, 1396); fols. 72r–v (Mar. 8, 1396), cited in López Pérez, *La Corona de Aragón*, 809n500; AHPB, Bernat Nadal, *Manual*, Sept. 30, 1396–Mar. 14, 1397, fols. 72r–73r (Feb. 5, 1397), cited in López Pérez, *La Corona de Aragón*, 808–9n497.

29. The contracts are those dated Feb. 24, 1396 and Mar. 8, 1396.

pounds, to another merchant, Francisco Folquet, who was negotiating Mayens's ransom in Málaga. Berenguer and Gabriel Barata had already paid 40 pounds and, according to the document,
still owed 35 to Serra. They would pay the debt when Mayens
was free.[30] Sometimes, the family or its agent set a price ceiling that the merchant was not to exceed, or they encouraged
the merchant to obtain a ransom for a lesser price.[31] The contract drafted for the liberation of Pedro Fabregues, a sailor from
Poblet, obligated his warrantor to pay the ransom price even if
Fabregues died or was unfortunate enough to fall into captivity
again after the ransomer had delivered him to the agent hired
by the family to handle the affair. This contract also had a time
limit. It expired five months after signing.[32]

Merchants were also responsible for many of the exchanges
that traded Muslim captives for Christian ones.[33] Their role in
these negotiations seems to have been limited to escorting the
captives back and forth and providing the necessary transportation and assurances for both sides engaged in the exchange.
As with the ransoms, it was a job for which they were ideally
suited with their access to ships, safe houses, and networks of
contacts in the Crown of Aragon and in the Muslim kingdoms.
Without them, it is not difficult to imagine a greater share of
the ransoming duties falling on family members—a task for
which most were not equipped.

The positive results of the merchant-ransomer's work sometimes appear in the sources. Unfortunately, we often meet the

30. See AHPB, Bernat Nadal, *Manual*, Nov. 20, 1393–June 3, 1394, fol. 82v
(May 6, 1394), published in Mitjà, "L'orde de la Mercè," doc. 8; AHPB, Bernat
Nadal, *Manual*, Nov. 13, 1395–Apr. 12, 1396, fols. 72r–v; AHPB, Bernat Nadal,
Manual, Sept. 30, 1396–Mar. 14, 1397, fols. 72r–73r (Feb. 5, 1397).

31. AHPB, Bernat Nadal, *Manual*, Nov. 14, 1394–May 9, 1395, fol. 7v (Nov.
21, 1394), published in Mitjà, "L'orde de la Mercè," doc. 11; AHPB, Bernat Nadal, *Manual*, Sept. 30, 1396–Mar. 14, 1397, fols. 72r–73r (Feb. 5, 1397).

32. AHPB, Bernat Nadal, *Manual*, Nov. 14, 1394–May 9, 1395, fol. 7v (Nov.
21, 1394), published in Mitjà, "L'orde de la Mercè," doc. 11.

33. For some examples, see Díaz Borrás, *El miedo*, 68.

ex-captives as paupers and beggars, trying to raise the immense sums that they owed as a result of their captivity. Such was the case of Marc de Venecia, a Sicilian merchant who had a difficult time in captivity. According to the begging license granted to him by Martin I, his captors had severed his left hand for refusing to convert to Islam. Eventually, some Christian merchants in Tunis advanced him the sum of 60 florins, and he negotiated his release. His freedom may not have been much better than his captivity, for it is likely that he spent many of his remaining days begging through the cities and villages of Aragon and Catalonia where the alms received from people who took pity on his missing hand paid off the merchants who had rescued him.[34] Nicolás Egidy from Valencia appealed to the king on similar grounds. Merchants had ransomed him from Granada at a cost of 125 duplas that he now saw himself obligated to pay, but, lacking the financial resources, he had to beg.[35]

These stories of destitution notwithstanding, hiring a merchant to negotiate a ransom had the distinct advantage of being much quicker than any other alternative available to family members. The poor conditions in which captives lived made a speedy ransom highly desirable. The tragic images of captives living in horrid conditions and on the verge of apostasy that were common in Aragon by the fourteenth century gave further urgency to the desperate campaigns that family members waged to free their captured relatives. Any subsequent penury was a problem to be dealt with when the time came. Moreover, the speed offered by the merchants was a stark contrast to the frustrations associated with navigating the bureaucratic machine that stood between petitioner and the crown or a local government. Relative quickness of action was also an advantage that the merchants enjoyed over the ransoming orders. The

34. ACA, C, reg. 2208:81v–82r (Apr. 16, 1410).
35. ACA, C, reg. 926:54v–55r (June 10, 1374).

orders, often strapped for cash or engaged in squabbles with the crown, ecclesiastical authorities, or each other, were not able to make ransoming expeditions every year. Granada, for example, did not receive any visits from Mercedarian ransomers between 1354 and 1368 or again between 1378 and 1397, even though the Nasrid kingdom was the most common destination for the orders (see chapter 5). Places such as Algiers, Bougie, or Fez entertained ransomers with far less regularity. A captive could spend years, even decades, waiting for the next ransoming expedition to come.

The price of expedience and convenience was typically a monetary one. The contracts discussed above reveal the large number of individuals involved when a family hired a merchant. All of these intermediaries had to be paid. There was the agent whom the family contracted to handle the negotiations. There may have been someone who lent the money. The agent then had to hire the merchant who negotiated the ransom, and, in many cases, the merchant-ransomer's factor was also involved. Notaries had to draft all the contracts to assure their legality. In addition, passage on board a ship had to be paid as well as lodgings and food at any place where there was a layover. Finally, Muslim authorities imposed custom duties on departing captives, raising the total price even more.[36] For those families with the necessary financial resources, the merchants were certainly a viable alternative. Moreover, in cases in which the orders, crown, or other ecclesiastical or local officials were unable or unwilling to help, merchants were the best option left for a captive or his family, and many selected this course of action even if it drove them to poverty.

For those lacking the financial resources to negotiate a ransom using merchants, the Mercedarians and Trinitarians may have given them their best chance for freedom. The orders con-

36. López Pérez, *La Corona de Aragón*, 807–12.

cerned themselves mostly with ransoming those individuals who did not have the personal or familial resources to bring about their return unaided, and they controlled some of the most highly organized ransoming operations in the Iberian Peninsula. A host of modern scholars has studied the origins of the orders and their charitable works, leaving little new to be added to the general understanding of their work.[37] However, the role they played in specific cases, those in which the family of a particular captive contracted them, requires and rewards more attention.

The typical ransoming method of the Mercedarians and Trinitarians was to liberate as many captives as possible at once, instead of trying to free specific individuals.[38] When they exhausted their money, they sometimes petitioned loans from local Christian merchants in order to effect the release of more captives.[39] On very rare occasions, the ransomers themselves may have taken the place of Christian captives.[40] On some missions, however, the orders had specific captives targeted for liberation, typically at the request of family members or others acting on the captives' behalf.[41] In September 1391, for example, John I asked the Mercedarians to do everything in their power to ran-

37. For the Mercedarians, see the many works of Brodman, specially *Ransoming Captives*; Dossat, "Les ordres de rachat, les Mercédaires"; Ferrer i Mallol, "La redempció," 269–74; Millán Rubio, *La Orden de Nuestra Señora de la Merced*; Mitjà, "L'orde de la Mercè"; Ramos y Loscertales, *El cautiverio*, 161–70; Sainz de la Maza, "Los Mercedarios en la Corona de Aragón." For the Trinitarians, the multiple works of Cipollone are a good start. His "L'ordre de la Sainte Trinité" provides a brief summary of the ransoming activities of the order. Other works to consult include Brodman, "Trinitarian and Mercedarian Orders"; and Porres Alonso's *Libertad a los cautivos.* The latter contains a general history of the order as well as over 350 source documents.

38. Brodman, *Ransoming Captives*, 114.

39. ACA, OR, MdeH 2704:4r–v (Sept. 10, 1361); published in Sáinz de la Maza Lasoli, "Los Mercedarios," doc. 9; cited also by Brodman, *Ransoming Captives*, 114.

40. See Brodman's discussion on this topic in *Ransoming Captives*, 112–13.

41. For a very brief overview of this practice, see Sáinz de la Maza Lasoli, "Los Mercedarios," 236.

som P. ça Fortesa, who had fallen into captivity six months earlier and whose expertise on Sardinia the king urgently needed.[42] Commissioning the services of the orders to ransom individual captives was not limited to kings. On June 15, 1385, the public crier of Mallorca made his rounds advertising an upcoming Trinitarian mission to Bougie. He announced to anyone who had a relative or friend in captivity that they could deposit a sum of money with Bernat Serda, a merchant, and the friars would do all they could to ransom their loved ones.[43] Similarly, Gabriela Tapiols, whose husband languished in captivity in Bone, arranged for the Mercedarians to free him, for which she advanced them the sum of 60 pounds.[44]

Some of these targeted missions were not ransoms but exchanges. On these occasions, the ransomers took with them Muslim captives whom they traded for Christian ones.[45] This was the case in 1361 when the Mercedarians purchased a Muslim slave belonging to Pere Bosch from Barcelona for 130 pounds. They then exchanged the Muslim captive for a Christian captive held in Tunis.[46] In 1389 John I ordered the governor of Ibiza to ensure that Jaume Abello, a resident of the island, agree to sell his slave, Alar Maymo, to the Mercedarians. The friars could then exchange Alar for Antoni Scola, a resident of Tarragona who was in captivity—the document does not say where. In this case, Muslim authorities were dictating the terms of the exchange. The letter from John makes it clear that Antoni's captors would not release him under any circumstances, except in

42. ACA, C, reg. 1961:112r (Sept. 16, 1391); published in Sáinz de la Maza Lasoli, "Los Mercedarios," doc. 37.

43. Porres Alonso, *Libertad a los cautivos,* doc. 3:144 (June 15, 1385); see also Le Blevec, "Le rachat des Provençaux captifs," 164.

44. AHPB, Joan Nadal, *Libre Comú,* Apr. 28, 1417–Aug. 12, 1417, fols. 49r–v (June 17, 1417).

45. Sixto Iglesias, "Emigrantes musulmanes y cautivos," 360.

46. ACA, OR, MdeH 2703:pergamino (parchment) 3 (July 20, 1361), published and discussed by Sáinz de la Maza Lasoli, "Los Mercedarios," 238 and doc. 7.

an exchange for Alar.[47] The local government of Ibiza was already experienced in these types of negotiations. Five years earlier Peter III, the Ceremonious, had entrusted a very similar case to the governor so that he could oversee the arrangements.[48]

Many relatives and friends also turned to the royal courts and town councils for assistance. Archival documents often mention family members and associates requesting aid, highlighting their central position in the ransoming process. Those who succeeded in having their pleas heard could expect three principal forms of help. The king or the town council could make an appeal to the foreign monarch whose subjects were holding the captive. They could make grants of money from the municipal or royal coffers or, alternatively, provide a Muslim slave whom the families of Christian captives could exchange for their loved ones. Or, most typically, the king or a high-ranking royal or ecclesiastical official could grant a begging license so that the family, or even the captive (after release), could raise the ransom money.

The sovereign and his lieutenants could be expected to use personal appeals to Muslim monarchs when individuals with good political connections, merchants, and associates of the crown were in captivity.[49] The king and his officials, however, did not limit their help to their favorites, often using the influence of their offices and the power of truce agreements for less well-connected captives. Moreover, these personal appeals were almost always reserved for cases of illegally seized captives—those taken while a truce was in effect.[50] (Captives taken during times of war—de bona guerra—had to look for other forms of as-

---

47. ACA, C, reg. 1842:23v–24r (June 1, 1389); published in Sáinz de la Maza Lasoli, "Los Mercedarios," doc. 35; Millán Rubio has also translated a part of the document in *La Orden de Nuestra Señora de la Merced*, 347–48.

48. ACA, C, reg. 1290:38v (Nov. 20, 1384); cited by Ferrer Ferrer i Mallol, "La redempció," 245n48.

49. See Ramos y Loscertales, *El cautiverio*, 170–88, for an overview.

50. Díaz Borrás, "Notas sobre los primeros tiempos," 344.

sistance.) Some of the responses that have survived from Muslim monarchs attest to the effectiveness of the royal involvement. In 1324 the sultan of Fez, Utmân Ibn Abî Yûsuf, agreed to release the Christian knight D'Armengal based solely on an appeal by James II.[51] Peter III obtained similar results from a petition he made, through an envoy, to Abd al-Rahmân ibn Abî-l-Hasan of Morocco in 1354. The Muslim monarch agreed to liberate twenty-two Christian captives, a group that included certain important people *(personages importantes)*.[52] The case of Mateu Mercer and his crew provides an example of how determined and prolific in its appeals the crown could be in trying to liberate captives. Between February 1361 and October 1373, Peter wrote at least twelve letters on behalf of Mateu and his crew. Some of the missives included threats against subjects of the sultan of Tlemcen, who was holding the men.[53] In the end, however, the most important letter, the one that tells us the outcome of the affair for the majority of the crew, is missing. Mateu himself apparently found his way to freedom, only to die at the hands of the Castilians shortly thereafter.[54]

The failure to bring about a quick resolution to the Mateu

51. Alarcón y Santón and Garcia de Linares, *Documentos Árabes diplomáticos*, doc. 86 (June 16, 1324).

52. Alarcón y Santón and Garcia de Linares, *Documentos Árabes diplomáticos*, doc. 100 (Dec. 18, 1354).

53. The twelve letters include one found in ACA, C, reg. 985:58v; see Ramos y Loscertales, *El cautiverio*, 177. The other eleven are in ACA, C, reg. 1389 and are found in the following folios (the numeration given to them by Dufourcq in "Catalogue chronologique et analytique du registre 1389" is included in brackets): 28v–29r (July 10, 1361) [doc. 19]; 29r–v (Nov. 5, 1361) [doc. 20]; 30r (Feb. 24, 1362) [doc. 21]; 30v (Feb. 24, 1362) [doc. 22]; 30v (Feb. 24, 1362) [doc. 23]; 31r (Mar. 18, 1362) [doc. 25]; 35r (June 30, 1362) [doc. 34]; 66v–67r (July 13, 1366) [doc. 94]; 75r (Apr. 15, 1369) [doc. 124]; 75v–76r (Apr. 15, 1369) [doc. 125]; 106r–7v (Oct. 19, 1373) [doc. 190]. One letter also survives from the Muslim point of view: a response to Peter's appeals written by the sultan of Morocco on Nov. 11, 1362. See Alarcón y Santón and Garcia de Linares, *Documentos Árabes diplomáticos*, doc. 113.

54. The Aragonese annalist Zurita thinks that Mateu found his way to safety, but he also cites a source that claims that the Castilians executed him along with many others: *Anales de la Corona de Aragón*, 9:29; see also Ramos y Loscertales, *El cautiverio*, 177–78.

Mercer affair certainly did not deter the Crown of Aragon from using its diplomatic powers again on behalf of other captives, especially when it was at the behest of distraught family members. Peter's efforts to liberate other Christians are numerous.[55] His successors kept up the practice. John I interceded on behalf of a student and of another captive who had spent fourteen years in the corral of Granada, among others.[56] Martin I, likewise, involved himself in obtaining the freedom of Christian captives. In one noteworthy case, he wrote at least eleven letters to try to obtain the release of the son, nephew, and son-in-law of one of his subjects, Pedro Marrades, whom the sultan of Granada was holding. The king sent two of the letters to Granada: one to the sultan and the other to one of his advisors in which he asked for the outright release of the captives. An additional three letters went to Christian officials—the master of Santiago, the baile of Xativa, and the bishop of Tortosa—asking for their help in the case. He asked the baile of Xativa to intervene personally in his capacity as ambassador to the Nasrid kingdom. The Muslim aljamas of Raval and Xativa received letters asking them to contribute 200 florins of gold to the ransom. Martin sent the last four letters to the kings of Navarre and Portugal and to two Portuguese nobles asking them to help Marrades as he passed through their realms, although the letters leave unclear why he was going in that direction.[57]

Later kings were equally or more active. Ferdinand I appealed on behalf of merchants, an itinerant priest, and a por-

55. See, for example, ACA, C, reg. 1389:32r (Apr. 6, 1362); 1389:51r–52r (Sept. 18, 1365); 1389:99r–v (Aug. 20, 1373).

56. ACA, C. reg. 1874:44r (Nov. 20, 1389) and reg. 1871:167r (Mar. 11, 1389). The latter is published in Ferrer i Mallol, *La frontera amb l'Islam,* doc. 152.

57. ACA, C, reg. 2187:45v–46r, three letters dated Jan. 11, 1409, to the sultan, to his advisor, and to the master of Santiago; reg. 2187:89r–v (Feb. 26, 1409), letters to the baile of Xativa and the bishop of Tortosa; reg. 2188:9r (Feb. 26, 1409), copy of two letters sent to the aljamas; and reg. 2188:9r–10v (Feb. 26, 1409): first document is a copy of the letters of introduction sent to the kings of Navarre and Portugal; the second is the letter of introduction sent to the two Portuguese nobles, the count of Narcella (?) and the constable of Portugal.

ter in a brief reign that witnessed vigorous royal participation on behalf of captives.[58] Alfonso IV, the Magnanimous, and his queen, María, who was regent of Aragon during Alfonso's long absences in Italy, invested substantial effort in obtaining the release of Genís Joan, captured by raiders from Granada in 1414 while a truce was in effect. Two and a half years later, after efforts by the man's father had failed, the baile of Valencia took an interest in his case and asked Alfonso to intervene on his behalf. The king immediately sent a letter to Yusuf III of Granada asking for Joan's release, noting that keeping him violated the truce agreement in effect at the time. The letter apparently accomplished little, since in July 1417 Joan again became the subject of a royal appeal. This time, Queen María sent a letter to her mother, Catherine of Lancaster, regent of Castile, asking for her help in the affair. A recent peace treaty between Castile and Granada obligated the Muslim kingdom to liberate one hundred captives every year. Maria was asking her mother to make sure that Joan was one of the one hundred captives released that year because "a poor and miserable old man," who "lives in great poverty," has "pleaded with me to appeal to you on the imprisonment of his son."[59] Alfonso and María also took special interest in the release of Felip de Boïl, a noble imprisoned in Granada, and in a group of Christians held in Málaga.[60] For this last

58. ACA, C, reg. 2391:46r–v (Nov. 26, 1415); reg. 2384: 36r–v (June 11, 1413); C, CR, Fernando I, box 11:1354 (May 5, 1414); C, CR, Fernando I, box 14:1652 (Oct. 30, 1414); C, reg. 2389:92v–93r (Sept. 10, 1415). The last three all deal with the release of the porter and are published in Salicrú i Lluch, "Cartes de captius cristians," docs. 5–7.

59. The documents involved are ACA, C, CR, Alfonso IV, box 3:300 (Sept. 4, 1416), letter from the baile of Valencia to Alfonso IV; ACA, C, reg. 2391:186r (Oct. 9, 1416), letter from Alfonso to Yusuf III; ACA, C, reg. 3162:73v–74r (July 16, 1417), letter from Queen Maria to Catherine of Lancaster. All the documents are published in Salicrú i Lluch, *Documents per a la història de Granada*, docs. 2, 3, and 19.

60. Salicrú i Lluch, *El sultanat de Granada i la Corona d'Aragó*, 172–76. For documents, see ACA, C, reg. 3163:70v (Nov. 13, 1420); reg. 3163:115v–16r (Feb. 25, 1421); reg. 3108:200r (Feb. 27, 1421); reg. 2575:3r (May 24, 1424). All are published in Salicrú i Lluch, *Documents per a la història de Granada*, docs. 68,

group of captives, Alfonso took time out from the siege of Bonifacio in Corsica to write a personal appeal to Muhammad IX of
Granada.[61]

A sovereign could sweeten his appeals with incentives for
the Muslim monarchs. In the summer of 1371, Peter III wrote
to the sultan of Granada asking for the release of three captives
held in that kingdom. The men had become prisoners while they
were part of a ship's crew returning some freed Muslim captives
to Granada. The Granadans had subsequently freed all the captured men except for these last ones, and now Peter demanded their release.[62] At about the same time that Peter sent off
this letter, an unrelated missive arrived from the Nasrid kingdom asking that the king help with the release of some Muslims taken captive during a truce. The king's officials quickly
found ten of the men, whom they immediately sent to Granada,
along with a royal official.[63] Peter may have been hoping that
his promptness and generosity would send a subtle message to
the sultan encouraging him to release the men whom he was
holding. In 1376, however, in the midst of negotiations with
Granada, Peter's approach was more direct. He instructed his
ambassador in Granada, the merchant Pere de Manresa, to assure the liberation of several captives before committing to any
peace treaty.[64]

When appeals to a Muslim ruler failed, or simply to increase
the odds that an appeal would be successful, the crown used

77, 78, and 95. For the group of Christian captives, see ACA, C, reg. 3222:30r–
v, 30v, 31r, 31r (all four dated Nov. 15, 1420); and ACA, C, reg. 2570:61r (Nov.
20, 1420), all also published in Salicrú i Lluch, *Documents per a la història de
Granada*, docs. 69–73.

    61. "Dado en el sitio de Bonifacio," in ACA, C, reg. 2570:61r (Nov. 20,
1420). See also Ryder, *Alfonso the Magnanimous*, 83.

    62. ACA, C, reg. 1389:86v–87r (June 10, 1371); cf. Dufourcq, "Catalogue
chronologique et analytique du registre 1389," doc. 151.

    63. ACA, C, reg. 1389:87r–v (June 14, 1371); cf. Dufourcq, "Catalogue chro-
nologique et analytique du registre 1389," doc. 152.

    64. ACA, C, reg. 1389:122r–25r (July 9, 1376); cf. Dufourcq, "Catalogue
chronologique et analytique du registre 1389," doc. 220.

well-positioned Muslim intermediaries to plead the case on its behalf. Sending multiple letters about the same captive to different officials within the administrative hierarchy was a common tactic. The episode above in which Martin wrote eleven letters appealing for the release of Pedro Marrades's family is but one example of this approach. In that case, Martin sent messages to both the sultan and to the alcayde of Granada. The communiqué to the latter is worth quoting: "Since we very much want to recover those [captives], we affectionately ask you, who are close to the king of Granada, that you would consider helping us in this matter. We are certain that if you wanted to help us we would recover the aforementioned captives."[65] Might a loyal assistant who had the ear of the sultan, indeed, one who was in his inner circle, convince the sultan to free the captives, if the king's more formal letter to the ruler himself did not succeed? Martin's successor used similar tactics. On June 5, 1415, Ferdinand I wrote to the sultan of Granada asking for the release of a group of merchants captured during a period of truce. He followed this up with an additional letter to one of the sultan's officials.[66] And, in a move designed to test the filial devotion of the sultan of Morocco, Ferdinand sent a letter to the sultan's mother, asking her to intercede on behalf of a group of captives.[67] Ferdinand's daughter-in-law, the queen Maria, repeated this approach. In a letter asking for the release of two young boys, Maria asked the sultan's mother for her help, urging her to use her "special way" with the sultan.[68]

Royal lieutenants and town councils also made appeals on behalf of their captured citizens, albeit on a smaller scale than the crown. The bailes of Valencia and Mallorca were among the most active, reflecting the frontline position of their territories

65. ACA, C, reg. 2187:45v–46r (Jan. 11, 1409).
66. ACA, C, reg. 2387:72v–73r and 2387:73r–v (Jan. 5, 1415).
67. ACA, C, reg. 2387:121v–22r (May 30, 1415).
68. ACA, C, reg. 3170:79v (Aug. 8, 1427), published in Salicrú i Lluch, *Documents per a la història de Granada*, doc. 151.

in the Mediterranean conflict. Berenguer Mercader, the baile of Valencia, mimicking royal tactics, wrote four letters on behalf of Martín Pérez, who was in captivity in Almeria. Besides the customary letter to the sultan, Berenguer wrote letters to three officials in Almeria asking for their help.[69] The baile of Mallorca made a similar appeal to the sultan of Tunis in 1337 to ask for the release of Jaime Cinchclaus, whose "parents and friends had come before [the baile]" and told him how some Saracens had captured Jaime and taken him to Tunis.[70]

The larger cities of the realms, which had considerable international influence of their own, also intervened for the benefit of captives. Both Barcelona and Valencia used their extensive commercial networks in Granada and North Africa to help captives. Barcelona, for example, intervened on behalf of a captured ship's captain by asking its consul in Tunis to help with his release in that kingdom.[71] And Valencia appealed directly to the sultan of Bougie for the release of one of its residents imprisoned in the North African realm.[72] When negotiations with a Muslim monarch proved fruitless, a city could ask its own monarch for help. This was the case in 1412 when the city councilors of Valencia asked the crown for help in obtaining the freedom of four Valencians who had been captured in Granada.[73]

The crown and other authorities could also help family members by providing them with Muslim captives who could be exchanged for their loved ones. Exchanges had been an integral part of the redemptive process since the earliest days of the Reconquest, and to this end truces between Muslim and Christian princes typically included prisoner swaps. By the late fourteenth and early fifteenth centuries, moreover, the ascendancy of the

---

69. Salicrú i Lluch, *Documents per a la història de Granada*, docs. 374–77 (all drafted on May 21, 1451).

70. Sancho y Vicens, "Documentos sobre cautivos," doc. 3 (Jan. 28, 1337).

71. Capmany y de Monpalau, *Memorias históricas*, doc. 120 (June 18, 1326).

72. Ivars, *Dos creuades*, doc. 12 (Oct. 16, 1403).

73. Rubio Vela, *Epistolari*, 2:doc. 142 (Sept. 20, 1412).

Christian kingdoms meant that the Muslim kingdoms, Granada in particular, had to pay tribute as part of many truce agreements. The tributes usually meant yearly payments of gold and captives. It was as part of tribute payments and prisoner swaps that many of the poorer prisoners, whose families did not have the resources to ransom them, attained their freedom. Truces, however, were complex affairs that were not always seen as desirable or attainable (see chapter 5). When truces and exchanges between nations were not a possibility, families could still initiate exchanges on their own, often with the king, royal officials, or cities providing the Muslim to be traded. This was a boon to the families, because in many cases it allowed them to acquire a Muslim captive free of charge. If the king did not have any Muslim captives available, he might force a private owner to sell one of his own captives to a needy family. We have already noted how the crown ordered Jaume Abello to sell one of his captives to the Mercedarians so that they could exchange him for a Christian. But a king could also promise future captives, as was the case in 1368 when at the king's order, royal officials promised the wives of seven Mallorcans enslaved in Granada that the next seven Muslim captives who arrived on the island would be used to free their husbands.[74] Some monarchs were quite generous. Between April and July 1415, for example, Ferdinand I ordered the donation of over thirty Muslim captives to the relatives of Christians held in different Muslim cities. The recent capture of a pirate galley from Bougie had presented the king with an opportunity to be magnanimous. The grants always came with a condition, namely that if the families could not negotiate the exchanges, they would return the Muslim captives to the crown. Otherwise, the family was obligated to reimburse the king 100 florins, the estimated market value of a Muslim captive.[75]

Families would have welcomed and appreciated all the help

74. Ferrer i Mallol, "La redempció," 244.
75. ACA, C, reg. 2388:82v (Feb. 23); 92v–93r (Feb. 22); 2415:68r–70r (Apr.

that came from merchants, the orders, and their government officials. Captivity was a terrible tragedy for a family to live through, yet the help that was available in the Crown of Aragon alleviated the suffering and desperation, if only a little, as these ransoming networks provided glimmers of hope. The small triumphs that could be experienced in hearing some news from a captured loved one, finding a merchant who would loan the money for a ransom, or getting an audience with the king occurred in the midst of drawn-out anguish and distress. Besides the long separation, uncertainty, and fear of loss, captivity also drove many families to poverty. It placed others in the unenviable position of having to beg, sometimes for years, while others had to make the miserable choice of whether to give up a son as hostage to free a father or wife. In a very tangible way, the capture of a loved one brought home the ongoing Muslim-Christian conflict in a way that talk about distant crusades or preaching campaigns aimed at converting Muslims could not. Tragically, for many families, almost surely the majority of them, all their efforts would come to nothing as their son, wife, brother, or father died in captivity or converted to Islam. The sacrifices made and the central role played by the family in many of the ransom negotiations remind us that captivity afflicted not only those in the mazmorras but also those who loved them.

---

23); 71r–72v (May 4); 119v (July 30). See also Salicrú I Lluch, "Cartes de captius cristians," 575–76.

CHAPTER 5

LIBERATING THE CAPTIVES
Communal and Institutional Responses

Besides the response that captivity generated from the victims' families and close associates, there were also communal and institutional responses. Town councils, royal officials, confraternities, religious figures and, of course, the crown often took up the plight of captives on their own. Although the primary responsibility for ransoming captives rested with the family, the larger Christian community was also bound to do all in its power to bring about their release.[1] This chapter will examine the efforts of the Christian community to help captives. These activities ranged from truce agreements to retaliatory raids designed to capture Muslims or rescue prisoners and from the work of the ransoming orders to the more modest negotiations undertaken by municipalities.

---

1. For an example of this communal responsibility, see Alfonso X, *Las Siete Partidas*, II:29:2–3.

THE CROWN, ROYAL OFFICIALS, AND CITIES

Exeas and *Alfaqueques*

The crown and the municipalities had a range of options when it came to helping captives. Among the earliest ransoming institutions to emerge in Iberia were the crown-appointed ransomers. Centuries of peninsular warfare had led the kingdoms of Iberia to appoint officials who facilitated and organized the exchange of prisoners and the ransoming of captives.[2] These individuals—Jews in the early years, but almost exclusively Christian and Muslim merchants by the fourteenth century—exchanged prisoners for both sides, and the kings and sultans allowed them a freedom of movement that very few others enjoyed. The position seems to have originated as early as the beginning of the twelfth century, when there is evidence of individuals empowered to deal with the exchange of captives.[3] In 1126 these individuals merited a collective name in the *carta-puebla* (town charter) of Belchite granted by Alfonso VII of Castile: the *exeas de moros et christianos*.[4] A second title, *alfaqueque*, from the Arab word for *redeemer*, soon emerged.[5] The influential town fuero of Aragonese Teruel, granted in 1179, recognized their importance and sought to codify their rights and obligations.[6] The equally significant fuero of Castilian Cuenca echoed these provisions. Among them was the duty of the exeas to "present legal bondsmen in the

2. For overviews on the exeas and alfaqueques, see Brodman, *Ransoming Captives*, 7–8; Ferrer i Mallol, "La redempció," 262–66; López de Coca Castañer, "Institutions on the Castilian-Granadan Frontier," 137–41; Ramos y Loscertales, *El cautiverio*, 154–56; Díaz Borrás, *El miedo*, 61–72; and Torres Fontes, "Los alfaqueques castellanos."

3. Verlinden, *L'esclavage*, 1:153.

4. Torres Fontes, "Los alfaqueques castellanos," 101.

5. Verlinden says *exea* was used in the Crown of Aragon, while the Castilians used *alfaqueque*: *L'esclavage*, 1:70. Sometimes this official was called a *mostolaf*, mostly in Catalonia. Bensch, "From Prizes of War to Domestic Merchandise," 71.

6. Caruana Gómez de Barreda, *El fuero Latino de Teruel*, ch. 507.

[town] council for the fact that the *requa* [expedition] that each leads should be secure."[7] This clause obligated the exeas to pay for any damage suffered during their missions. A further stipulation called for them to be thrown from a cliff if they ever betrayed the trust of the council that appointed them.[8]

The *Siete Partidas* further clarified their status and added new qualifications to the positions: "First, they should be sincere, for from this they derive their name; second, they should be without covetousness; third, they should be as familiar with the language of the country to which they go as with their own; fourth, they should not cherish ill-will; fifth, they should be courageous; sixth, they should own property."[9] The *Partidas* also required the alfaqueques to carry always the royal standard; to travel on the most direct roads; to do everything possible to protect the dependents with whom they were traveling and their property; and to notarize a list of everything in their possession as a record in case they fell victim to brigands and thieves.[10] These regulations ensured that others could recognize them easily and that they themselves would be above suspicion should calamity befall their mission. The great importance given to the selection of the exeas and alfaqueques and the high qualifications that they had to have attest to the significance of their position. Even with all the possible pitfalls that might occur along the way and for which the alfaqueques and exeas were responsible, many coveted the position because of its money-making potential. The profit for the exeas came from, among other things, the fee that captives owed them for their redemption, that is, a tenth of the ransom price in the case of Christian captives and one gold coin, an *aureus*, for Muslim captives. The

7. Powers, *Code of Cuenca*, 41:2.

8. For more punishments that could be levied against alfaqueques, see Torres Fontes, "Los alfaqueques castellanos," 112.

9. Alfonso X, *Las Siete Partidas*, II:30:1.

10. Ibid., II:30:3.

bulk of their earnings came from more traditional mercantile transactions: the fact that they were sometimes the only individuals allowed to cross frontiers placed them in a unique position to turn tidy commercial profits.[11]

José María Ramos y Loscertales has argued that the exeas and alfaqueques served mostly at the behest of families, who made contracts with them similar to those with the merchants discussed in chapter 4. However, this seems to hold true only until the thirteenth century.[12] In the fourteenth century, the role of these officials became more fluid. They rarely appear as caravan leaders, trudging back and forth across the frontier amid trains of pack animals and recently liberated captives. Instead, in Aragon in particular, the exeas emerge as the crown's point men in handling difficult negotiations, and their duties resemble very closely those of royal envoys and ambassadors. In 1366–67, for example, a Catalan exea led an expedition to return a group of Muslim captives to Granada. The mission began well enough and even enjoyed a safe-conduct from the sultan. As soon as the ship arrived in the Nasrid kingdom with the Muslim captives, however, things started to go wrong. The authorities arrested all the Christian crewmen and the exea. Upon verifying his safe-conduct, they released the exea but kept the sailors in prison, where most of them died. Subsequent negotiations for the release of three survivors were still under way in 1372.[13] In another case, the crown sent an exea to pick up Miguel del Abat, who had spent fourteen years in captivity in Granada.[14] The same exea may have handled the negotiations for the three sailors and the release of Miguel del Abat, although

11. Dufourcq, *L'Espagne Catalane*, 76–77.

12. Ramos y Loscertales, *El cautiverio*, 156.

13. ACA, C, reg. 1389:86v–87r (June 10, 1371); 91v (July 10, 1372); 93v–94r (Oct. 7, 1372); 94r–v (Oct. 15, 1372); 94v–95r (Oct. 16, 1372); cf. Dufourcq, "Catalogue chronologique et analytique du registre 1389," docs. 151, 163, 167–69.

14. ACA, C, reg. 1871:167r (Mar. 11, 1389); published in Ferrer i Mallol, *La frontera amb l'Islam*, doc. 152.

they are seventeen years apart.[15] If this is the case, it suggests either continuity in the position or the crown's trust in certain individuals to handle difficult cases. This is confirmed by the grant given to another exea in 1450 by Alfonso IV: he appointed Manuel de Mena to the position for life to ransom Christians from Granada and Muslims from Castile and Aragon.[16]

There are numerous other examples from the late fourteenth and fifteenth centuries of merchants, ambassadors, and royal envoys negotiating for, ransoming, and escorting captives back to Christendom in the name of the crown.[17] These individuals were performing in fact, if not in name, the same duties that the exeas had done. Indeed, the merchants discussed in the previous chapter were likely performing their ransoming duties as exeas. Muslim alfaqueques and exeas were also active in Aragon in the fourteenth and fifteenth centuries. The city of Valencia, for example, often hired Jucef Xupió, a Muslim merchant, to handle its ransoms and exchanges.[18] And in 1424 Alfonso IV granted a safe-conduct to Said al-Amin, "*alfaqueque mayor* of the king of Granada," so that he could "come, go, be, and return throughout our lands."[19] The safe-conduct also applied to those who succeeded him.

Truces and Peacemaking

Crown-brokered truces were another institutional response to captivity and among the most common ways for captives to gain their freedom. There was a long history of truces and peacemaking in medieval Iberia. The conflict between Christianity

15. The name of the exea in the first case is Jacme Roig and in the second is Jayme Rois.

16. Salicrú i Lluch, *Documents per a la història de Granada,* doc. 368 (Mar. 24, 1450).

17. Among the examples, see ACA, C, reg. 1389:119v (June 17, 1376); 1389:125v (July 15, 1376); 2385:18v (Feb. 7, 1414).

18. Díaz Borrás, *El miedo,* 69.

19. ACA, C, reg. 2591:186v–87r (Dec. 30, 1424); published in Salicrú i Lluch, *Documents per a la història de Granada,* doc. 105.

and Islam was such that war was the norm and truces were negotiated to give the two sides a chance to recuperate their energies before the next invasion or raid.[20] The exchange of prisoners was a critical part of truce agreements, as Muslim law allowed the *fida'*—prisoner exchange—as a legitimate reason to conclude treaties.[21] In fact, by the late fourteenth century the truces negotiated between the Crown of Aragon and the neighboring Muslim polities were mostly for the purpose of exchanging captives.[22] Moreover, truces between Muslims and Christians in medieval Iberia were between the respective sovereigns and not their respective states. This meant that every time a king died or, as was common in the Maghrib, was overthrown, any truce agreement that was in place immediately expired and a new one had to be negotiated. These regular rounds of negotiations between Aragon and the numerous Muslim polities (see table 1 in chapter 1) created ample opportunities for captives to be released. Some truces simply appended exchanges of specific captives to the body of the document. The truce signed between Aragon and Granada in 1377 obligated Aragon to release twenty-four Muslim sailors from Almeria, while Granada liberated thirty men captured on two galleys from Mallorca and Barcelona.[23] More commonly, the truces called for the liberation of most or all of the captives in any one particular kingdom. In a five-year truce negotiated between Aragon and Bougie in 1309, the third clause stipulated that the king of Bougie would release all the Aragonese captives under his control. The king of Aragon, James II, would do the same with all the subjects of the king of Bougie he or his subjects held. The Muslims were to turn the captives over to the king's envoys, who would escort them back

20. Khadduri and Liebesny, *Origin and Development of Islamic Law,* 358–60.

21. Friedman, *Encounter between Enemies,* 34; Khadduri and Liebesny, *Origin and Development of Islamic Law,* 366.

22. López Pérez, "Las relaciones diplomáticas y commerciales," 167–68.

23. Giménez Soler, "La Corona de Aragón y Granada," 30:342–44 (May 27, 1377).

to their homeland.[24] It is unclear how effective the treaty was in liberating captives, since in 1314, when the two sides renewed the truce, there was again a clause calling for the liberation of Aragonese captives in Bougie.[25] However, this time, the negotiators relegated this provision to the latter part of the document (clause 13 out of sixteen), perhaps confirming that the earlier accord had succeeded in freeing most of the captives. A similar treaty between Aragon and Granada in 1382 committed both sides to freeing all captives that each held within six months of the signing, including the Jewish subjects of both monarchs.[26] Like the treaty with Bougie in 1309, the treaty with Granada in 1382 apparently did not succeed in liberating *all* the Aragonese captives. When the two kingdoms renewed their peace agreement in 1386, there were more than 150 captives from Catalonia, Valencia, and the Balearics in Granada.[27]

The importance of releasing captives as a critical goal of truce agreements is made evident in numerous negotiations and treaties. An embassy sent by James II to Tlemcen in 1319 serves as an excellent example. James had sent his envoys with the primary intention of gaining the release of Christians in the North African kingdom. A set of instructions to his ambassadors, however, allowed for a backup strategy. The king had empowered the embassy to negotiate a truce with Tlemcen if the Muslim king wished. The catch was that the number of captives freed would determine the length of the truce. A release of three hundred captives would mean a ten-year truce. Fifty captives, on the other hand, would bring peace for only two or three years.[28] At other times the unwillingness of one of the parties to release captives could delay agreements and intensify heated

24. Capmany y de Monpalau, *Memorias históricas,* doc. 82 (May 8, 1309).
25. Ibid., doc. 88 (Jan. 7, 1314).
26. Dufourcq, "Catalogue chronologique et analytique du registre 1389," doc. 267.
27. Canellas, *Aragón y la empresa del estrecho,* doc. 19 (June 26, 1386).
28. Masía de Ros, *La Corona de Aragón,* doc. 155 (Apr. 24, 1319). This contains both the letter to the sultan and the instructions to the ambassadors.

negotiations. In 1413 Ferdinand I refused to sign a peace treaty with Yusuf III of Granada unless the sultan released all his Christian captives. Ferdinand based his argument on a previous arrangement he had made with the Nasrids while he was regent of Castile. In that accord, Granada agreed to release three hundred captives in exchange for a truce. In the most recent agreement, the Nasrids were not as charitable. Because they were allowing the release of only eight or ten Christians, Ferdinand felt that they were insulting his royal dignity. He reasoned that if Granada had released three hundred captives when he was still an uncrowned prince (ante que nos fuessemos en la dignidat reyal), then they certainly ought to do better now that he wore the crown of "so many kingdoms." In a disappointed voice, the king admonished the sultan that he had "expected much more from him," and he finished his letter by refusing to sign any truce agreement unless Yusuf released all the captives.[29] When Ferdinand signed the truce two months later, however, he failed to secure the release of the captives that he had been so adamant about earlier.[30] Captives could also be used as leverage by one side when the other was unwilling to come to the negotiating table and suspend hostilities. In 1323 the ruler of Tlemcen sent a letter to James II agreeing to release those captives whose return James was demanding, but only if the king of Aragon would consent to a peace treaty. The sultan finished the letter in no uncertain terms: "if you refuse to do as we say . . . the negotiations between us are at an end."[31]

Beyond the immediate freedom that truces brought for many captives, they also had a very positive long-term consequence: truces gave Christian monarchs a diplomatic and moral position from which to appeal to their Muslim counterparts,

29. Ramos y Loscertales, *El cautiverio,* doc. 29 (Mar. 15, 1413).
30. Arribas Palau, *Las treguas entre Castilla y Granada,* doc. 8 (May 31, 1413) and p. 24.
31. Alarcón y Santón and Garcia de Linares, *Documentos Árabes diplomáticos,* doc. 88 (Feb. 9, 1323).

especially when captives were taken while a truce was in effect.[32] For example, the truces signed by Aragon and Granada in 1382 and in 1405 called for the immediate freedom of anyone from either realm captured while the truce obtained.[33] Treaties with other Muslim countries contained similar provisions. Thus, in 1371, when Peter III wrote to the sultan of Tlemcen, he asked for the release of one of his Mallorcan subjects solely based on the truce that existed between the two realms.[34] Some years later, Peter's son, Martin I, made a similar request using the same argument when Tunisians seized one of his compatriots during a truce.[35] During these negotiations, the king did not have to offer anything in return, as it was made clear that the Muslim ruler—or, more likely, his subjects—had broken a truce agreement, and Martin was merely asking to have that agreement enforced. Other parties negotiating on behalf of captives also used truces as the basis of their appeals. This was the case in 1403 when the city council of Valencia wrote to the sultan of Bougie seeking the liberation of one of its citizens. The Valencians reminded the sultan that he had recently signed a truce with the king of Aragon calling for the freeing of Christian captives under the control of the sultan or of his subjects. Thus, they continued, the sultan, "who was famous and renowned for his justness, should observe the conditions of said peace."[36]

Cities, towns, and regional lords also worked out local truces between themselves and the neighboring Muslim munici-

32. Muslim rulers also invoked existing truces when they asked for the liberation of their illegally seized subjects. See Alarcón y Santón and Garcia de Linares, *Documentos Árabes diplomáticos*, docs. 43 (Aug. 23, 1335), 58 (Sept. 22, 1344), 67 (Oct. 16, 1344).

33. For the truce of 1382, see ACA, C, reg. 1389: (July 29, 1382); cf. Dufourcq, "Catalogue chronologique et analytique du registre 1389," doc. 267. For the treaty of 1405, see Bofarull y Mascaró, *Colección de documentos inéditos*, 1:25–34 (May 4, 1405).

34. ACA, C, reg. 1389:90r (Sept. 25, 1371); cf. Dufourcq, "Catalogue chronologique et analytique du registre 1389," doc. 161.

35. ACA, C, reg. 2177:9r (Oct. 2, 1403).

36. Ivars Cardona, *Dos creuades*, doc. 12 (Oct. 16, 1403).

palities.[37] This process was particularly evident in Castile due to its shared land frontier with Granada and the proximity between Christian and Muslim towns.[38] Municipalities in the Aragonese Confederacy, in spite of not having a land frontier with Granada, also employed considerable efforts on diplomacy.[39] Even without a common land frontier, raiders from Aragon and Granada routinely attacked one another's territories by crossing through Castilian Murcia. These raiders were often brigands and thieves acting without the support or permission of their own sovereigns. Frontier defenders did their best to stop the intrusions and, as was the case with pirates, captured raiders faced the death penalty. Many Christian town councils even paid bounties for the heads of Muslim raiders.[40] The measures, however, provided small respite to the residents of the frontier. The Christians also suspected, sometimes with reason, that many of the Mudejar communities in southern Valencia lent aid to the raiding parties, which in turn created a sense of hostility between the Christian communities and their Muslim neighbors.[41] The hostility could extend to local officials, who then turned their power against their Muslim subjects. In 1388 John I had to order the governor of Xixona to release some Muslims who stood accused of aiding Muslim raiders. An inquiry had determined that they were innocent but the governor refused to release them, prompting the king to intervene on their behalf.[42] Murcia further complicated the situation. Besides the obvious problems created by the initial raids, Aragon was

37. Municipalities in Iberia had a long history of semiautonomy from the crown and many would have considered treaties such as these to be well within their authority; see O'Callaghan, *Medieval Spain*, 435–49.

38. Torres Fontes, "La frontera de Granada," 194–95.

39. For a brief overview, see Ferrer i Mallol, "La redempció," 249.

40. Ferrer i Mallol, *La frontera amb l'Islam*, 53–62 (for punishments) and 208–9 (for bounties); also Torres Fontes, "La frontera de Granada," 195–98.

41. See Hinojosa Montalvo, "Crevillente."

42. ACA, C, reg. 1835:19v–21r (Sept. 8, 1388) and 72v–73v (Oct. 8, 1388); published in Ferrer i Mallol, *La frontera amb l'Islam*, docs. 148–49 and discussed on p. 194.

often limited in its options to retaliate since any such attack would have to cross Castilian territory. Thus, Aragonese reprisals against Granada often brought down counterstrikes from Granada on the Murcian towns. This, in turn, led to recriminations, accusations, and increasing animosity between Murcian and Aragonese towns.[43]

As a way to resolve the problem posed by the raiders, some communities in southern Valencia negotiated their own accords with Granada. In 1391 Oriola, which bore the brunt of many of the raids, tried to reach an agreement with Muslim towns in Granada that obligated each municipality to return the other's illegally seized captives.[44] A later pact penalized the offending side 200 florins if the marauders killed anyone during an incursion.[45] More effective in dealing with attacks across the frontiers were the *hermandades* (brotherhoods) created in southern Valencia in 1394.[46] These sought to impose collective civic responsibility on the Christian towns and Muslim aljamas within the borders of Valencia, holding each accountable for the activities of raiders from their respective side.[47] Thus, if Muslim brigands captured Christians, the aljamas were responsible for paying the ransom. A similar obligation fell on the Christian communities if Christian raiders took Muslim captives.[48] Although the system favored the Christians—aljamas had to pay 2,000 sous for a captured Christian and received only 1,200 sous for a captured Muslim—and the Muslims complained about having to pay for events they could not control, the hermandades survived for

---

43. Torres Fontes, "La hermandad de moros y cristianos," 499–500.

44. Bellot, *Anales de Orihuela*, 176.

45. Ibid., 185.

46. Torres Fontes, "La hermandad de moros y cristianos," 500, gives 1399 as the starting date for the hermandades in Oriola. However, Ferrer i Mallol, working with the richer materials of the Aragonese chancery, has found a royal charter approving an hermandad in 1394. See *La frontera amb l'Islam*, 198n43 and doc. 167 (June 4, 1394).

47. Ferrer i Mallol, *La frontera amb l'Islam*, 196.

48. Torres Fontes, "La hermandad de moros y cristianos," 501–2.

over fifteen years and proved very successful.[49] Martin I praised the "great good" that had come as the result of the hermandades and lobbied for their continuance.[50] Eventually, however, the pacts that kept them going expired without much effort by either side to renew them, and the situation on the frontier deteriorated until the growing weakness of Granada in the mid-fifteenth century put an end to the problem—at least from the point of view of the Crown of Aragon.[51]

Defensive Measures

When the olive branch of diplomacy failed, the crown and other government officials had recourse to the shield and the sword to help captives or to keep their subjects from captivity. The shield came in the form of defensive fortifications, coast-watching networks, and anti-pirate patrols, while the sword unleashed its fury in *cavalgadas* (raids), privateering activity on the part of Aragonese corsairs and, in its fiercest form, in a crusade or all-out war.

Defensive measures were a common feature of frontier activity. A look at the Castilian-Granadan frontier reveals a multilayered network of fortifications anchored in frontier cities such as Seville and Jaén and buttressed with castles and towers.[52] The coastlines and the southern cities of the Crown of Aragon possessed similar strongholds.[53] A system of coast watchers and mes-

49. Ferrer i Mallol, *La frontera amb l'Islam*, 205 for the payments made by either side, 199–200 for Muslim opposition to the hermandades, and 201–2 for their success. On this last point, see Torres Fontes, "La hermandad de moros y cristianos," 502–3.

50. Ferrer i Mallol, *La frontera amb L'Islam*, doc. 225 (Dec. 14, 1403).

51. There is again disagreement between Ferrer i Mallol and Torres Fontes as to the length of time that the *hermandades* were active. Professor Ferrer i Mallol suggests that they probably lasted until the death of King Martin when the pacts to renew them were allowed to expire: *La frontera amb l'Islam*, 220. Torres Fontes suggests that opposition by Oriola kept them from being renewed beyond 1404: "La hermandad de moros y cristianos," 504–5.

52. García Fernández, "La defensa de la frontera de Granada," 40–44.

53. Ferrer i Mallol, *Organització i defensa*, chs. 5–6; for the defensive measures against pirates undertaken by Mallorca, see López Pérez, *La Corona de*

sengers augmented the mortar and brick fortifications, as towns frequently warned one another of potential danger. The Consell de Cent, the city council in Barcelona, routinely received messages from other municipalities alerting it to the presence of pirates in the waters of the realm. A warning could make its way up and down the coast, alerting cities and towns as it went, with each locale adding its name to the dispatch before it proceeded to the next destination. In 1410, to give just one example, the Consell received a missive from the councilors of Tarragona, who were passing on a message received from Tortosa, which in turn was forwarding a letter sent from Peñiscola that contained a warning issued by Valencia about a pirate raid reported from Alicante.[54] The message had traveled from one of the southernmost points in the Aragonese Confederacy to its upper reaches, and everyone in between had received the warning. More typically, the notifications came from closer afield, as was the case in 1439 when the town of Blanes, a short distance to the northeast of Barcelona, warned the Consell twice within the expanse of two months about pirates lurking off the coast.[55]

The crown and municipal governments also sponsored and helped to equip galleys and other coast-watching vessels to counter the threat posed by pirates. This was most evident in the second half of the fourteenth century, when the pirate menace was relentless, prompting coastal cities and towns to maintain their defensive systems in a constant state of alert. Barcelona, Valencia, and Mallorca led the way, arming vessels on a regular basis and capturing their fair share of pirates.[56] Some, including King

Aragón, 748–63, and for Barcelona, 763–71; for Valencia, see Díaz Borrás, *Los orígenes de la piratería islámica,* 95–100; for Sicily, see Bresc, "Course et piraterie," 752.

54. AHCB, CC, LCO, X-4, no. 1 (Dec. 9, 1410).

55. AHCB, CC, LCO, X-9, no. 186 (May 28, 1439) and no. 197 (July 4, 1439).

56. For Mallorca and Barcelona, see López Pérez, *La Corona de Aragón,* 748–63 and 763–71 respectively; for Valencia see Díaz Borrás, *Los orígenes de la piratería islámica,* 95–110; and Hinojosa Montalvo, "Piratas y corsarios," 106–8.

Martin the Humane, even argued that this defensive strategy was the best way of helping captives. Bemoaning the fact that ransoms only encouraged Muslim raiders and pirates to continue their activities, Martin suggested that all the money received by the ransoming orders should instead be spent on a fleet of ships specifically devoted to minimizing the pirate menace.[57]

For those pirates who were captured by these coast-watching patrols, the penalties were swift and harsh, as a captured Muslim pirate had little hope to expect anything but a summary execution. The city of Valencia, in particular, made extraordinary efforts to bring Muslim buccaneers to justice, routinely paying large sums of money to buy pirates from the merchants and privateers who had captured them and then putting the brigands to death.[58] As one recent scholar has noted, in the 1380s "Valencia became a center of acquisition and execution" for captured pirates.[59] This plan of action, judging from piratical activities in the fifteenth and sixteenth centuries, does not seem to have succeeded very well. For many potential pirates, the promise of quick riches offered by capturing and selling human beings outweighed the risks they faced.

The authorities, moreover, could not resolve all the piracy cases with the hangman's gibbet, and the pirate threat sometimes posed thorny predicaments for them. A letter written by the baile of Valencia to Ferdinand I in 1414 illustrates some of the problems. Among the items covered in the letter was the news that the Valencians had recently captured a group of Muslim pirates in the seas off the southern kingdom. The pirates were likely aware of their poor future prospects, knowing Valencia's well-established reputation for executing their kind. They, however, had plans for this eventuality. They offered the

57. Ferrer i Mallol, "La redempció," 274.
58. Díaz Borrás, *Los orígenes de la piratería islámica,* 100–105. In one noteworthy case, the Valencian city council paid the large sum of 900 pounds for eighteen pirates, subsequently beheading eleven of them.
59. Díaz Borrás, *Los orígenes de la piratería islámica,* 103.

Christian authorities an exchange: the thirty pirates for fifty-two Christian captives whom the pirates held. They also promised a sum in excess of 4,500 doblas to make the offer more attractive—a sum that illustrates how lucrative piracy could be.[60] This episode underscores two points. First, it suggests that pirates and other raiders might have been planning for the possibility of their capture—in this case, by holding a group of Christians whom they could exchange for themselves. Second, it highlights the dilemma faced by Christian authorities when confronted with the prospect of setting pirates free, even if captives consequently achieved their liberation. Was long-term coastal security more valuable than obtaining the freedom of fifty-two captives? In the majority of cases, the local authorities seem to have favored the former, as suggested by their tendency to execute pirates instead of trying to exchange them.

Christians on the Offensive

The crown and cities also went on the offensive from time to time. Just as Muslim pirates terrorized Christian shipping and seamen, subjects of the king of Aragon raised similar havoc in Islamic regions. Private businessmen financed many of the privateering expeditions, but the royal government and municipal councils also sanctioned raids by granting privateering licenses, the *licensias de corso*. The crown and its officials, moreover, fostered the growth of privateering by progressively decreasing the "royal share" of the booty from one-fifth in 1357 to one-fortieth by the last quarter of the fourteenth century.[61] This created "an ad-hoc naval militia" of Aragonese corsairs acting with the consent of the crown.[62] The case of Mallorca attests to the regularity with which the crown or its lieutenants *(lugartenientes)* granted the privateering licenses: between 1375 and 1419,

60. ACA, C, CR, Fernando I, box 14:1739 (Nov. 7, 1414).
61. López Pérez, *La Corona de Aragón*, 636.
62. Backman, *Decline and Fall of Medieval Sicily*, 271.

the governors of the island granted at least seventy-six licenses.[63] Each document included the names of the corsair captain and of the members of his crew, the type of ship, amount of bond and its guarantors, and a clause that noted any group or kingdom that was excepted from the aggression of the corsairs. The crown required the bond and noted exceptions as assurances that the corsairs would not rob or capture innocent people or the subjects of friendly kingdoms.[64] This did not always work, and we often find the king complaining to local governors about corsair activities that had gone too far.[65] In 1366 perhaps trying to prevent future "misunderstandings," Peter III sent a letter to the baile of Valencia outlining his restrictions for Valencian corsairs. He forbade them from attacking any ship or subject of the kingdoms of Tlemcen, Tunis, Bougie, and Morocco due to prevailing or possible truces. On the other hand, the king encouraged the corsairs to attack the ships and men of Granada with impunity because of the state of war that existed between the two kingdoms.[66]

The city councils also involved themselves in the activities of corsairs. In 1384, after years of suffering piratical attacks, the city of Valencia outfitted a galley for the dual purpose of coastal protection and raiding against the Barbary Coast.[67] When the

63. López Pérez, *La Corona de Aragón,* table 36.

64. Ibid., 594, 618–24.

65. In 1378 Peter III complained to his officials in several letters that acts by Christian pirates were violating a peace with Granada, and in 1389 John I ordered the governor of Mallorca to crack down on Christian piracy. See ACA, C, reg. 1389:138r, 138v–39r, 139v–40r, 140v–41r (the first three are dated Mar. 3, 1378 and the last one is from Mar. 8, 1378); see also Dufourcq, "Catalogue chronologique et analytique du registre 1389," docs. 244–47. For John's letter, see ACA, C, CR, Juan I, 2:121 (Oct. 1, 1389).

66. ACA, C, reg. 1389:59r (June 7, 1366); cf. Dufourcq, "Catalogue chronologique et analytique du registre 1389," doc. 80. See a similar license granted by the baile of Valencia to Miquel Segarra that allowed him to go privateering as long as he did not attack Christians, Jews, or Muslims who came from Barbary: Hinojosa Montalvo, *Textos para la historia de Alicante,* doc. 146 (Apr. 24, 1448).

67. Díaz Borrás, *Los orígenes de la piratería islámica,* 122–25; see also Hinojosa Montalvo, "Piratas y corsarios," 103–6.

raids proved to be unprofitable, the city awarded the captain a grant to compensate his losses.[68] The following year, a more impressive flotilla of three galleys descended upon the North African coast to raid and loot. Valencia again rewarded the corsairs, this time by buying the Muslim captives they had seized for the sum of 1,000 pounds.[69] Mallorca sanctioned similar expeditions, although, as noted above, the corsairs from the island proved to be a source of concern for the crown, for they consistently violated truces and attacked the vessels of friendly kingdoms.[70]

The corsair attacks served a double purpose. First, they enriched the Christians who carried them out. Under advantageous circumstances, using a ship for piracy could be more profitable than using it for legitimate commercial transactions.[71] Second, the activities of corsairs created a pool of Muslim captives who could be used in exchanges for Christians. Of course, attacks by Christian corsairs often forced Muslim rulers to apprehend Christians in their realms or launch their own piratical raids in retaliation, making the attacks a questionable tactic from the point of view of freeing captives and creating a situation in which "piracy begat more piracy."[72] These retaliatory raids, although perhaps helping some captives in the short term, served to further destabilize the frontier and increase the insecurity for those who lived there.

Land attacks against Granada also formed part of the Christian countereffort against Muslim raiders. Although the crown usually frowned on these measures because of the reprisals they generated, the requests of local officials or continued attacks on frontier municipalities sometimes forced the monarch to retali-

68. Díaz Borrás, *Los orígenes de la piratería islámica,* doc. 22 (Dec. 22, 1384).

69. Ibid., 126–27.

70. See, for example, ACA, C, reg. 1389:52v–53r (Nov. 20, 1365) and 58v (May 27, 1366); cf. Dufourcq, "Catalogue chronologique et analytique du registre 1389," docs. 67 and 78.

71. López Pérez, *La Corona de Aragón,* 818.

72. Ibid., 817.

ate against the Nasrid kingdom. In 1312 one of James II's officials in Xixona informed the king that although Muslim raiders
frequently killed and captured many Christians in the region,
he could not license any counterstrike without royal approval.[73]
While James does not appear to have retaliated in 1312, he did
order attacks against Granada in 1315 and 1316.[74] In 1393, after some years of relative peace between Aragon and Granada,
maintained by truce agreements, a lapse in the last pact gave
John I an opening to launch a raid into Granada. In the spring of
that year, over the course of twenty days, John granted licenses
for two small Christian expeditions. Both licenses pointed to the
problem of captives as the motivating factor behind each raid.
On April 21, John allowed Joan de Castre to lead a party into
Muslim territory to capture Muslims whom the raiders could
sell or exchange for Christian captives imprisoned in Granada.[75]
A fortnight later, the king accorded a similar license to Antoni Baró due to the trials and tribulations that Christian captives
were suffering in Muslim lands.[76] Legal and illegal raids mounted by frontier municipalities, such as Oriola, augmented those
sanctioned by the crown. As with the activities of the pirates
and corsairs, however, raiding parties did more to undermine the
stability of the frontier and to create animosity between Christians and Muslims than to ameliorate the fate of captives.

Captives also played a crucial role when the crown sought
to launch more grandiose military campaigns. Whether the intent was to help captives or to achieve another end entirely,
Christian authorities often pointed to their plight as a justify-
ing factor in their wars or crusades against their Muslim neighbors. James II invoked this concern when he was trying to con-

73. Ferrer i Mallol, *La frontera amb l'Islam*, doc. 40 (Apr. 2, 1312).
74. Ibid., 108–9.
75. ACA, C, reg. 1884:19r–v (Apr. 21, 1393); published in Ferrer i Mallol, *La frontera amb l'Islam*, doc. 162.
76. ACA, C, reg. 1882:197v–98r (May 8, 1393); published in Ferrer i Mallol, *La frontera amb l'Islam*, doc. 163.

vince the papacy, preoccupied with launching a crusade to the east, to support the Castilian-Aragonese crusade against Granada in 1309.[77] He informed the pontiff that in constant invasions and raids, the Muslims had captured an "infinite" number of men and women and led them into captivity, forcing them to "relinquish our [religious] laws and accept their sect." They then "took the women for concubines and had many children with them."[78] James may have had a genuine concern for the captives, perhaps believing that a crusade was the strategy that would help them the most—he even asked the papacy to divert all of the Mercedarian and Trinitarian funds to the royal coffers so that he could better finance his campaign against Granada.[79] On the other hand, a cynical interpretation of James's actions would conclude that he was only using the captives' plight to generate support and funds for his territorial ambitions, but it would miss the point that captives were an integral part of Aragonese foreign policy; the desire to set them free commingling with other necessities and objectives. Ultimately, captives were one of many reasons that compelled the Aragonese monarch to move against his onetime ally the sultan of Granada when he did.[80] The crusade, which began with high hopes, ended in almost total failure, as only Gibraltar fell to the Christian armies.[81] In 1340 Peter III also conjured up the image of captives renouncing their faith while in Muslim servitude to convince Benedict XII to grant crusading indulgences for the coming war against Morocco.[82] And again the pope authorized a crusade, which eventually ended in a Christian victory at the battle of

77. See Housley, "Pope Clement V and the Crusades of 1309–10."
78. Giménez Soler, "La Corona de Aragón y Granada," 22:353 and n1.
79. Brodman, "Ransomers or Royal Agents," 248.
80. Giménez Soler, "La Corona de Aragón y Granada," 22:341.
81. Although the capture of Gibraltar was significant, particularly in giving the Christians control over the straits, the crusade, which combined the might of Aragon and Castile, had set out to conquer Granada completely, and the two Christian sovereigns had already agreed to its partition. See Ferrer i Mallol, *La frontera amb l'Islam*, 99–101.
82. Canellas, *Aragón y la empresa del estrecho*, doc. 9 (1340).

Salado. The immediate impact of this battle on captives is difficult to measure. However, there is little doubt that a Moroccan victory would have left hundreds if not thousands of Christian soldiers in captivity and opened up a longer stretch of the frontier to the depredations of raiders.

Crusades and captives would converge again in 1397. Late in the summer, the Valencian village of Torreblanca was the site of a celebration to welcome a new priest. Visitors and guests had come from neighboring communities to share in the festivities and to add their voices in greeting the new cleric. As Torreblanca rejoiced, off the coast, four North African galleys prepared to unleash their pirates on the unsuspecting festival. Torreblanca offered a tempting target, filled with visitors and caught up in the spirit of the celebration. The attack was devastating. The pirates captured 108 people and ravaged the town. In the midst of the assault, they broke into the local church, vandalized it, and removed the Host kept inside. With this act, the pirates had literally taken Christ captive, prompting a swift and decisive Valencian reaction.[83] In a matter of days, the governor appeared before the Consell bent on a plan of ambitious retaliation. He wanted to build a fleet of five galleys, five galliots, and additional supply ships to mount a mortal strike against the pirates of Barbary. The pope approved the expedition by granting a crusading bull and corresponding indulgences for the participants.[84] The crown also endorsed the enterprise, although it provided very little in the way of material aid.[85]

In the meantime, word had spread that a Jew had given

83. The capture of the Host was not an isolated incident. In 1454 the elders of Valencia wrote a letter to the bishop in which they listed, among other transgressions committed by Muslim raiders, the theft of several consecrated forms. See Rubio Vela, *Epistolari*, 2:doc. 41 (Mar. 8, 1454).

84. For the crusading bull issued by Benedict XIII, see Ivars Cardona, *Dos creuades*, doc. 25 (Mar. 1, 1398).

85. See Díaz Borrás, *Los orígenes de la piratería islámica*, 155–57, for the lukewarm support of Martin I, for whom the crusade was of secondary importance in comparison to his ongoing dispute with the count of Foix. The king's intention to attack the count also kept Barcelona from participating in the cru-

the Muslim pirates intelligence on the town, allowing them to mount the raid when it would achieve optimal damage. To add further fuel to the fires of vengeance that burned within the Christian populace, a second rumor surfaced that a Christian renegade had led the raid. In early 1398 Mallorca, which had also suffered from the same raid, lent its support to the expedition. Mallorcan help and that of other cities and towns in the Crown of Aragon boosted the number of ships to seventy.[86] By late summer the expedition was ready to go.

The leaders chose the village of Tedeliz, which was under the suzerainty of the sultan of Tunis, because it was one of the most active staging points for Muslim piracy in the western Mediterranean. Almost a year to the day after the assault on Torreblanca, the Christian fleet, with its seventy-five hundred crusaders, fell on the coastal community and sacked and pillaged it for almost two days. The plundering even extended into the funduqs of Christian merchants in the city, where the crusaders looted several warehouses and storage facilities. The expedition had limited success, costing little in Christian casualties and reaping a bountiful cache of Muslim captives and goods, but failing to recover the precious Host. Its results inspired a second armada one year later. This one, however, was a total failure, owing to the well-prepared defenses that the Muslims had set in place.[87]

A few points about this event are worth considering beyond the basic facts. Valencia had been suffering repeated incursions by pirates for most of the previous two decades and had never responded with the resolution that it did in 1397. Mounting an expedition such as this one required vast sums of money,

---

sade since it could not meet royal demands for ships and take part in the expedition at the same time.

86. For an example of one local response, see Martínez Ortiz,"Gentes de Teruel." For a breakdown on the naval expedition, see Díaz Borrás, *Los orígenes de la piratería islámica,* 182.

87. For full descriptions of the crusades, see Cardona, *Dos creuades;* and Díaz Borrás's critique and reevaluation of Cardona's work in *Los orígenes de la piratería islámica,* 142–94.

manpower, and organization, which the municipal government could never manage on its own. A recent work on the topic has argued that Valencia had wanted to launch such a strike against the pirates for a long time, but the circumstances had never favored it.[88] This was not an impetuous reaction by the authorities to another attack by Muslim pirates, but one that had years of planning behind it and had never materialized due to a lack of public support. The captivity of so many Christians in a single raid, and especially the capture of the Host, had been the turning point in securing popular support. In fact, the people clamored for vengeance. It was during this period of intense emotional outpouring that the city's leaders saw their chance to move against the pirates. The proponents of the expedition had been able to tap into a long tradition of Christian society aiding captives and of launching crusades to redeem them. In this case, the captured Host added a highly charged symbolic element to the enterprise. The crusaders were redeeming the Redeemer. Indeed, how could they face their Judge on the Day of Reckoning and answer the reproach "I was in prison and you did *not* come to visit me?" All the elements necessary for the holy war were in place, and at its center was the resolve to liberate the captive men, women, children, and Christ from the hands of the infidels. Spiritual enthusiasm played a much lesser role in the second campaign, which was little more than a plundering expedition born out of the success of the first attack. By this point, the crown had a diplomatic initiative in place to recover the captured Host. It appears to have failed, and like many other captives, the Host of Torreblanca never returned home.

RANSOMING ORDERS

The problem of captivity stimulated not only secular but also ecclesiastical responses. Leading the church's effort to re-

88. Díaz Borrás, *Los orígenes de la piratería islámica*, 152–54.

deem captives were specialized orders founded for the sole purpose of ransoming Christians. The origins of these ransoming
orders date back to the military orders that thrived in Spain and
the Levant in the twelfth century. It was one of these orders,
the Knights of Santiago, which first "attempted the systematic
liberation of non-members" at the encouragement of the king
of Castile, Alfonso VIII (r. 1158–1214).[89] In 1180 Alfonso donated a hospital in Toledo to the order "to serve all Christian captives, not just those affiliated with Santiago itself."[90] In Aragon,
the Hospital of the Holy Redeemer, associated with the military Order of Mountjoy, served a similar purpose.[91] Although
the ransoming work of Santiago grew to include nine hospitals by 1227, its duties were slowly taken over by two new orders founded specifically to handle the problem of captivity: the
Trinitarians and the Mercedarians.[92]

The battle of Hattin in 1187 was a major turning point for
Christendom. Saladin's victory outside of Jerusalem led to the
recapture of the city by Muslim forces—after almost ninety
years under Christian control—and to a staggering number of
Christian captives in the crusader states. Indeed, the disaster at
Hattin was likely responsible for the foundation of the French
Trinitarian Order a decade later in 1198.[93] Although the Trinitarians were founded in response to events in the Levant, it soon
became obvious that the order would also become involved in
ransoming captives in Iberia, and it would be in Iberia, particularly in Castile, where the order would enjoy its greatest suc-

89. Brodman, "Military Redemptionism," 24–25.
90. Ibid., 25.
91. Ibid.; Ramos y Loscertales, *El cautiverio*, 156–61; for a good overview of
the Order of Mountjoy, see Forey's "Order of Mountjoy."
92. Other military orders were also active in the ransoming process, but
they mostly limited their activities to ransoming for profit, as opposed to ransoming for charity. See Delaville le Roulx, *Cartulaire*, docs. 1410 (May 16, 1212),
1434 (Feb. 1215), and 1861 (May 8, 1227) for some representative examples of
the ransoming work conducted by the Knights Hospitallers. For a more nuanced
study of the ransoming activities of the military orders, see Forey, "Military Orders and the Ransoming of Captives."
93. Friedman, *Encounter between Enemies*, 87.

cess. By 1201 it had a house in Lleida, to the east of Barcelona, and by 1207 additional houses had been established in Toledo and Burgos.[94] The Mercedarians were founded a couple of decades later (1235) in Barcelona as a Catalan order and also with the express goal of ransoming captives.[95]

The thirteenth century was a time of growth and achievement as the orders acquired property, coherence, and popular support. The panegyrics written about their early years recount exemplary successes as Mercedarian and Trinitarian brothers swept through the slave pens of the Muslim kingdoms and lifted the dwellers from their tragic captivity. Hagiographers credited Pere Nolasc, the founder of the Mercedarians, with no fewer than fourteen hundred ransoms. Other friars suffered painful martyrdom as they strove to complete their appointed ransoming duties.[96] Although the degree of their accomplishments is questionable, there is no doubt that the orders did do a great deal of ransoming during this first century.

The fourteenth century was more turbulent, as internal discord, conflicts with the crown, and mutual competition severely limited the orders' effectiveness. The Mercedarians, for example, underwent a total reorganization in the early part of the century by which the clerical arm wrested power away from the lay brothers, who had, until then, controlled the mastership of the order as well as many of the local chapters.[97] The Black Death, in 1348, further debilitated both orders by killing many of the brothers and, perhaps more damaging, many of the benefactors. Four Mercedarian houses disappeared around this time, presumably from lack of members and secular support.[98] The death of many of the brothers in the plague also led to a breakdown in discipline and leadership, as unfit candidates assumed the top

94. Porres Alonso, *Libertad a los cautivos*, 1:106–7.
95. Brodman, *Ransoming Captives*, 16–17.
96. Ibid., 108.
97. Ibid., 69–76.
98. Vásquez Núñez, *Manual de historia de la Orden*, 1:229.

positions in many of the local chapters. Their incompetence—and, at times, open delinquency—led to the loss or theft of property, rents, and alms.[99] The order reached its nadir in the 1380s. In 1382 the king chastised the order for misappropriating the alms given to it for ransoms and, consequently, failing to mount a ransoming expedition in three years.[100] More aspersions were cast on the order in 1386 when the sovereign ordered the governor of Valencia to investigate the local Mercedarians, who, "[i]n the middle of the day, while the men are working at their labors and [doing] other things, and absent from their homes . . . , enter the homes of said men and commit adultery with their wives and do not hesitate to commit many other great crimes."[101] By 1389 these accusations were being made in public at the order's own general chapter.[102] The transgressions led to increased dissatisfaction and open aggression, and attacks against Mercedarian brothers and possessions mounted as the century progressed.[103]

Equally damaging were the continued conflicts between the two orders over the collection of alms and testamentary bequests. Scandalous scenes were played out in the streets and churches of the realms as brothers from one order forced members of the other to hand over their collection of alms and tipped over one another's begging bowls, presumably alienating many prospective donors.[104] A vacillating crown, which banned an order one year, only to welcome it back the following, further complicated the situation. In Aragon, for example, royal preference for the Mercedarians was not enough to impose an outright ban on Trinitarian begging, for the latter had the full approval of the papacy and the king found himself backtrack-

99. Sáinz de la Maza Lasoli, "Los Mercedarios," 239–40.

100. ACA, C, reg. 1274:51v–52r (Apr. 30, 1382); published in Sáinz de la Maza Lasoli, "Los Mercedarios," doc. 28.

101. Sáinz de la Maza Lasoli, "Los Mercedarios," doc. 32 (July 30, 1386).

102. Taylor, *Structures of Reform*, 49–52.

103. Sáinz de la Maza Lasoli, "Los Mercedarios," 241–43.

104. Porres Alonso, *Libertad a los cautivos*, doc. 3:40 (Oct. 12, 1382).

ing each time he tried to restrict their activities.[105] Nonetheless, the Brothers of Merced tried at different times to prevent the Trinitarians from receiving alms or inheritances, usually claiming that they had absolute right to the alms given for captives in Aragon due to their unique relationship with the crown.[106] In 1477 the Mercedarians succeeded in gaining a monopoly over alms and bequests in Aragon, in effect putting an end to the activities of the Trinitarians in that kingdom.[107] The Order of the Trinity fared somewhat better in Castile, where it fought the Mercedarians to a stalemate: the orders split the money given by the faithful for the redemption of captives.[108]

When the orders were able to fulfill their mission, they could be very effective ransomers. Their skills as fund-raisers ensured that they could liberate captives en masse, without separating the rich from the poor and the favored from those without political connections. They often represented the best hope for needy captives whose families could not afford to pay large ransoms. Captives whose whereabouts were unknown back home and whose families could not initiate any ransom for lack of information presumably also viewed the orders as their best means of salvation. Providing hope to those who had none may have been the orders' single greatest contribution to the captives.

A ransoming expedition usually began in the orders' general chapter. The Mercedarians held their meeting at the beginning of May on the feast of the Holy Cross.[109] The Trinitarians

105. Sáinz de la Maza Lasoli, "Los Mercedarios," 230.
106. The Mercedarians claimed that James I's central role in the foundation of the order gave them a special privilege with the Aragonese Confederacy: Porres Alonso, *Libertad a los cautivos*, 1:163–64.
107. Ibid., 1:165.
108. The Trinitarians did much better in their home country of France, where they received the lion's share of funds earmarked for captives. For an overview of the struggle between the two orders, see ibid., 1:161–73, 277–81, with a brief summary on 172–73; see also Sáinz de la Maza Lasoli, "Los Mercedarios," 228–31.
109. Brodman, *Ransoming Captives*, 128.

held theirs at roughly the same time, as they gathered on the fourth Sunday after Easter.[110] With all the brothers assembled, the orders organized their ransoming expedition for the year and named the ransomers, who usually came from the higher ranks—commanders or priors. Two ransomers were the norm, but one or three brothers going on an expedition was not unheard of.[111] Through most of the fourteenth century, Mercedarian expeditions usually departed very soon after the general chapter, as attested by letters of introduction written by the royal chancery on their behalf. These were often dated from late May to June.[112] In the fifteenth century, the trend was toward departures in the late summer or fall, perhaps to time them with the winding down of piracy, which hit its high point during the summer months.[113] Not only would the ransomers arrive in Granada and North Africa when the slave corrals were at their fullest, they also avoided the pirates themselves, who could destroy an expedition before it was able to carry out its duty. In 1423, for example, Christian pirates from Marseilles attacked a ship carrying two Mercedarian ransomers and their gold on the way to the North African city of Bone. The buccaneers took the two friars to their hideout, where they robbed them and then sent them on their way half naked. The total

110. Gross, *Trinitarian's Rule of Life*, 32 (rule of 1267). The Trinitarians had confirmed two previous rules, 1198 and 1217, which called for the general chapter to be held on the Octave of Pentecost in the late spring.

111. "The master of the order in our province of Aragon has ordered [the following brothers] to go to your lands and kingdoms: Brother Michael d'Othion, commander of Pamplona, Brother Bernat Esmar, commander of Agramunt, and Brother Joan Gras, of the house of Tolosa, bearers of this letter"; letter from Peter III of Aragon introducing the ransoming expedition to Muhammad V of Granada, in ACA, C, reg. 1389:7r–v (May 20, 1368). See also Brodman, *Ransoming Captives*, 108–9.

112. See, for example, Ribera, *Real patronado*, 564 (May 18, 1342); ACA, C, reg. 555:112v–13r (May 22, 1349); ACA, C, reg. 1389: 7r–v (May 20, 1368); ACA, C, reg. 1389:97r (June 20, 1373).

113. See, for example, Ribera, *Real patronado*, 154 (Nov. 23, 1395); ACA, OR, MdeH 2703:1r–v (Nov. 26, 1412); ACA, C, reg. 2577:44v (Sept. 15, 1427), published in Salicrú i Lluch, *Documents per a la historia de Granada*, doc. 160; Ribera, *Real patronado*, 73 (Aug. 8, 1437).

failure of the expedition led many of the donors who had contributed to the ransoming effort to demand the return of their
money. The Mercedarians resorted to a loan to pay off the donors, damaging the prospect of future expeditions.[114] There is no
other confirmed mission until 1427.[115]

The orders did most of their ransoming in the large Muslim
cities of Granada and North Africa: Algiers, Bone, Bougie, Málaga, Granada, and Tunis. Unlike the legends woven by some of
the historians of the orders, who often numbered the freed captives in the hundreds, archival sources suggest ransoms that
were more modest.[116] The Mercedarians, for example, ransomed
12 captives from Bone in 1366.[117] In 1388 two other friars ransomed "38 captives out of the enormous multitude of Christians who are held in the city of Bougie in chains . . . and who,
in said ransom, spent 3,840 doblas of gold."[118] Between 1443 and
1445, three small expeditions ransomed a total of 37 captives.[119]
And in 1478 they liberated 56 captives from Granada.[120] The
only time the sources indicate that they exceeded these humble
figures was in 1462, when they ransomed 186 captives.[121] The
Trinitarians seem to have fared slightly better. Between 1450
and 1454 they ransomed 84 Castilians from Granada. A very
successful expedition, also from Castile, in 1462 yielded 110
captives.[122] Unfortunately, the archival evidence that relates to
Trinitarian ransoming expeditions launched from the Crown of
Aragon is capriciously ambiguous concerning number of cap-

114. Ribera, *Real patronado*, 77.
115. ACA, C, reg. 2577:44v (Sept. 15, 1427); published in Salicrú i Lluch,
Documents per a la historia de Granada, doc. 160.
116. As an excellent example of these larger figures, see table 5 in Ferrer i
Mallol, "La redempció."
117. ACA, OR, MdeH 2703, no. 4 (July 8, 1366); published in Sáinz de la
Maza Lasoli, "Los Mercedarios" doc. 13.
118. Millán Rubio, *La Orden de Nuestra Señora de la Merced*, 344.
119. ACA, OR, MdeH 2703:14r–14v.
120. Arié, *El reino Nasrí de Granada*, 139.
121. Ibid.
122. Porres Alonso, *Libertad a los cautivos*, doc. 2:69 (Nov. 23, 1462).

tives ransomed.[123] The seemingly greater success of the Trinitarians may be explained by two factors: they did the bulk of their begging in the larger and richer kingdom of Castile, and they also concentrated their ransoming on the more numerous Castilian captives.

After freeing the captives, the Mercedarian and Trinitarian brothers began the long trip home. Before leaving the Muslim kingdoms, they had to pay "innumerable gavels and taxes" that served to further increase the ransom price.[124] Since the orders did not charge individual captives for their ransoms, they had to devise other ways of filling their coffers to support their massive expenditures. (For fuller details on the financing of a mission, see chapter 6.) Consequently, the raising of funds for the next expedition typically began before the current one left the Maghrib or Granada. Before leaving, the friars made the released captives "swear an oath and do homage to the master."[125] In exchange for their release, the captives promised to serve the orders for six months to one year and help the friars beg for alms. The captives became tangible centerpieces that testified to the orders' successes and the merit of their work before prospective donors.

One of the most descriptive of these contracts survives in the Archive of the Crown of Aragon, written on parchment and dated from 1366.[126] The document begins with a long section in Latin in which the baile of Mallorca explains how the two ransomers had come before him with a sheet of paper and asked him to include the contract in the book of the curia and to have it read by the notary in public. The text then shifts to Catalan and the voice becomes that of the captives as they testify

123. See, for example, ibid., doc. 3:35 (May 13, 1371), "plures captivos christianos," or doc. 3:83 (Feb. 5, 1444), "christianos a manibus et posse infidelium agarenorum."

124. Millán Rubio, *La Orden de Nuestra Señora de la Merced,* 344.

125. "Mercedarian Constitution," ch. 21; published in Brodman, *Ransoming Captives,* app. B.

126. ACA, OR, MdeH 2703, no. 4 (July 8, 1366).

to their willingness to enter into the agreement. The captives identify themselves by name and provenance, "I, Francesc Goday from the city of Barcelona, and I, Francesc Bisern, from the city of Mallorca, and I, Domingo Ferrer and I, Johan Lanssol, from the city of Tortosa," and so on. They continue by praising the efforts of the ransomers who had "come to Barbary and had bought, ransomed, and brought out of captivity from the power of the Saracens . . . the above named [captives]." The captives recognize the debt they owe to the order and proceed to bind themselves to their ransomers: "we wish to be truly obedient to God and to the said order, and to you sirs, we promise to follow and serve . . . on travels for six months . . . and to begin counting those six months the first day that we are placed on land, either in Catalonia or in the kingdom of Valencia." The captives then took an oath in the name of "God and the Holy Gospels" that they would abide by their agreement or bear the burden of being "liars and traitors." The document concludes with a list of Christians who witnessed it in North Africa, including a ship captain (perhaps from the vessel that brought the ransomers and the captives to Mallorca) and the merchant who drafted the contract. Such legalistic requirements were a necessity since some captives, once freed, went back on their obligations to the orders and deprived the ransomers of their most valuable pieces of propaganda.

Captivity was a wide-ranging social problem that engaged the efforts of the Crown of Aragon, municipal councils, and other institutions. The comprehensive approach that evolved to free Christian captives meant that captivity touched most people living in the Aragonese confederacy at one time or another. At no point was this more true than when captives or those acting on their behalf spilled out into city streets to beg for money that would pay for their ransoms and to tell their stories to anyone who would listen. It was in this act of giving that most Christians came face to face with captivity.

CHAPTER 6

THE FINANCES OF RANSOMING

A certain worthy lady had a husband whom she greatly
loved, and he had been in captivity, and with a large
sum of money had been redeemed. This lady sold all
her possessions and those of her husband that she might
pay the ransom, and, since this sufficed not, she went
through the chief squares begging. . . . As she begged
she wept, and related to a great company of notable
citizens the story of the captivity of her husband and
the torment which he suffered in prison. Together with
her she led four small children. All the citizens had pity
upon this lady, giving her money, and consoling her in
her tribulation.[1]

The image depicted by Ramond Llull in *Blanquerna*
repeated itself many times over in the cities of the Crown
of Aragon: captives and their families begging to pay off a
ransoming debt or to secure the liberation of a loved one.
Their pleas were augmented by the begging work of the
ransoming orders, the church, and individual municipalities. Their combined efforts collected the huge sums of
money that ransoms demanded from a Christian populace

1. Llull, *Blanquerna,* 71:3.

that was well inclined to give alms to the needy. In this way, captivity afflicted not only the captive and his family. Nor was it solely the duty of kings, bishops, and friars to help captives in need. Instead, captivity provoked and received a response from the entire Christian community, bound as it was by charity to its most disadvantaged members. This chapter will explore the money-raising efforts conducted on behalf of captives and argue that it is through these efforts that the full extent of Aragon as a ransoming society becomes evident, offering a clear indication of just how widespread a response captivity generated.

MEDIEVAL CHRISTIAN CHARITY

Captives depended on the good intentions and charitable donations of other Christians to gain their freedom. The alms they received were predicated on a calculus of salvation that promised enormous returns for relatively small investments.[2] Biblical stories provided the basis for this spiritual arithmetic.[3] Jesus had promised his followers that "every one that hath forsaken houses, or brethren, or sisters, or father, or mother or wife, or children, or lands, for my name's sake, shall receive a hundredfold, and shall inherit everlasting life."[4] The hundredfold return was, not coincidentally, one of the promises made by the begging licenses in an opening clause where they encouraged Christians to help captives.[5] The parable of the Last Judg-

2. For an introduction, see Rosenthal, *Purchase of Paradise,* esp. ch. 2.

3. For more on the metaphor of the "arithmetic of salvation," see Chiffoleau, *La comptabilité,* esp. part 2, "La mathématique du salut."

4. Matthew 19:29; see also Luke 18:29–30: "Verily I say unto you, there is no man that hath left house, or parents, or brethren, or wife, or children from the kingdom of God's sake who shall not receive manifold more in the present time, and in the world to come life everlasting."

5. "Vobisque dictis officialibus et subdtis nostris dicimus et mandamus de certa sciencia et expresse quatenus ob Dei reverenciam, caritativis erogacionibus misericorditer renumeracionem in centumplum tribuentis," in ACA, C, reg. 2205:140r–v (Apr. 10, 1408); published in Ferrer i Mallol, *La frontera amb l'Islam,* doc. 238. This, moreover, was not an isolated example but part of a formulaic opening exultation; see also ACA, C, reg. 2206:11v–12r (June 6, 1408) and 49v–50r (Sept. 18, 1408).

ment in the Gospel of Matthew (25:36–41) clarified the ways in which Christians could help their own salvation by helping those less fortunate: a group that included captives or prisoners. The Beatitudes further defined the hierarchy of salvation by giving privileged positions to those in the direst need of charity and promising them everlasting rewards.[6] Christian theologians from Caesarius of Arles to Thomas Aquinas recognized the central role that charity played in the Christian worldview. Caesarius called it the *vinculum societatis*, or the "bond of society," adding that without it other virtues were insufficient.[7] Aquinas defined it in similar terms: "Charity is likened to a foundation or root because it sustains and nourishes all other virtues."[8]

Many of the most popular medieval saints exemplified these ideals and set the standard for the societies that emulated them and prayed for their intercessory powers. The image of St. Martin of Tours giving half of his cloak to the poor man was a common one in medieval art and literature, and especially popular in the iconography of the Crown of Aragon.[9] Spanish holy men and women also lived up to these charitable ideals by providing multiple examples of aiding the poor and those in need.[10] Monasteries and nobles followed the models set by the "soldiers of Christ" and engaged their energies in charitable activities, distributing alms on a regular schedule—sometimes, as at Cluny, on a tremendous scale. The religious houses and the church also acted as administrators of large legacies and donations, functioning as a "screen" between the poor and the donors.[11]

This framework, however, was soon to change. The twelfth and thirteenth centuries witnessed the development of individual giving and the birth of the mendicant movements, which

6. Matthew 5:3–16.
7. Klingshirn, *Caesarius of Arles*, 189.
8. Aquinas, *Summa Theologiae*, vol. 34 (charity $2^a 2^{ae}$), 23:8.
9. Buxó Massaguer, "Iconografía de la pobreza en la pintura catalana," 72–78.
10. López Alonso, *La pobreza en la España medieval*, 254–56.
11. Geremek, *Poverty*, 36–40.

had important repercussions for medieval charity.[12] Increasingly, donors gave their alms "in response to specific requests . . . [and thus] the act of charity became almost a mass phenomenon."[13] It was not, moreover, a one-sided transaction, with a donor providing alms to a beneficiary who returned nothing. Instead, it consisted of an exchange wherein the rich provided material goods—alms—to the poor who, in turn, prayed for the souls of their wealthy benefactors or accompanied their funeral processions.[14] Likewise, it was hoped that the act of giving to the less fortunate would provoke a similar reaction from Christ toward the donor. The tradition behind these exchanges also required that donations be reserved for the deserving poor *(pobres vergonzados)*, a group that in Iberia included the sick, orphans, widows, unmarried girls, and captives.[15] A typical donor would include in his or her will as many of these groups of deserving poor and other charitable institutions as resources allowed.[16] The will of the Catalan merchant Philip Prestador is a good example of this approach. Philip bequeathed funds to the Hospital of the Holy Cross, the cathedral chapter of Barcelona, six of the seven parish churches in the city, two other churches, the Franciscans and Dominicans, two convents, two confraternities, and the Mercedarians, a total of seventeen charitable bequests.[17] He also chose the pauper cemetery as his burial site, although he could have afforded a more reputable location. Other donors left the specific decisions about the distribution of their legacies up to their executors, simply alluding to "pious causes and charitable works."[18]

12. Ruiz, *From Heaven to Earth*, ch. 1.

13. Geremek, *Poverty*, 41.

14. Chiffoleau, *La comptabilité*, 305–7; Geremek, *Poverty*, 47–48.

15. López Alonso, *La pobreza en la España medieval*, 44–82; Brodman, *Ransoming Captives*, 11.

16. Chiffoleau, *La comptabilité*, 215.

17. AHPB, Pere de Folgueres-Menor, *Liber Testamentorum*, Oct. 13, 1405–Aug. 30, 1442:23v–25r (Dec. 3, 1426).

18. See, for example, the will of Maria, wife of Guillem de Busqueris, AHPB,

Giving to the poor was not reserved solely for the hour of death. Those who were able gave alms on a regular basis and accentuated a lifetime of giving with the will at the end. Many of these individuals made their charitable contributions in begging bowls found in local churches or gave them to ex-captives or their families begging in the streets. Their generosity went unrecorded—but then again, with God keeping score, human record keeping was not a requirement. Much of the money raised for captives came in this manner, with donors giving their money directly to captives or their families as they begged on the streets. Donors also made significant deposits in the begging bowls found in the cities of the Aragonese Confederacy as they attended mass or went to mill their grain. The proceeds from these begging bowls typically went to the ransoming orders, but the orders also raised substantial funds by begging through the streets of the realm, often accompanied by ex-captives as a triumphant testimony of the successes of their charitable mission. This chapter will examine each of these methods in detail, but first it is important to make a few observations about prices, wages, and ransoms in the Crown of Aragon.

PRICES AND WAGES

Ransoms were costly and beyond the means of most people who needed them. Commenting on the high prices that his fellow Muslims set for Christian captives, the Tunisian scholar Ibn Khaldun noted that the prices were often very high, making it exceedingly difficult for the Christians to raise the amount.[19] The many factors that could affect the ransom price—social station of the captive, who his captors were, location of captivity, age, sex, and skills, among others—make it particularly chal-

---

Pere Pellisser, *Liber Testamentorum*, July 7, 1395–May 28, 1435, 54r–56r (Oct. 8, 1414).

19. Ibn Khaldun, *Histoire des Berbères*, 3:117.

lenging to give specific figures that can stand for all captives during the period covered here. Thus, the following figures are only guidelines based on a small number of captives for whom a ransom amount has survived. Between 1374 and 1399, the median ransom price for Aragonese captives was around 2,230 sous (111 pounds), although the average was much higher, hovering around 3,066 sous (153 pounds). By the first quarter of the fifteenth century, the median ransom price had increased to about 2,380 sous (119 pounds), but the average price had come down to 2,722 sous (136 pounds).[20] A ransom price of 2,500 sous (125 pounds) will do here for our purposes, providing a baseline against which to measure the economic price of captivity for an average family.[21]

In the early fifteenth century, an unskilled laborer might earn about 2.5 sous a day—a wage that could add up to about 750 sous (39 pounds) of annual income if he was lucky enough to work over three hundred days a year, an almost impossible proposition.[22] A master carpenter could command over 5.5 sous a day, but this rate was at the high end of craftsmen salaries. More typical were the wages of master stonecutters and masons, who earned between 4 and 4.5 sous per day. The income of other workmen and journeymen mirrored those of the unskilled laborers. Salaried public officials had more stable incomes, but few of them got rich from their wages. A granary guard, for example, received about 500 sous (25 pounds) in annual income.

20. The discrepancy in the averages may be explained by two unusually high ransoms between 1374 and 1399, one valued at 8,500 sous (425 pounds) for a courtier and the other at 9,000 sous (450 pounds) for another government official.

21. This figure may well be on the conservative side since it is based on amounts listed in the begging licenses. The licenses recorded the amount of money that the family needed to raise and not the actual price of the ransom.

22. This estimate is based on the figures provided by Hamilton, *Money, Prices, and Wages,* apps. 9 and 10. The estimate assumes three hundred workdays, and the figures are for Valencia. Laborers earned less in smaller cities or areas with more modest economies. In Aragon proper, for example, an unskilled laborer earned around 25 pounds a year in 1405.

A warehouseman made about 600 sous (30 pounds), and a notary could command about 1,600 sous (80 pounds) a year. At the other end of the pay scale, janitors, trumpeters, and messengers earned 90, 180, and 240 sous a year respectively, although these were probably part-time jobs that allowed the individual to have another source of income.

Sailors, who made up a significant portion of those who fell into captivity, had a compensation system that depended on their position in a ship's hierarchy. Oarsmen were the worst paid, receiving between 40–60 sous a month in the 1380s and 66 sous a month in 1415.[23] By comparison, the wages of the craftsman responsible for the upkeep of the ship's oars, the *remolar*, began at 120 sous a month; the barber-surgeon could command about 100 sous; while the captain earned about 200 sous a month.[24] Daily allotments of rations augmented the sailors' income. Complicating this assessment of sailors' wages was the fact that many hired on for a share of the profit of a voyage. This could be very profitable, especially if they engaged in contraband or piracy, but it could also be disastrous. Not only did sailors have to contend with the perils of sea travel cutting into their gains, but if the expedition made no profit, the law obligated the seamen to pay the ship's owner for the rations he had provided them.[25] And, of course, all these salaries assume steady employment year-round, which would have been very difficult to maintain.

The next question that arises concerns the buying power of these incomes. In the early fifteenth century, the household of a Catalan merchant spent about 200 sous (10 pounds) a year feeding and clothing each family member, a figure that did not include expenditures on wine or spices.[26] It is reasonable to sug-

23. See López Pérez, *La Corona de Aragón*, 824–25, for the figures from the 1380s; Guiral Hadziiossif, *Valence*, 230 for 1415.
24. López Pérez, *La Corona de Aragón*, 824–25.
25. Jados, *Consulate of the Sea*, ordinance 247.
26. Vinyoles i Vidal, *La vida quotidiana*, 185–86.

gest that less affluent families spent between 120 and 150 sous a year on each family member, for a total of between 480 and 600 sous for a family of four. This sum does not take into account rents (an extra 100–200 sous a year) or extraordinary expenses. A few simple calculations show that when we allow for expenses, some households with single incomes had very little additional money to divert to emergencies such as ransoming a captive family member. Admittedly, many households had other sources of income, but usually these would have been secondary and not nearly as great as the wages earned by the head of the household. With these figures and exceptions, it is possible to suggest a yearly sum of 650 sous (32.5 pounds) as the minimum living expenses needed by a family of four. Table 2, which subtracts the living expenses from the salaries calculated above, shows the disposable income that could be used for an emergency like captivity.

It is now possible to make rudimentary observations on the impact that captivity had on a working family in the Crown of Aragon around 1400. Based on the ransom price of 2,500 sous (125 pounds), an unskilled laborer would have needed about twenty-five years to ransom a loved one or to pay off the debt

Table 2. Salaries in the Crown of Aragon, c. 1400

Profession	Yearly salary (sous)	Disposable income (sous)
Laborer/journeyman	750	100
Master carpenter	1,650	1,000
Master mason	1,200–1,350	550–700
Guard	500	−150
Warehouseman	600	−50
Notary	1,600	950
Janitor	90	−540
Trumpeter	180	−470
Messenger	240	−410
Oarsman	480–720	−180 to +70
Remolar	1,440	790
Barber-surgeon	1,200	550
Captain	2,400	1,750

of his own ransom if he was the unlucky one who fell into captivity. A master craftsman had to save from two to five years to reach the necessary amount. A well-paid oarsman had almost no chance to raise the money in his working lifetime, since it would have required over thirty-five years of saving to ransom someone based on his salary. A ship's captain, on the other hand, could raise the necessary money in less than a year and a half. Individuals engaged in the least paying professions would have found it next to impossible to acquire the necessary sum for a ransom from their own wages. Although unskilled laborers and those at the bottom of the earning hierarchy probably had smaller ransoms to pay, the difference in price was not great enough to be a big relief, knocking off perhaps five or ten years. Of course, in times of emergency families could cut back on spending, other family members could take jobs, or relatives could be persuaded to help. But how far would that go? Could it cut in half the time needed to raise the ransom? Ten or fifteen years in the case of the poorer families is still a very long time. Moreover, since the majority of captives were male, the man's income is what was often lost when a family member fell into captivity. The rest of the family would have had a difficult time feeding themselves, let alone raising a large ransom. The loans discussed in chapter 4 could help, but only the most generous or foolish merchants would extend a loan to a family that had almost no chance of repaying it. Moreover, loans had to be repaid. The point here is that for most families, having to raise a ransom equaled economic disaster and hardship. It was under these overwhelming circumstances that families turned to begging and charitable donations.

RAISING THE MONEY

Raising a ransom was often a long and difficult process for captives and their families. For those who lacked independent means, the bulk of the ransom would be raised by begging on the streets, by soliciting secular and ecclesiastical officials for aid, by appealing to the executors of estates, and sometimes by asking the ransoming orders for funds. Most ransoms were raised by combining money from all of these sources. Thus, a typical ransom would include whatever contribution the captive's family could make as well as alms collected from the faithful, donations received from wills that set aside money specifically for ransoming, and in some cases contributions provided by civic groups, municipal councils, ecclesiastical officials, the orders, and royal grants.

Begging was a regulated activity in the Crown of Aragon. Before taking to the streets, a captive or his family had to acquire a begging license, an authorization granting the bearer the right to beg for money without interference. Licenses were typically issued by the king, one of his lieutenants, or by ecclesiastical officials. They were formulaic documents that included the name of the beggar—if a family member or friend was doing the begging—and the name of the captive. They usually recorded the ransom amount and often had a time limit, expiring two to three years after the date of issue.[27] The licenses were also the most common type of aid that the crown furnished, turning up often in the royal registers. One of the scribes working in the chancery of Alfonso IV (r. 1416–58) captured their frequency and his bureaucratic boredom by indifferently titling one "another begging license."[28]

The licenses reveal other information. They highlight the hardships that captives endured, intending thereby to convince the faithful of the captives' need. Among the most frequent torments that the licenses listed were hunger, thirst, cold, and

27. ACA, C, reg. 1895:105r–6r (Dec. 4, 1388), published in Ferrer i Mallol, "La redempció," doc. 3.
28. "Alia licencia acaptandi," in ACA, C, reg. 2585:112v–13r (Sept. 22, 1416).

chains.[29] A good example that can stand for many is the license given to Berengar Cristofol: "Berengar Cristofol, neighbor of Valencia, who was recently captured by faithless Saracens while sailing in the sea off Alicante and led captive to the city of Bougie, where he suffers diverse hardships, and he wishes to ransom himself at any price so that he may be able to free himself and not abjure the faith of Christ, but his own resources do not suffice for paying off this ransom since he is a pauper unless the faithful of Christ help him with alms."[30]

The evocation of these torments and the specter of religious conversion were intended to resonate with the Christian donors upon whom the captives depended for their alms, for those who fed the hungry, gave drink to the thirsty, and clothed the naked would "inherit the kingdom prepared for [them] from the foundation of the world." On the other hand, the Gospel promised "everlasting punishment" in a "fire prepared for the devil and his angels" to those who turned away from the needy in their hour of distress.[31] Echoing this not so subtle, and frightening, suggestion, the licenses often reminded Christians of their moral responsibility to captives in an opening clause that linked their eternal salvation to their charitable deeds.[32]

Ecclesiastical officials granted begging licenses as well, although with less frequency than the royal chancery. These licenses tended to be more restricted in scope, typically limited to the boundaries of the issuing diocese. They were similar to the royal licenses, including sections highlighting the captive's suffering, the reasons for his capture, the place of captivity, and the amount of the ransom. In 1431 the bishop of Barcelona granted

29. See, among the many examples, ACA, C, reg. 2180:59v–60r (June 8, 1406); ACA, C, reg. 2208:81v–82r (Apr. 16, 1410); ACA, C, reg. 2586:149v (Jan. 25, 1418); ACA, C, reg. 3150:74r–v (undated).

30. ACA, C, reg. 2204:53v–54r (Oct. 8, 1406).

31. Matthew 25:31–46.

32. See, for example, ACA, C, reg. 1895:105r–6r (Dec. 4, 1388), published in Ferrer i Mallol, "La redempció," doc. 3; also ACA, C, reg. 2206:11r–12r (Jan. 27, 1409).

a license to Pedro Corneller, who was languishing in a Bougiot prison and whose faith was apparently wavering.[33] A license issued the same year to Bernardo Puig, whom slavers had taken to Tunis, allowed begging for the rather large sum of 270 pounds.[34] The registers of the bishopric of Zaragoza also show the local bishops dispensing numerous licenses to captives and their families.[35] The interest taken by the bishops of Zaragoza suggests that aid for captives was not limited to the crown and frontier or coastal cities but was spread throughout the realm and penetrated deep inland.

Church officials gave additional aid by promising indulgences to the faithful who gave alms to captives. As early as 1245, Pope Innocent IV had promised a penitential reduction for anyone who gave alms to the Mercedarians and Trinitarians.[36] For the remainder of the thirteenth century the papacy continued to offer newer and typically more generous indulgences to anyone who contributed alms to the ransoming orders.[37] By the fourteenth century, the practice had spread and the church was granting indulgences to anyone who gave money for ransoms, not just those who gave alms to the ransoming orders. Thus, in 1370 the bishop of Barcelona gave indulgences to anyone who helped the bearer of one of his begging licenses to ransom his wife, son, and father-in-law from captivity in Granada.[38]

Many licenses were valid only for a limited time. This often meant that captives who needed to raise large sums of money had to request new licenses or extensions. This was the case of Stefan Moliner, who received a begging license on July 31, 1417 to raise 600 doblas (510 pounds) to ransom his mother and

33. ADB, *Gratiarum*, 1431–32:71r (Sept. 17, 1431).
34. ADB, *Gratiarum*, 1431–32:11v (undated, but considering its place in the register, certainly from 1431).
35. Pueyo Colomina, "Litterae 'pro captivis,'" 361–66.
36. For the Mercedarians, see Brodman, "Rhetoric of Ransoming," 47; for the Trinitarians, see Porres Alonso, *Libertad a los cautivos*, 1:135.
37. Brodman, *Ransoming Captives*, 100; Porres Alonso, *Libertad a los cautivos*, 1:145–47.
38. Puig y Puig, *Episcopologio*, doc. 122 (Oct. 21, 1370).

six brothers who were being held in Bougie. Moliner and his wife, Isabel, had also been among those captured, but had been able to pay 400 doblas (340 pounds) for their release. Once released, they set about to ransom the other family members.[39] One and a half years later, their task was apparently still unfinished, as the king granted them a second license. The first one was due to expire in July 1419, two years from the date of its granting. The king, perhaps realizing the difficulty of their mission, granted the second license for three years.[40] Moliner and his family may have been well off as the initial, and considerable, sum of 400 doblas paid for the ransom of Stefan and his wife suggests. However, when confronted with ransoming nine family members, none but the richest of families could hope to cope with such a demand.

Sometimes the licenses bear proof of their own effectiveness in helping raise money. In April 1408 Martin I gave a license to Yvany Garcia for 210 doblas (178.5 pounds).[41] This was not Garcia's first license. In 1406 he had received his first begging license, which was to last for two years.[42] By September 1409 he was the recipient of a third license issued in his name. As was the case with Stefan Moliner, the time afforded by the original license was insufficient for Garcia to raise the full amount of his ransom, and he requested two extensions. The third license does suggest that Garcia was making impressive progress since it explicitly states that he needed only another 46 doblas (39 pounds) to finish paying off his debt.[43] These three docu-

---

39. ACA, C, reg. 2587:97r–v (July 31, 1417).

40. ACA, C, reg. 2588:166r–v (Feb. 4, 1419).

41. ACA, C, reg. 2205:140r–v (Apr. 10, 1408). At the bottom of a license granted to a Bartomeu Grimalt appears the following: "Similis licencia acaptandi fuit concessa sub eisdem data, signo atque mandato pro Yvanno Garsie dicte ville Oriola et pro simili rescato ducentarum duplarum." Although this description specifically says "200 doblas," the other two licenses issued to Yvany put the ransom price at 210 doblas.

42. ACA, C, reg. 2180:59v–60r (June 8, 1406); published in Ferrer i Mallol, *La frontera amb l'Islam,* doc. 229.

43. ACA, C, reg. 2206:180r (Sept. 24, 1409).

ments also allow us a glimpse into the time required to raise a ransom. Martin had granted the first license in April 1406, and the third one was due to expire in September 1411. In this case, slightly less than five and a half years of begging and, we may assume, additional fund-raising were needed to raise the ransom for one person.

Captives also benefited from testamentary bequests. Since at least 1255, the church had been including captives among the "poor of Christ" and encouraging testamentary bequests to aid them.[44] Donors contributed their money in different ways. In some cases, testators left a specific amount for ransoming as part of *pro anima* bequests, for the expiation of sins.[45] The notary Johan de Trillea, for example, assigned 30 sous for the ransom of captives in his will.[46] And Antonia, the wife of a merchant of Barcelona, made a similar provision in her will, leaving 10 sous for "redeeming Christian captives."[47] Others left bequests that were linked to burial expenses. A typical will contained a clause in which the testator assigned a certain amount of money to cover the cost of his or her funeral and memorial masses. Since these expenditures varied, there was usually money left over. Many people willed this money to charitable causes, including the redemption of captives. Johanna, the wife of a painter, instructed her executors to give, at their discretion, whatever remained from the 10 pounds she had set aside for her burial for "celebrating masses, redeeming captives, helping poor girls marry, and other worthy causes."[48] Morgano Castello left similar instructions for the surplus money from his burial.[49]

44. Brodman, "Rhetoric of Ransoming," 46.

45. For more on pro anima bequests, see Brodman, "What Is a Soul Worth?"

46. AHPB, Francesc de Manresa, *Llibre de Testaments*, Oct. 4, 1401–Sept. 3, 1424:83v–86r (May 13, 1416).

47. AHPB, Pere de Pellisser, *Liber Testamentorum*, July 7, 1395–May 28, 1435:32r–33v (May 19, 1410).

48. AHPB, Bernat Pi, *Llibre de Testaments*, Mar. 17, 1408–Apr. 10, 1430:42v–43v (May 29, 1417).

49. AHPB, Bernat Pi, *Llibre de Testaments*, Oct. 13, 1405–Aug. 30, 1442:85r–86v (Aug. 9, 1434).

In many of these wills, donors grouped captives and unmarried poor girls together in their lists of beneficiaries.[50] Alfonso Garcia, after setting aside some money for his parish church, funding masses for his soul, and paying his executors, ordered the executors to sell his remaining assets and distribute the money "celebrating masses for [his] soul, ransoming Christian captives in the power of the Saracens, and helping poor girls marry."[51] Elisenda, the wife of a farmer, had the remnants of her chattels divided into three equal parts, one of which went to ransoming captives and another bequeathed to unmarried girls.[52] In these transactions, the captives and the unmarried girls formed a second tier of beneficiaries that clearly fell behind paupers and religious institutions in the hierarchy of giving. This may be because donors did not consider captives to have the same intercessory capacity in the afterlife that paupers or mendicants had. For example, much of the money given to the poor required that paupers pray for the soul of their benefactor or escort his or her funeral bier. Captives never had any of these preconditions imposed on them. In other words, although certainly worthy of charity, captives do not seem to have delivered the same returns as did paupers in the calculus of salvation.

A question also arises as to how money from wills made its way to those families that needed it. In reality, it appears that most of the money wound up in the coffers of the ransoming orders. The orders could then use the money for their own ransoming expeditions or turn it over to individual captives as the need arose and resources permitted. This issue, however, has been little studied in the secondary literature. I would tentatively suggest that by the fourteenth and fifteenth centuries,

50. For a brief study of the relationship between captives and unmarried girls in charitable donations, see Sánchez Herrero, "La acción benéfica de las cofradías."

51. AHPB, Bernat Pi, *Llibre de Testaments*, Mar. 17, 1408–Apr. 10, 1430:23v–24v (Aug. 16, 1414).

52. AHPB, Pere de Folgueres, *Liber Testamentorum*, Oct. 13, 1405–Aug. 30, 1442:89r–v (Feb. 4, 1417).

the orders preferred to use the monetary resources that they controlled in their own ransoming expeditions (see below).

Not all the money set aside in wills went directly to the ransoming orders, however. Some donors left the dispensation of the funds up to their executors. In these cases we may assume that captives or their agents had to apply to the executor for the funds. A good example comes from Valencia, where the city council was helping to raise the ransom of Pere Alfonso, a captive in Algiers. The city had already provided all the help that it could; yet that had not been enough to complete the formidable ransom of 241 doblas (205 pounds). Consequently, the council wrote to the executors of the will of a lady from Terol asking that they turn over to Pere the 10 pounds that the deceased had set aside for ransoming captives.[53] A similar process may have taken place after the death of Elisenda, the wife of a Catalan merchant. She instructed her executors to set aside the very generous sum of 100 pounds for the ransom of captives. The executors would then distribute 1 pound to each supplicant.[54]

Finally, some donors left money for individual captives, typically family members. When Raymond Eimeric notarized his will, he assigned 11 pounds to "Francisco Macanet, a sailor of Barcelona who was being held captive by the Saracens in Bougie."[55] In the spring of the following year, Raymond's wife, Francisca, also left money to Francisco Macanet—in this case, 50 sous.[56] The document is not explicit, but Francisco and Francisca may have been related.[57] In a similar case, Clara Gelat as-

53. Rubio Vela, *Epistolari*, 2: doc. 145 (May 25, 1441).
54. AHPB, Pere de Pellisser, *Liber Testamentorum*, July 7, 1395–May 28, 1435:40r–46r (July 21, 1412).
55. AHPB, Bernat Nadal, *Liber Testamentorum*, July 1385–Dec 1397:93r–94r (Aug. 22, 1394).
56. AHPB, Bernat Nadal, *Liber Testamentorum*, July 1385–Dec. 1397:101v–3r (Apr. 3, 1395).
57. Francisca also left money to a Pedro Macanet, whom she identifies as "consanguineo germano meo."

signed 100 sous to Gabriel Ponc, her brother, who was a captive in Algeciras.[58]

Aside from the begging done by captives and their families and the money left in wills, there were other sources of revenue available for ransoming. Many captives turned to their monarch for aid. By far the most common type of monetary aid that a captive could expect from the crown were the aforementioned begging licenses. However, on certain occasions, the supplicant could persuade the monarch to help with money, sometimes enough to raise the entire ransom. In 1377 Peter the Ceremonious granted the large sum of 20,000 sous (about 1,000 pounds), to Gueraldo Cevilione, a member of his court (domicellus).[59] John I gave 50 pounds to a man from Oriola to aid in his "ransom and redemption, since Saracens had captured and imprisoned him."[60] And in 1415 Ferdinand I ordered the baile of Valencia to turn over 30 pounds to the wife of Guillem Tallada so that she could ransom him from captivity in Tunis.[61]

When these large quantities were not forthcoming from the king himself, families turned to the royal almoner. The alms they received were pitifully small, and families had to request the aid in writing.[62] The typical donation given out in 1383 was 1 florin (11 sous).[63] In one case, the petitioner received 5 florins, but the unfortunate man was raising money to pay for his ransom and that of his wife and children.[64] The amount given also

58. AHPB, Bernat Nadal, *Liber Testamentorum,* July 1385–Dec. 1397:60r–61r (Aug. 20, 1390).

59. ACA, C, CR, Pedro III, box 54:6616 (Jan. 7, 1377).

60. ACA, C, reg. 1888:116r (Oct. 11, 1395), published in Ferrer i Mallol, *La frontera amb l'Islam,* doc. 172.

61. ACA, C, reg. 2415:44r (Feb. 9, 1415), "donets e paguets a dona Guillermona mullier d'en Guillem Tallada trenta doblas d'or los quals per vos li bolem . . . donats en aiuda del rescat d'en Guillem Tallada fill d'en Guillem Tallada de la vila d'Almatora qui es preso et captiu en la ciutat de Tuniz terra de moros."

62. Altisent, *L'almoina reial,* xxxviii–xxxix; see also Gual, "La asistencia a los pobres," 479–81.

63. Altisent, *L'almoina reial,* 183, 186, 190.

64. Ibid., 171.

fluctuated based on the availability of funds. In 1384 and 1385, for example, the typical grant was 5 florins. Even with these greater sums, it would have taken a great deal of additional begging to raise the ransoms.

The crown also indirectly provided money for families by asking, or sometimes forcing, the ransoming orders to turn over some of their funds for the ransoms of specific captives.[65] Kings ordinarily employed these strong-arm tactics when close associates of the crown were in captivity. In 1389 John I demanded that the Mercedarians and Trinitarians provide 150 doblas (127.5 pounds) toward the ransom of the son of Pedro Morera, a royal councillor whom pirates from Barbary had captured and who had subsequently left his son as a hostage while he raised the ransom. The king's request left the orders little recourse since he pointed out that it was *his* decision that they turn over some of the money they were collecting in *his* realm to aid Morera (emphasis mine).[66] In 1395 he asked the Mercedarians for 500 florins (275 pounds) for the ransom of Berenguer de Lacera *("domèstich e familiar nostre")*. The order, for unknown reasons, did not provide the money promptly, causing John to threaten the master with retaliation if he did not comply.[67] About two months later, but with less thunder in his voice, John again asked the Mercedarians to contribute to a private ransom; this time the sum was 200 florins (110 pounds) for two captive Franciscans.[68]

In spite of these philanthropic examples (even if it was the

65. For a brief overview, see Sáinz de la Maza Lasoli, "Los Mercedarios," 238; Brodman, "Ransomers or Royal Agents," 248.

66. "Havem acordat que es nuestra voluntat que del accapte que se fa en la senyoria per reaure catius cristians de la terra de moros per les fratres de la vostra orde sien donads al dit mossen P. Morera cent cinquanta dobles d'or en ayude de pagar son rescat," ACA, C, reg. 1871:146r–v (Feb. 1, 1389).

67. ACA, C, reg. 1967:25r–v (Apr. 29, 1395), published in Sáinz de la Maza Lasoli, "Los Mercedarios," doc. 41.

68. ACA, C, reg. 1887:135v–36r (June 17, 1395), published in Sáinz de la Maza Lasoli, "Los Mercedarios," doc. 43.

forced philanthropy of others), spending money for ransoming captives was not always a top priority of the kings of Aragon. At a time when the families of Christian captives were begging for ransom money through the kingdom, and captives themselves were pleading for help from their prisons in Tunis or Granada, John I's queen, Yolande de Bar, was giving 300 florins to a court favorite for his upcoming wedding.[69] John himself gave 1,000 florins to another member of his court as a gift, money that could have gone for the ransom of five or six captives.[70] Martin I (r. 1395–1410) endowed one of the queen's ladies with a 1,000-florin gift for her wedding.[71] A few days later he awarded 500 florins to a sergeant at arms for a recent promotion.[72] Two weeks after that, he presented 160 florins to a councillor for the purchase of a horse, an amount that would have sufficed to free one or two captives.[73] Captives and their families did receive financial aid from the crown, but acquiring the freedom of a captive often competed with, and lost out to, other "needs."[74]

Other groups and institutions also raised money for captives or contributed to their ransoms. Civic confraternities and guilds were among the most active.[75] The shoemakers' guild in Valencia, for example, stipulated in its bylaws that if "any member, through his sins or due to disaster, became a captive and in good faith was unable to pay his ransom, then each member, for the love of God and in the name of charity, would contribute 2 sous for the ransom."[76] Other guilds in other cities in the Aragonese Confederacy had similar requirements, including tai-

69. ACA, C, CR, Juan I, box 6:617 (Jan. 10, 1392).
70. ACA, C, CR, Juan I, box 6:621 (1392).
71. ACA, C, CR, Martin I, box 2:181 (May 15, 1399).
72. ACA, C, CR, Martin I, box 2:187 (May 26, 1399).
73. ACA, C, CR, Martin I, box 2:190 (June 10, 1399).
74. For a similar criticism, see Gual, "La asistencia a los pobres," 463.
75. Sánchez Herrero, "La acción benéfica de las cofradías," 163–91; Verlinden, L'esclavage, 1:538–39.
76. Bofarull y Mascaró, Colección de documentos inéditos, 40:doc. 17 (Sept. 1329).

lors, blacksmiths, leather workers, butchers, ironsmiths, silversmiths, and carpenters.[77] One interesting example was the Cofradía Real de Barcelona para hacer cruzada contra sarracenos (Royal Confraternity of Barcelona for Crusading against Saracens). The rich citizens *(rich homens)* of Catalonia founded it to "exalt the holy Catholic faith and for battling and to the detriment of the evil sect of Mohammed."[78] Should the confraternity dissolve, however, all its revenues would devolve to ransoming. Even confraternities linked to universities had clauses that guaranteed their members aid should they fall "in the power of the Moors, enemies of the faith."[79]

Some cities were very active in their efforts to ransom their citizens. Valencia, due to its exposed position on the coast in the southern reaches of the kingdom, led the way. The city had an organized municipal ransoming system from 1323. It raised money through the traditional methods of collection plates distributed throughout the city's parishes, wandering alms collectors, and testamentary bequests. The two citizens in charge of the program investigated each appeal for aid and, if it were found worthy, paid out a sum that was not to exceed 300 sous (15 pounds). In order to qualify, the captive had to be a Christian, from Valencia, and had to show a financial need. The city did not engage itself in the actual ransom, which more traditional ransomers such as the orders, exeas, or merchants handled. Valencia's archival records show that between 1375 and 1399, the city handed out 24,000 sous (1,200 pounds) to help over sixty captives, some of whom received more than one grant of money.[80] Beyond these efforts, the city council could

77. Ibid., docs. 4, 14, 17–23, 26–27, 45–47, 52, 59, 64. The dates range from 1298 to 1392.

78. Ibid., 40:doc. 14 (1315).

79. Sánchez Herrero, "La acción benéfica de las cofradías," 167.

80. For a full account, see Díaz Borrás, "Notas sobre los primeros tiempos," 337–54, and "La organización de la caridad redentiva," 157–75.

also give out money in unusual circumstances.[81] Valencia's concern for its captive sons and daughters was extraordinary but not unique. In 1391, for example, the town council of Oriola voted to give 100 florins for the ransom of one of its residents.[82] And in a similar situation in 1404 the southern town of Asp gave 100 florins to Bartomeu Grimalt to help him with the ransom of his son Pere, who had been captured in a raid.[83] Other frontier communities have also left records of underwriting the cost of ransoms.[84] Town fathers could also use their influence to encourage the population at large to contribute alms for the sake of captives, since this was one of "the best works of charity that a Christian could do."[85]

Individual captives had to compete for the ransom dole with the ransoming orders—not to mention other religious orders and secular clergy—as the orders' begging drew on the same limited funds and functioned on the same principles of almsgiving and charity that sustained the begging efforts of individual captives.[86] The orders, moreover, benefited from a long history of fund-raising that allowed them to be much more effective than individuals. Their appeals for funds were aided by a display designed to draw attention to themselves and their cause in a performance that negotiated a fine line between the ritualistic and the pragmatic. The centerpiece of this act were the ex-captives who had indentured themselves to the orders for six months to a year as part of their ransom agreement. The cap-

81. Díaz Borrás, "Notas sobre los primeros tiempos," 348.

82. Bellot, *Anales de Orihuela*, 175–76.

83. The same raid claimed the life of Pere's wife, and subsequently the town council gave Grimalt an additional 100 florins as a gracious gesture for the death of his daughter-in-law. The money, however, was not enough, and in 1408 Martin I granted him a begging license for 200 pounds (3,400 sous) to help with his son's ransom. See Ferrer i Mallol, *La frontera amb l'Islam*, 217–18 for the background and doc. 238 for the published begging license. The original license is in ACA, C, reg. 2205:140r–v (Apr. 10, 1408).

84. Carriazo, "Relaciones fronterizas," 41–45.

85. Rubio Vela, *Epistolari*, 1:doc. 15 (Mar. 27, 1399).

86. Taylor, *Structures of Reform*, 26.

tives were clothed in white tunics, mimicking the clothes worn by the brothers but also alluding to martyrs and martyrdom.[87] Accompanying the two or three brothers who led the begging effort and their attendant ex-captives were the blare of trumpets and flying pennons.[88] One can easily imagine one of these white-clad troops, probably numbering a dozen individuals, entering the square in front of the local church and regaling passersby with sermons about the virtues of Christian charity and stories detailing the horrors of captivity. If nothing else, they differentiated themselves from the many other beggars and mendicants who competed for the dole handed out by donors by providing a spectacle that people would come out and see. The returning captives were also potential fonts of information for those in the community who had family members in captivity.[89] In coastal cities in Valencia and Mallorca, this alone is likely to have drawn people to the exhibition being put on by the orders. The attention, moreover, served to highlight the story that the captives told and to create a triumphalist image of the orders that had saved the poor Christians from the terrible fate that awaited them. These performances placed the obligation for ransoming squarely on the shoulders of the faithful, since it was only with their contributions that the merciful work of the brothers could continue.

The orders also used more mundane methods to raise capital. One of the preferred tactics was to place begging bowls in strategic locations where they confronted people in their daily activities.[90] In 1363, for example, Peter the Ceremonious granted permission to the Trinitarians to circulate collection plates

87. For the clothing of captives, see Vásquez Nuñez, *Manual de historia de la Orden*, 273; for the clothing of brothers, see Brodman, *Ransoming Captives*, 131; Gross, *Trinitarian's Rule of Life*, 29.

88. Porres Alonso, *Libertad a los cautivos*, doc. 2:52 (Jan. 23, 1453).

89. See also Weiss, "From Barbary to France," 794.

90. Begging bowls, *bací* or *plats*, were common in medieval churches in the Crown of Aragon. Some churches had multiple bowls, each collecting alms for a different cause. Laymen administered some of them, such as the *bací dels*

in churches.[91] Two years later, Peter extended the privilege, allowing the order to place begging bowls within and outside of churches to aid them in their fund-raising.[92] Later that same year, Peter again extended privileges to the Trinitarians. In a document dated May 18, 1365, the king conferred permission for brothers "to preach to the Christian people and to describe for them the calamities and miseries the Christian captives, who are held by the Barbarians, suffer."[93] All of these royal decrees also emphasized the right of the Trinitarians to place their begging bowls in mills and ovens, where they would have been strategically placed amid the constant traffic of prospective donors with loose change in their pockets.

The many properties that the orders had accumulated since their foundation were also an important component of the fund-raising, as the brothers drew substantial rents and other incomes from them. In Valencia, for example, the Mercedarian patrimony "comprised . . . over 160 acres of farmland, eleven gardens, three other fields, eighteen groups of houses, five vineyards, a farmstead, a mosque, a fonduk, an olive grove, two castles, a mill, two plazas, eight villages, three hamlets or groups of hamlets, five workshops and a parish church."[94] The order drew substantial sums from these properties that served to subsidize the ransoming expeditions.[95] The Trinitarians collected similar benefits from their landed property.[96] The rents the orders collected, besides serving to underwrite many of the ransoming expenses, also gave them capital with which to make further acquisitions and augment their holdings.

Two smaller sources of revenue also deserve mention: re-

pobres vergonyants, which became entities in themselves with substantial patrimonies; see Riu, "La ayuda a los pobres," 789–93.

91. Porres Alonso, *Libertad a los cautivos*, doc. 3:29 (Feb. 15, 1363).

92. Ibid., doc. 3:31 (Jan. 20, 1365).

93. Ibid., doc. 3:32 (May 18, 1365).

94. Brodman, *Ransoming Captives*, 80.

95. Ibid., 92–94.

96. Porres Alonso, *Libertad a los cautivos*, 1:156–57.

quiem masses and burial in the orders' cemeteries and trade. Mercedarian acquisition of churches afforded them the opportunity to perform masses, invite patrons to give endowments, and offer burial services.[97] This put them in direct competition with other religious houses and monasteries, not to mention parish churches. The merchant Ferrario Soares provides a good example of the options the dying had to ensure salvation in the afterlife. He bequeathed 15 sous each to the Franciscans, Dominicans, Augustinians, Carmelites, and Mercedarians for pro anima masses.[98] Eulalia, the wife of another merchant, made a similar request, leaving 10 sous apiece to the Augustinians, Franciscans, Dominicans, and Mercedarians in return for "celebrating masses for [her] soul after [her] death."[99] The cultivation of patrons by the orders could pay significant dividends when these patrons drew up their wills, as evidenced, for example, by the bequests of the notary Vicente Lugneti. He began his will by selecting Johan Olmeri, the subprior of the Mercedarian house in Barcelona, as one of his executors. He also requested burial in the order's cemetery as well as permission to receive the Mercedarian habit in death. Finally, and most important, after making other provisions, he instructed that the remnants of his estate be distributed among captives, unmarried girls, and other pious causes.[100]

Small-scale trade also figured into the fund-raising efforts of the orders as they turned profits into ransoms—profits that sometimes attracted covetous eyes. Ferdinand IV, king of Castile, had to order his officials to stop extorting the Mercedarians as they passed through Castilian cities. Other times, local offi-

97. Brodman, *Ransoming Captives*, 96–97.
98. AHPB, Bernat Nadal, *Liber Testamentorum*, July 1385–Dec. 1397:161v–63v (Aug. 26, 1397)
99. AHPB, Bernat Nadal, *Liber Testamentorum*, July 1385–Dec. 1397:12v–14r (July 6, 1388).
100. AHPB, Bernat Pi, *Llibre de Testaments*, Mar. 17, 1408–Apr. 10, 1430:65r–66r (Nov. 13, 1419).

cers of the crown took the beasts and trinkets that Mercedarians carried with them to sell in Muslim lands. Henry II, another Castilian king, had to issue a similar order in 1373 forbidding rapacious officials from taking the mules or other animals that the order brought with it to sell. Castilian officials sometimes went even further in their greed, taking the cloth that the Mercedarians usually carried to make crude clothing for captives and miscellaneous items that the captives brought back with them from captivity.[101]

In considering the many ways that captives or their agents raised money, we should not forget that most of these methods were fraught with potential pitfalls that made the process much more difficult and in many cases hampered the ability of those collecting the alms to do their work. Oftentimes, the different options that were in place to aid captives canceled each other out, as they and other deserving groups competed for a finite amount of charity. The conflicts that arose between the Mercedarians and Trinitarians in the fourteenth century and warnings inscribed in begging licenses that forbade the orders from interfering with the begging of individual captives are but two examples of this struggle over limited resources.[102] Individuals who assumed the guise of captives in order to capitalize on the public pity, having never endured a day of captivity, stretched the resources even further.[103] Problems even arose in the case of testamentary bequests as relatives contested wills or refused to

101. Vázquez Nuñez, *Manual de historia de la Orden*, 272–76.

102. The ransoming orders, which considered any charitable donation for captives to belong to them rightfully, sometimes proved to be the most troublesome obstructions to families or captives begging for money. Noting this, the crown sometimes warned them about interfering with the begging efforts of captives on the begging licenses themselves. For warnings on the licenses, see ACA, C, reg. 926:54v–55r (June 10, 1374); 55r (June 10, 1374).

103. In 1389, for example, the crown ordered the capture and punishment of fake captives, who were usually fit young men: see ACA, C, reg. 1895:243v–44v (May 4, 1389), published in Sainz de la Maza, "Los Mercedarios," doc. 34. For an example from Castile, see Porres Alonso, *Libertad a los cautivos*, doc. 2:10 (Feb. 27, 1311).

turn over funds to the orders or to the captives' families.[104] The biggest hurdle, however, may have been the inescapable penury into which captivity drove many individuals and families. In the end, many captives and their loved ones probably experienced the same hardships as Ramond Llull's "worthy lady." Faced with the possibility of their loved ones dying in captivity or converting to Islam, many turned to begging and the other options that were available to them and tried to raise the ransoms by whatever means necessary, hoping that their fellow citizens would take pity upon them, give them money, and console them in their tribulations.

104. Porres Alonso, *Libertad a los cautivos*, doc. 2:16 (Sept. 22, 1360); ACA, C, reg. 2132:156v–57r (Nov. 22, 1401), published in Ferrer i Mallol, "La redempció," doc. 6.

EPILOGUE

Freedom and Reintegration

In 1485, during Holy Week, a pitiful group of people slowly made its way from the captured city of Ronda to Córdova in southern Spain. The crowd, numbering over four hundred men, women, and children, was in a poor state. Many showed the signs of malnutrition; others were sick; the clothing of most confirmed the wear and tear of having gone for years unchanged; only a few lucky ones rode animals or enjoyed the comforts of a cart; some even carried chains or wore hair the length of many seasons' growth. Most probably considered themselves lucky and even in their current situation were experiencing a joy they had not felt for some time. A few days earlier they had been captives in Ronda. That was before King Ferdinand, leading joint Castilian-Aragonese forces, had come with his army and conquered the city, liberating them in the process. Their arrival in Córdova was a happy affair. Queen Isabel and her daughter turned out to greet them, and each of the ex-captives proceeded to kiss the royal hand in reverence. They proceeded to the cathedral where they received 8 reales each (about 10 sous) and were left to make their way back to their homes and families as best they could.[1]

1. Bernáldez, *Historia de los reyes católicos,* 1:207–8; the amount dispensed to each captive is confirmed by Isabel's treasurer, Gonzalo de Bae-

The story of the captives of Ronda provides a brief but useful look into the lives of captives after their release. It highlights their initial joy, the way that institutions such as the crown and the ransoming orders used them for purposes of propaganda, the ceremonies employed to incorporate the returnees into the Christian body social, and the uncertainty of life after their release symbolized by the long, ambiguous road that lay ahead for many on their journey home. The episode, moreover, is indicative of the fate of medieval captives in the historical sources. The efforts undertaken on their behalf while they were imprisoned and the parchment and paper trail this process created made them historical figures and brought their struggles to the eyes of the modern historian. Yet, after gaining their freedom, a shroud of obscurity descended upon most of them, hiding them from view. They disappeared into everyday life. The lack of sources is not absolute, and periodically we get glimpses of captives reclaiming their lives or trying to put the pieces back together. A begging license here, a dispensation from an almoner there, and perhaps a contract or inclusion in the text of a chronicle: tantalizing clues about specific captives. For the most part, however, we are left to reconstruct their experience from very scattered fragments and educated inferences.

Before captives could begin to recover their former lives, they had to somehow get out of captivity.[2] In spite of the extensive efforts organized on their behalf, only a small minority of Aragonese captives ever returned home. Using the figures given in chapter 1 of 2,300 Aragonese citizens in captivity in any given year, it is possible to work our way backward and to roughly approximate how many may have gotten out. Truces and wholesale prisoner exchanges were responsible for a large

---

za, in his account book, but he says that only 125 captives received alms from the queen: De la Torre and De la Torre, *Cuentas de Gonzalo de Baeza*, 86.

2. See also Friedman, *Encounter between Enemies*, 130; Cipollone, *Cristianità-Islam*, 223.

share of the liberations. The truce negotiations between Aragon and Tlemcen in 1319 discuss the release of some 300 Christians, while a similar negotiation with Granada in 1386 mentions 150 captives.[3] Other negotiations were not so fruitful, and exchanges that numbered only a couple of dozen captives were common.[4] Moreover, as truces typically lasted three to four years, even the larger figures do not represent annual exchanges but must be spread out over a number of years. Consequently, even the most sanguine estimate could not be much larger than some 50 captives a year released as the result of truces and prisoner exchanges. To this figure must be added those captives ransomed by the religious orders. Mercedarian historians have noted that the order ransomed some 7,000 captives throughout the fourteenth century, which would average out to 70 redemptions a year. As noted earlier, I believe this number is too high; 50 may be a more accurate figure which, when combined with those captives who were freed due to truces, gives us a total of 100. The ransoms of the Trinitarians are even more difficult to estimate.[5] Since the bulk of their ransoming efforts were carried out from Castile, relegating Aragon to a secondary theater, the number of Aragonese captives they ransomed was likely smaller than what the Mercedarians were able to accomplish; perhaps an average of 25 a year. We can optimistically assume another 100 were ransomed by their families, escaped, or otherwise found their freedom, for a grand total of 225 captives liberated in any given year. When this figure is compared to the 2,300 Christians who were in captivity in any given year, it yields a release rate of 9.8 percent.[6] As a result, even by hopeful calcula-

3. For the negotiations with Tlemcen, see Masía de Ros, *La Corona de Aragón* doc. 155 (Apr. 24, 1319); for Granada, see Canellas, *Aragón y la empresa del estrecho*, doc. 19 (June 26, 1386).
4. For example, Giménez Soler, "La Corona de Aragón y Granada," 30:342–44 (May 27, 1377); Ramos y Loscertales, *El cautiverio*, doc. 29 (Mar. 15, 1413).
5. For an overview, see Porres Alonso, *Libertad a los cautivos*, 1:277–84.
6. This figure is similar to the release rate that Davis has computed for cap-

tions only 1 in 10 captives ever found his way home. The rest of these men, women, and, in some cases, children converted to Islam or died in captivity.

The majority of those who were freed were passive participants in their own redemption, leaving their freedom in the hands of others. The most many of these captives did was to contact their family and hope that it could arrange a ransom. Others, less fortunate, who had no choice but to wait for the ransoming orders, faced even more uncertainty. Their freedom depended on one of the orders launching an expedition to the area where they were held, and then, if ransomers did come, on the chance that they would be among those chosen for liberation. Captives must have viewed the arrival of the ransoming friars with excitement and joy, but also doubt and fear. Cash reserves were usually insufficient to free everyone and while selection for ransom was a cause for celebration, exclusion would have been devastating. Once freed, captives waited for the ransomers to finish their mission in a safe house or other location set aside by the Muslim authorities specifically for that purpose. Before leaving Muslim territory, they had to pay a customs fee. The same fee was also imposed on those captives freed by merchants. Passage back to Christendom was on Christian ships that disembarked the captives in one of the major ports such as Mallorca, Valencia, or Barcelona. Some of the unluckier captives sometimes ran into pirates on the way home and, with freedom so close, returned to captivity.[7]

For those who opted to take matters into their own hands,

---

tives in the sixteenth and seventeenth centuries. Davis has argued that ransoms and escapes reduced the captive population by about 4 percent. However, truces do not appear to have been common at this time and do not enter into Davis's equation. When we add truces into our calculations, then the disparity between my figures and Davis's are not significant. See *Christian Slaves, Muslim Masters*, 21.

7. AHPB, Bernat Nadal, *Manual*, Nov. 14, 1394–May 9, 1395:fol. 7v (Nov. 21, 1394), published in Mitjà, "L'orde de la Mercè," doc. 11.

rather than waiting for a ransom or exchange that might never come, there were two options: flight or apostasy. Escape was always an option, although success was more likely from Granada than from North Africa, and the price of failure was great.[8] Captives escaping from Granada had to get across the border to Christian territories. Considering the shackles and the prisons it was not an easy task, but not an altogether impossible one either. Surprisingly, local Muslims helped the prisoners at times. An entry in the royal almoner's register for November 20, 1382, describes the recipient, N. Bafumet, as "a Moor who had rescued a friar of St. George."[9] The registers of the Kingdom of Valencia contain a similar example with a much more harrowing tale. Fernando de la Guzalera had been a captive in Almeria. Cilim, a black servant of the ruler of Almeria, had helped in his escape because he wanted to convert to Christianity. The two men stole a boat, hoping to make their way to Castile, but bad weather thwarted their plans and eventually the two were recaptured, this time by Christians who sold Cilim to a man from Cartagena who promptly sold him again. While with his second master, Cilim converted to Christianity and took the name of Johan. He endured one more sale, this time to Pere Roig, a Valencian. In the meantime, Fernando had been trying to free his companion. The king of Castile heard his appeals and asked the governor of Castilian Murcia to do what he could. By this time, Johan had passed on to Aragonese territory. So the governor wrote to the baile of Valencia, Johan Mercader, to petition his help. The baile finally worked out an exchange in which Johan's master received another black slave in return for Johan's freedom.[10]

8. For an overview of escapes by both Christians and Muslims, see Salicrú i Lluch, "En busca de una liberación alternativa," 703–13.

9. Altisent, L'almoina reial, 149.

10. Salicrú i Lluch, Documents per a la història de Granada, doc. 320 (Nov. 12, 1438); see Carriazo, "Relaciones fronterizas," 32, for a similar example.

.

Local Christians could also help escapees, but they faced imprisonment, or worse, if they were found out. Shortly before Christmas in 1417, as Alfonso IV celebrated the season in Valencia, he wrote a letter to Muhammad VIII, sultan of Granada, in which he asked for the liberation of Rodrigo Martínez and his wife, Benita, who stood accused of helping a Christian ship captain smuggle some Christian captives out of the Nasrid kingdom.[11] They were languishing in prison in place of those whom they had allegedly helped to escape. It is doubtful, however, this example notwithstanding, that Christian merchants were of much value in helping escapees. Their ships were under watch in port, and customs officials coming on board to inspect cargoes also complicated matters. Finally, penalties like those imposed on Rodrigo Martínez and his wife discouraged assistance.[12]

Captives who escaped by land had a daunting time finding their bearings and determining in what direction freedom lay, especially at night, when many escapes took place. To help them, the Castilians built a beacon in Alcalá la Real, marking the boundaries of their territories and signaling to lost captives where freedom lay. Although battered by storms, "many Christian captives escaped through the light of the said beacon."[13] In 1392 the Castilian king, Henry III, ordered its repair. One year later, it was still damaged, and Henry again gave orders to fix it, this time by asking the royal treasurer to track down craftsmen and workmen who could do the job.[14] Apparently at this point progress began to be made, and a few days later the king approved an outlay of annual funds for oil, wicks, and tenders to keep the beacon burning.[15]

---

11. ACA, C, reg. 2563:71r–v (Dec. 23, 1417), published in Salicrú i Lluch, *Documents per a la història de Granada*, doc. 20.

12. Khalilieh, *Islamic Maritime Law*, 147.

13. Juan y Lovera, *Colección diplomática medieval*, doc. 37 (July 10, 1392).

14. Ibid., doc. 43 (May 24, 1395).

15. Ibid., doc. 44 (June 3, 1395).

The Mediterranean made flight from North Africa a much more difficult endeavor. Captives had the monumental task of escaping from their chains and prisons, eluding the pursuers who followed, and finding transportation across the sea. The captive in *Don Quixote* accomplished such an escape, but he had the help of a Muslim woman and a Christian renegade and was leading a numerous party that could man a large vessel. Captives acting on their own did not have these options. Consequently, individual escape from Tunisian or Bougiot prisons was rare. The *Cantigas de Santa María* does include the escape of a captive from Muslim-held Mallorca; unfortunately, the text elides the details of the escape, other than that the escapee used a boat.[16]

Harsh punishments further discouraged escape attempts. The breakout planned at Montefrio (discussed in chapter 2) brought the captives severe beatings from their jailers when it was discovered. Recaptured fugitives in Tlemcen had their noses or ears severed and suffered whippings as punishment for their escapes.[17] A captive who failed in his escape from Tunis was beaten with over five hundred blows and the king also sentenced him to have his nose and ears cut off. More exemplary or, perhaps, sadistic punishment followed, and he was ordered to cut off the arms and legs of those who had tried to escape with him.[18]

Conversion to Islam may have created other opportunities for escape, but it was a dangerous course of action, with the renegade walking a tightrope of quickly changing alliances between enemies and friends. Some captives saw conversion as a way to join in raids against their former homes in order to slip away from their fellow raiders once they were in Christian ter-

16. Alfonso X, *Cantigas de Santa María*, no. 176.
17. ACA, C, CR, Alfonso III, box 24:3669 (Oct. 1327), published in Masiá de Ros, *La Corona de Aragón*, doc. 173.
18. AMG, Codice 8: 67r.

ritory. Others used the freedom they gained upon conversion to escape from Muslim territories into Christian regions.[19] Even if successful, they still had to deal with suspicious Christian authorities upon their return. Some of them carried letters from other captives and from Christian friars attesting to the superficiality of their conversion, undertaken as a means of escape or under duress.[20] In other situations, character witnesses interceded on behalf of renegades once Christian authorities had captured them. "Johan d'Albalat," wrote the town council of Valencia, "was a native of Valencia, who was in the power of the Moors, whence he was a captive, reneging the faith, but he was now reconciled."[21] Christians who converted to Islam also ran the risk of outsmarting themselves. A letter sent by the emir of Tunis to James II of Aragon provides a useful example. According to the Muslim monarch, he was refusing to release some Christian captives on whose behalf James had interceded because they were no longer Christians.[22] They had apostatized and their conversion had negated the diplomatic initiative of the king of Aragon.

Freedom did not mean an immediate return to home and family. The men and women ransomed by the Mercedarians and the Trinitarians were indentured to the orders for six months to a year. This servitude certainly had its advantages, as these captives did not emerge from their imprisonment with the crippling debts that many other captives contracted. Moreover, the orders fed them, clothed them, and even cared for them if they were sick.[23] But it also meant more time away from home and

19. See the story of the three Christian renegades who ransacked the palace of the sultan of Granada before escaping to Alicante. The sultan complained to James II, who tactfully avoided returning the renegades on the grounds that as Christians they would be tried under Christian law: Ferrer i Mallol, "La redempció," 243.

20. Bunes Ibarra, *La imagen de los musulmanes*, 195.

21. Rubio Vela, *Epistolari*, 1:doc. 114 (Aug. 17, 1401).

22. Giménez Soler, "Documentos de Túnez," doc. 19 (1315).

23. Millán Rubio, *La Orden de Nuestra Señora de la Merced*, 100.

family. Many other released captives became the subjects of ritualized pilgrimages and ceremonies that reintegrated them into Christian society and helped them to begin the process of recovering their lives, but were also time consuming. The captives freed from Ronda went through such a ceremony upon their return that included meeting the king and queen.[24] They were not the only captives to have this honor. It seems that almost every group of captives freed by the final campaigns of the Reconquest (1482–92) met at least one of the monarchs in a carefully staged ceremony.[25] The conquest of Málaga and the subsequent liberation of its captives were followed by an elaborate welcoming ceremony. The king ordered his workmen to erect the royal pavilion near the gate that led to Granada and there prepared to receive the captives in the company of the queen and their daughter.

> And by the gate where they [the captives] came out, there were many other people with crosses and royal pennons who processed with them to where the king and queen waited. When they arrived in the presence of Their Highnesses, they all humiliated themselves and fell to the floor wanting to kiss their feet, but the monarchs would not allow it, giving them their hands instead, and everyone who saw this gave praises to God, and cried tears of joy. . . . And the king ordered that the captives be given food and drink, and ordered their shackles removed, and they were given clothing and alms so that they could go wherever they pleased.[26]

By the time Granada fell in 1492, the ceremony had conventional elements and encompassed two days of rituals and celebrations. On the day of their release, the captives marched towards the assembled Christian host and met the monarchs and

24. For an excellent treatment of similar processions and ceremonies in the early modern period, see Weiss, "From Barbary to France."

25. Gozalbes Cravioto, "La liberación de los últimos cautivos."

26. Bernáldez, *Historia de los reyes católicos,* 1:249–50.

other dignitaries. On the second day, all the Christians, including the newly freed captives, made a procession to the nearest
church to celebrate mass. Eyewitnesses to the fall of Granada
recalled the details of these ceremonies. Bernard Roi, an Italian
who played a central role in the reception of the captives, wrote
a letter detailing the events a few days after they occurred. Roi
noted that following their entrance into the city after its conquest, the monarchs ordered

> [t]he captives who were imprisoned by the Muslims to be
> released, and they came in procession with the cross and
> an image of the blessed Virgin, which they carried with
> their chains, and I led them to the king, who as a Catholic
> prince received them kindly, and he ordered me to wait for
> the queen, who was following behind with other people, and
> with her was the cardinal of Spain; and said queen received
> [the captives] with great reverence and ordered that they be
> transferred to the castle of Santa Fé. . . . The next day we
> made the procession from the castle [inside Granada] to the
> city of Santa Fé, and the king and the queen were there with
> friars and clerics numbering four hundred; and there came
> the prisoners, seven hundred in number, who were dressed
> and given gifts by the king and queen, and in all these events,
> I was present.[27]

The meetings between recently freed captives and members
of the royal family were not limited to moments immediately
after conquests. The captives received by Diego Zurita in Jerez
de la Frontera were recuperating their strength before going on
to meet the king and, presumably, offer their thanks.[28] A Trini-

---

27. Garrido Atienza, *Las capitulaciones para la entrega de Granada,* doc.
68 (Jan. 7, 1492). Santa Fé was the camp set up by the Christians when they
besieged Granada. The procession was going to the church within the camp;
Gozalbes Cravioto, "La liberación de los últimos cautivos," 757–65, here see
761–62. See also Pescador del Hoyo, "Cómo fué de verdad la toma de Granada,"
326–28.
28. Torres Delgado, "Liberación de cautivos," 646.

tarian ransoming expedition from 1371 brought freed captives to meet with John, prince and future king of Aragon, prompting the prince to grant the order permission to seek alms within the realm.[29] A similar event took place in 1444 when María, queen of Aragon, took under her protection another recently released group of captives.[30]

Captives also participated in other ceremonies associated with their return. The collected miracles of Santo Domingo exist because captives who believed that the saint had freed them made pilgrimages to his monastery at Silos to tell their story. A similar desire to thank their intercessor in person drove those escaped captives who went to the shrine of the Virgin of Guadalupe. The monastery also recorded their stories of miraculous escapes. Pilgrimages of thanksgiving are also evident in the *Cantigas de Santa María* that involve captivity.[31] And we should not forget the processions staged by the ransoming orders when they returned with the freed captives to Christian cities.

How should we read these events? The meetings with the monarchs were opportunities for the captives to offer their thanks, but they also gave the monarchs the chance to highlight the role they had played in the liberation. The power of Iberian kings resided in a social contract with the people over whom they ruled. Implicit among the kings' obligations "was a commitment to fight the Moors and recover the lands once held by the Visigoths."[32] Consequently, victory celebrations typically followed the conquest of new regions, demonstrating to the people that the monarch was fulfilling his obligations. In the ceremonies described above, the crown co-opted the deliverance of the captives into a larger celebration of victory that was a mainstay of royal propaganda in the medieval

29. Porres Alonso, *Libertad a los cautivos*, doc. 3:34 (Feb. 24, 1371).
30. Ibid., doc. 3:83 (Feb. 5, 1444).
31. See, for example, *Cantigas* 83 and 176.
32. Ruiz, "Unsacred Monarchy," 123.

kingdoms of Spain.[33] This propaganda aimed to depict a martial king who was leading the Christian armies of Spain to victory over the Muslims, and the captives, needful of liberation, played a role not unlike that of damsels in distress in romances whom the chivalric king had come to rescue. Additional elements in these ceremonies also served to enhance royal prestige and mark the presence of royal power. The pennons are the most obvious signs, symbolizing royal authority and the central role the king played in setting the captives free.[34] Another good example was the kissing of the royal hands and feet, which had antecedents in the feudal kiss of homage found in northern Europe and also in Muslim customs, which implied submission and established a bond of loyalty between the grateful captives and the monarch.[35]

The sacred symbols are also important, as they were necessary for the ceremonies of thanksgiving that took place after successful battles. As Michael McCormick has pointed out, "armies and kings which expended such efforts to secure success could not fail to thank the divine author of victory after the battle."[36] The captives shared with the king and his soldiers a debt to divine intercessors. Many captives spent their time in captivity praying for deliverance, and it was natural that they would want to express their gratitude to the "divine author" of *their* "victory." From their perspective, the presence of the Virgin had a special significance, since she was the recipient of many of the prayers that many associated with their freedom. For the captives, processing with the Virgin, the saints, and even the monarchs was an opportunity to offer thanks to those who had made their freedom a reality. The liturgical elements

33. For an introduction, see Nieto Soria, *Ceremonias de la realeza*, esp. 145 58 for victory ceremonies; see also Ruiz, "Festivités, couleurs et symboles du pouvoir," 522–23 and 533–39.

34. Nieto Soria, *Ceremonias de la realeza*, 193–94.

35. Ruiz, "Unsacred Monarchy," 125–26.

36. McCormick, *Eternal Victory*, 355; see also Kempers, "Icons, Altarpieces, and Civic Ritual in Siena Cathedral," 102.

and the highly ritualized processions may also have served to bring back from the precipice of apostasy those captives who had been considering conversion.[37] Indeed, we should not forget the Mercedarian strategy of ransoming those captives who were contemplating conversion to Islam before any others. The aim here was twofold: to remove the captives from those surroundings that made conversion a tempting choice and subsequently, to place them in a setting where the sacred symbols of Christianity could restore their faith in Christ.

Marching together under the crosses, Marian images, and the royal pennons gave coherence to a varied group that included the monarchs, nobles, clerics, friars, common soldiers, and the captives. These postconquest processions and others like it glossed communal identities.[38] They identified who was "in" and who was "out" of any given group and helped define the social structure of a community.[39] This was of special importance to the captives, who, at least physically and geographically, had been torn away from the community of the faithful. The processions served to reincorporate them into the Christendom from which they had been absent for so long. As Robert Darnton has noted, a procession "was a statement unfurled in the streets, through which the city [community, society, etc.] represented itself to itself."[40] In a similar fashion, the processions in which captives participated after their release announced to the world that these men and women were again part of Christendom.

The procession, moreover, was but one of a series of rites of passage that the captives performed during this period of reinte-

37. Weiss, "From Barbary to France," 800.
38. Processions have received a lot of attention from scholars, especially of the early modern period. Among the better examples, see Darnton, "A Bourgeois Puts His World in Order"; Davis, "The Sacred and the Body Social"; Weiss, "From Barbary to France"; Zika, "Hosts, Processions, and Pilgrimages."
39. Muir, *Ritual in Early Modern Europe*, 3–4.
40. Darnton, "A Bourgeois Puts His World in Order," 120, is addressing specifically an eighteenth-century procession in Montpellier, but the point can be made about processions in general; see also 122–23.

gration.[41] In the case of the captives, the rites defined the transition from captive to free: a change of status from that of one who has been away to that of one who has returned. The masses may be the most obvious of these rites, as they performed a function analogous to the procession. They were the symbols of incorporation par excellence in Christianity, as evidenced by their use in baptisms, marriages, and coronations. The new clothes that the captives received also played a role in their reintegration. New outfits served to dress them with a spirit of renewal and belonging. The newly dressed captives were no longer the poor unfortunates clothed in tattered garments but members returned to a community in which people dressed like their brethren.[42] Even the geography of the ceremonies described above facilitated the move from one state to another: from slaves to freed men and women. The captives who emerged from the gates of Málaga and processed to where the king and queen waited offer a good example. The gate served as a "threshold which separate[d] two distinct areas, one associated with the subject's pre-ritual or pre-liminal status, and the other with his post-ritual or postliminal status."[43] Finally, these ceremonies of reintegration did not need to be collective. Those captives who made the pilgrimages to Silos or Guadalupe were not only offering thanks but also participating in self-imposed rites of reintegration as they made journeys to the sacred centers of Christendom and restaked their place in Christian society.[44]

41. Van Gennep identified three major phases in human ceremonies associated with these rites: separation, transition, and incorporation. For a brief overview of van Gennep's model, see Solon Kimball's introduction to the English language edition of *Rites of Passage*, vii–x.

42. Van Gennep, *Rites of Passage*, 94–95; see also Douglas, *Purity and Danger*, 114. For the importance of clothing to symbolize different stages of life or inclusion in a group, one only has to think of a bride's wedding dress, the black clothing of mourners at funerals, or uniforms, which by their very name imply the uniformity of a vast range of social groups from armies to softball teams; see Piponnier and Mane, *Dress in the Middle Ages*, 108–13.

43. Turner, *From Ritual to Theater*, 25. Turner is following van Gennep, *Rites of Passage*, 15–25.

44. Turner and Turner, "Pilgrimage as a Liminoid Phenomenon," 9, 34–

Flying pennons, processional crosses, and thresholds had powerful symbolic meanings, but they also had practical purposes. One immediate and tangible effect of the processions and other rites were the alms they stimulated and that the captives received: food, new clothes, and perhaps enough money to find their way home. The ceremonies that signified their symbolic return to the Christian community also marked them as eligible for further charitable assistance. Indeed, we can view the king and queen as setting an example for the rest of their subjects with the initial donations they made to the captives. In this case, the ritual became a model, "a standard or a simplified miniature for society to follow."[45] There is also no doubt that the ceremonies arranged by the ransoming orders were aimed at helping with their fund-raising efforts.[46] Monasteries associated with redemptions benefited from the popularity of their patron saints, especially as captives on pilgrimages of thanksgiving told their stories as they made their way to the sacred shrines, in turn spreading the popularity of the cults. Likewise, the irons and shackles that many captives donated to the religious houses, an act that in itself had strong symbolic overtones, gave additional credence to the cults of Santo Domingo in Silos and the Virgin Mary in Guadalupe and to the miraculous powers of these saints.[47]

The eventual homecoming must have been a moment of profound joy for the captives and their families, yet it was a happiness that was quickly tempered by the realities of life after captivity. How does one pick up the pieces of a shattered

35; for the pilgrimage as a unifying and centralizing institution, see Turner and Turner, "Locality and Universality in Medieval Pilgrimages," 188–89, 192–93; along similar lines, see Weiss's argument that as captives moved toward sacred centers, "they symbolically reclaimed their identities as subjects of the crown and children of God," in "From Barbary to France," 790.

45. Muir, *Ritual in Early Modern Europe*, 5.

46. Weiss, "From Barbary to France," 789–90.

47. García de la Borbolla, "Santo Domingo de Silos," 546–47.

life? For many who had received loans or pawned their possessions to raise their ransom, poverty awaited. We have already
met a few of them in the begging licenses: Stefan Moliner, trying to ransom his mother and six brothers; Anthony Sanc, a
captive who had left his son as hostage in Granada while he
raised the ransom and then found himself penniless; and Yvany
Garcia, who spent almost six years begging in order to pay off
the debts of his ransom. The wives and children of other captives appear in the dole lists of charitable institutions, although
the reasons for their poverty are often hidden under the general
heading of "deserving poor."[48] Other poor captives appealed to
the royal almoner for help: "Given to Berenguer Denadeu from
Mallorca, released from captivity, 2 florins," or to "Guillem de
la Abadia from Valencia to help with the ransom he has to pay,
5 florins."[49] The data from the almoner's roll, which lists only
one repeat petitioner over a seven-year period, seems to suggest
that captives got back on their feet relatively quickly.[50] However, this is misleading, since captives seem to have had one
chance to get money from the almoner, after which they had to
fend for themselves.

Many captives returned with health problems, which the
documents mention explicitly or which we can deduce from
their treatment in captivity. Antony Jorda had crippling injuries serious enough that Martin I allowed him to beg to sustain himself.[51] Other captives who lost limbs or suffered disfig-
urement during their imprisonment found it difficult to resume
their former lives.[52] Indeed, the royal almoner in Aragon had

48. i Fort and Claramunt, "El 'Plat des Pobres,'" table 9, 198–200.
49. Altisent, *L'almoina reial*, 174, 210.
50. The captive in question is Matheu Lombart, who received 1 florin on
two separate occasions, April 5 and 23, 1383; Altisent, *L'almoina reial*, 182,
183.
51. ACA, C, reg. 2208:9v–10r (Nov. 28, 1409), cited in Ferrer i Mallol, "La
redempció," 239n12.
52. For some examples, see ACA, C, reg. 2208:81v–82r (Apr. 16, 1410);
ACA, C, reg. 2593:67r–v (Feb. 28, 1424).

a special category for the *espunyats*, or those individuals who had lost their hands. They received substantial donations and their numbers were so great that they formed their own confraternity.[53] Those captives who were malnourished contended with illnesses and diseases brought on by the chronic lack of food, with many likely suffering lifelong morbidity. Studies on the effects of malnutrition suggest that prolonged starvation can lead to "altered heart muscle mass and function, decreased pulmonary mechanical function and a diminished response to stimuli to breathe . . . and immunodeficiency," among other ailments.[54] The immunodeficiency may have been the most dangerous, since it made captives susceptible to fatal diseases or left lasting damage on their bodies. Among pathogens, tuberculosis may have struck the captive populations with particular ferocity, since there is a clear link between the disease and sustained lack of food.[55] The description of "gaunt and pallid" captives offered by one chronicler might indicate consumption as much as the malnutrition the writer was highlighting.[56]

Perhaps the biggest cost was the psychological impact on captives and their families. Descriptions of the effects of separation are largely absent from the sources, and the effects would be unmeasurable even if this were not so. Earlier chapters have alluded to some of the indirect effects of separation, such as chil-

53. Gual suggests that some of these "espunyats" were victims of the war between Peter the Ceremonious and Peter the Cruel of Castile in the mid-1360s. Peter the Cruel had ordered the amputation of the hand of some of his prisoners. However, he allows that not all of the "espunyats" in the almoner's roll lost their hands under these circumstances: "La asistencia a los pobres," 475–76.

54. Hoffer, "Starvation," 936.

55. Malnutrition does not have the same positive effects on all contagious diseases. Although it is clearly implicated in the spread of tuberculosis, cholera, leprosy, and others, lack of food plays almost no role in the dissemination of malaria, the plague, or typhus: Rotberg and Rabb, *Hunger and History*, 308. See also the study conducted on two groups of World War II prisoners, one consisting of Danish policeman and the other of members of the resistance movement in Denmark. The policemen received food supplements while in captivity and as result contracted tuberculosis at about one-third the rate of the resistance members, whose rations were more meager: Bang, "Role of Disease," 66–67.

56. Bernáldez, *Historia de los reyes católicos*, 1:250.

dren begging for the ransom of their fathers or for their own daily bread, wives coming to terms with the disappearance of their husbands and the associated uncertainty, and parents grieving over sons and daughters who perished in captivity. Captives who returned after decades of enslavement would have found a world very different from the one they left behind. How many family members and friends would be alive or residing in the same region after an absence of fifteen or twenty years? Children would have been born, parents would have died, and the long absence could mean returning to a wife or husband who had remarried or an inheritance that had passed on to someone else. The joys of repatriation would have been brief as many of these realities sank in.

Captives also had to deal with the memories of their experience. All the details, from being taken from their beds in the middle of the night in a raid to beatings and rapes suffered at the hands of their captors to pangs of conscience experienced by those who abandoned their faith in moments of weakness, were locked in the captives' minds to torment them as they tried to recover their lives.[57] Many of the captives are likely to have experienced what we would today diagnose as post-traumatic stress disorder, which would manifest itself in an inability to readjust, depression, anxiety, anger, and alcoholism. These psychic scars, moreover, could remain with them for the rest of their lives.[58] And, lest we forget, these were the supposedly fortunate ones—the ones who had been freed and not left to die in captivity or converted to Islam. They were the survivors of an experience that was repeated incessantly in the late Middle Ages as Christians and Muslims continued locked in their struggle for dominion. Their legacy remains with us to this day.

57. For an example of former renegades wanting to expiate their sin, see Bennassar, *Los cristianos de Alá*, 509–16.
58. Studies conducted on prisoners of war in the Pacific theater during World War II reveal many of them still suffering psychological problems fifty years after their release: Ursano and Rundell, "The Prisoner of War," 440.

BIBLIOGRAPHY

ARCHIVAL SOURCES

Barcelona: Arxiu de la Corona d'Aragó

Cancillería Real

  Registers

    Pedro III (the Ceremonious)
      Guerre Sarracenorum: 1377, 1378, 1389
      Regum Sarracenorum: 555
      Commune (Diverse registers)
      Gratiarum (Diverse registers)

    Juan I (the Hunter)
      Commune: 1825–66
      Commune Sigilli Secretum: 1867–89
      Gratiarum: 1890–1911
      Diversorum: 1922–28
      Curiae Sigilli Secretum: 1952–69
      Peccuniae: 1971–85

    Martin I (the Humane)
      Commune: 2111–65
      Commune Sigilli Secretum: 2166–88
      Gratiarum: 2189–208
      Diversorum: 2209–16
      Peccuniae: 2253–62

    Fernando I (d'Antequera)
      Commune: 2359–80
      Commune Sigilli Secretum: 2381–91
      Gratiarum: 2392–95
      Diversorum: 2397
      Curiae Sigilli Secretum: 2401–10
      Peccuniae: 2411–12
      Diversorum (Alfonso IV): 2446–49

    Alfonso IV (the Magnanimous)
      Commune Sigilli Secretum: 2560–84
      Gratiarum: 2585–97

Commune Sigilli Secretum (regency of Queen Maria): 3108–13
Diversorum (regency of Queen Maria): 3116–61

Cartas Reales
  Jaime II
  Alfonso III
  Pedro III
  Juan I
  Martin I
  Fernando I
  Alfonso IV

Monacales, Hacienda de Barcelona
  Folio Volumes
  Parchment Rolls
  Parchments

Barcelona: Arxiu Històric de Protocols

Notaries
  Francesc Bernat: 1407–29
  Antoni Brocard: 1406–45
  Bartomeu Eiximenis: 1374–1413
  Joan Eiximenis: 1362–1407
  Berenguer Ermengol: 1366–1405
  Mateu Ermengol: 1399–1407
  Joan Ferrer, major: 1405–67
  Pere de Folgueres, menor: 1393–1443
  Joan Franc, major: 1406–56
  Francesc Fuster: 1387–1418
  Felip Gombau: 1370–1406
  Francesc de Manresa: 1401–24
  Bernat Nadal: 1385–1432
  Joan Nadal: 1384–1431
  Bernat Pi: 1408–50
  Pere de Pou: 1389–1421
  Pere Soler: 1411–60
  Gabriel Terrassa: 1401–48
  Joan de Vilagaia: 1402–28

Barcelona: Arxiu Històric de la Ciutat de Barcelona
Barcelona: Arxiu Diocesà de Barcelona

PUBLISHED PRIMARY SOURCES

Abellán Pérez, Juan. *Documentos de Juan II.* Murcia: Academia Alfonso
  X el Sabio, 1984.
Africano, Juan León. *Descripción de África y de las cosas notables que
  en ella se encuentran.* Madrid: Imperio, 1952.
Alarcón y Santón, M. A., and R. Garcia de Linares. *Los documentos*

árabes diplomáticos del Archivo de la Corona de Aragón. Madrid:
Imp. de E. Maestre, 1940.

Alfonso X. *Las Cantigas de Santa María: Códice Rico de el Escorial.*
Edited by José Filgueira Valverde. Madrid: Editorial Castalia, 1985.

———. *Las Siete Partidas.* 5 vols. Edited by Robert I. Burns. Translated
by Samuel Parsons Scott. Philadelphia: University of Pennsylvania
Press, 2001.

Al-Qalqasandi. *Subh al-a'ša fíkitâbât al-inša.* Translated by Luis Seco de
Lucena. Valencia: Anubar, 1975.

Antolínez de Burgos, Justino. *Historia eclesiástica de Granada.* Edited by
Manuel Sotomayor. Granada: Universidad de Granada, 1996.

Aquinas, St. Thomas. *Summa Theologiae.* 60 vols. Edited by R. J. Batten.
New York: Cambridge University Press, 1974.

Armengol Valenzuela, P. *Obras de San Pedro Pascual, martir obispo de
Jaén y religioso de la Merced.* 4 vols. Rome, n.p.,1906–8.

Augustine of Hippo. *Concerning the City of God against the Pagans.*
Translated by Henry Bettenson. 1972. Reprint, London: Penguin, 1984.

Baird, Joseph. *The Chronicle of Salimbene de Adam.* Binghampton, Eng.:
Medieval and Renaissance Texts and Studies, 1986.

Baratier, Edouard. *Documents de l'histoire de la Provence.* Toulouse:
Privat, 1971.

Bellorini, Theophilus, and Eugene Hoade, ed. and trans. *Visit to the Holy
Places of Egypt, Sinai, Palestine, and Syria in 1384 by Frescobaldi,
Gucci, and Sigoli.* Jerusalem: Franciscan Press, 1948.

Bellot, Pedro. *Anales de Orihuela.* Edited by Juan Torres Fontes. Alicante:
Academia Alfonso X el Sabio, 1954.

Bermúdez de Pedraza, Francisco. *Historia eclesiástica de Granada.*
Granada: Universidad de Granada, 1989.

Bernáldez, Andrés. *Historia de los reyes católicos Don Fernando y Doña
Isabel.* 2 vols. Seville: Imprenta que fue de Don Jose Maria Geofrin,
1870.

Bofarull y Mascaró, Próspero de. *Colección de documentos inéditos del
Archivo General de la Corona de Aragón.* 41 vols. Barcelona: J. E.
Montfort, 1847–1910.

Brunschvig, Robert. *Deux recits de voyage inedits en Afrique du Nord
au XV e siècle: Abdalbasit b. Halil et Adorne.* Paris: Larose Editeurs,
1936.

Burns, Robert. *Diplomatarium of the Crusader Kingdom of Valencia:
The Registered Charters of Its Conqueror James I, 1257–1276.* 3 vols.
Princeton, N.J.: Princeton University Press, 1991.

Camarena Mahiques, José. *Colección de documentos para la historia de
Gandía y su comarca.* Gandía: Casa Ferrer, 1959–61.

Canellas, Vidal de. *Traducción aragonesa de la obra "In Excelsis Dei
Thesauris" de Vidal de Canellas.* 3 vols. Edited by Gunnar Tilander.
London: H. Ohlssons, 1956.

Canellas López, Ángel. *Colección diplomática del concejo de Zaragoza.*
Zaragoza: "Cátedra Zaragoza" en la Universidad, 1972.

Carriazo y Arroquia, Juan de Mata, ed. *Colección diplomática de Quesada.* Jaén: Instituto de Estudios Giennenses del C.S. de I.C., 1975.
———. *Hechos del Condestable Don Miguel Lucas de Iranzo (crónica del siglo XV).* Madrid: Espasa-Calpe, 1940.
Caruana Gómez de Barreda, Jaime. *El fuero latino de Teruel.* Teruel: Instituto de Estudios Turolenses de la Excma, Diputación Provincial de Teruel, 1974.
Cervantes Saavedra, Miguel de. *The Adventures of Don Quixote.* Translated by J. M. Cohen. London: Penguin, 1950.
Chodorow, Stanley, and Charles Duggan. *Decretales Ineditae Saeculi XII.* Vatican City: Biblioteca Apostolica Vaticana, 1982.
Cicero, *De Officiis.* Edited by M. Winterbottom. New York: Oxford University Press, 1994.
Corpus Iuris Civilis. 3 vols. Edited by Paul Krueger et al. Dublin and Zurich: Weidmann, 1970.
De la Torre, Antonio, and E. A. De la Torre. *Cuentas de Gonzalo de Baeza: Tesorero de Isabel la Católica.* 2 vols. Madrid: Consejo Superior de Investigaciones Científicas, Patronato Marcelino Menéndez Pelayo, 1955.
Delaville le Roulx, Joseph. *Cartulaire general de l'ordre des Hospitaliers de Saint Jean de Jerusalem.* 4 vols. Paris: E. Leroux, 1894–1906.
Donna, Sister Rose Bernard. *Saint Cyprian: Letters (1–81).* Washington, D.C.: Catholic University of America Press, 1964.
Eanes de Zurara, Gomes. *Crónica dos feitos notáveis que se passaram na conquista da Guiné por mandado Do Infante D. Henrique.* 2 vols. Edited by Torquato de Sousa Soares. Lisbon, 1978. Translated by C. R. Beazley and Edgar Prestage in *The Chronicle of the Discovery and Conquest of Guinea,* 2 vols. (New York: Hakluyt Society, 1896).
Eimeric, Nicolas. *El manual de los inquisidores.* Edited and translated by Louis Sala Molins and Francesco Martin. Barcelona: Muchnik Editores, 1983.
Eno, Robert. *Saint Augustine: Letters, Volume VI (1*–29*).* Washington, D.C.: Catholic University of America Press, 1989.
Estal, Juan Manuel del. *Corpus documental del reino de Murcia bajo la soberanía de Aragón.* Alicante: Instituto de Estudios Juan Gil-Albert, 1985.
García Guzmán, María del Mar. *Colección diplomática del adelantamiento de Cazorla (1231–1495).* Cádiz: Universidad de Cádiz, 1991.
Garrido Atienza, Miguel. *Las capitulaciones para la entrega de Granada.* Edited by José Enrique López de Coca Castañer. Granada: Universidad de Granada, 1992.
Giménez Soler, Andrés. "Documentos de Túnez: Originales y traducidos del Archivo de la Corona de Aragón." *Anuari de l'Institut d'estudis Catalans* 3 (1909–10): 210–59.
Golubovich, P. Girolamo. *Biblioteca bio-bibliografica della Terra Santa e dell Oriente franciscano.* 8 vols. Florence: Collegio di S. Bonaventura, 1913.

Gorosch, Max. *El fuero de Teruel.* Stockholm: n.p., 1950.

Gran crónica de Alfonso XI. 2 vols. Edited by Diego Catalan. Madrid: Seminario Menéndez Pidal, Universidad Complutense de Madrid: Editorial Gredos, 1976.

Gross, Joseph. *The Trinitarian's Rule of Life: Texts of the Six Principal Editions.* Rome: Trinitarian Historical Institute, 1983.

Haedo, Diego de. *Topografía e historia general de Argel por el Maestro Frey Diego de Haedo.* 3 vols. Madrid: Sociedad de Bibliófilos Españoles, 1927.

Hinojosa Montalvo, José. *Documentación medieval alicantina en el archivo del reino de Valencia.* Alicante: Instituto de Estudios Juan Gil-Albert, 1986.

———. *Textos para la historia de Alicante: Historia medieval.* Alicante: Instituto de Cultura Juan Gil-Albert, 1990.

Hoare, F. R. *The Western Fathers: Being the Lives of SS. Martin of Tours, Ambrose, Augustine of Hippo, Honoratus of Arles, and Germanus of Auxerre.* New York: Sheed and Ward, 1954.

Hood, A. B. E., ed. and trans. *St. Patrick: His Writings and Muirchu's Life.* London: Rowman and Littlefield, 1978.

Housley, Norman. *Documents on the Later Crusades, 1274–1580.* London: Macmillan, 1996.

Ibn Battuta. *The Travels of Ibn Battuta, AD 1325–1354.* 4 vols. Edited and translated by H. A. R. Gibb. London: Hakluyt Society, 1956–94.

Ibn Jubayr. *The Travels of Ibn Jubayr.* Translated by R. J. C. Broadhurst. London: J. Cape, 1952.

Ibn Khaldun. *Histoire des Berbères et des dynasties musulmanes de l'Afrique septentrionale.* 4 vols. Translated by Baron de Slane. Paris: P. Guthner, 1934.

———. *The Muqaddimah: An Introduction to History.* Edited by N. J. Dawood. Translated by Franz Rosenthal. 1967. Reprint, Princeton, N.J.: Princeton University Press, 1989.

Itinerarium Symonis Semeonis ab Hybernia ad Terram Sanctam. Edited by Mario Esposito. Dublin: Dublin Institute for Advanced Studies, 1960.

Jados, Stanley S. *The Consulate of the Sea and Related Documents.* Tuscaloosa: University of Alabama Press, 1975.

Juan y Lovera, Carmen. *Colección diplomática medieval de Alcalá la Real.* 2 vols. Alcalá la Real: Esclavitud del Señor de la Humildad y María Santísima de los Dolores, 1988.

Lewis, Bernard, ed. and trans. *Islam: From the Prophet Muhammad to the Capture of Constantinople.* 2 vols. New York: Harper and Row, 1974.

Llull, Ramon. *Blanquerna.* Edited by E. A. Peers. London: Dedalus, 1987.

Marineo Sículo, Lucio. *Vida y hechos de los reyes católicos.* 1587. Reprint, Madrid: Atlas, 1943.

Martínez Ferrando, J. E. *Catálogo de la documentación relativa al antiguo reino de Valencia.* Madrid: Imprenta Góngora], 1934.

Masía de Ros, Ángeles. *Jaume II: Aragó, Granada i Marroc: Aportació documental.* Barcelona: Consejo Superior de Investigaciones Científicas, 1989.

Medina, Pedro de. *Libro de grandezas y cosas memorables de España.* In *Obras de Pedro de Medina,* edited by Ángel González Palencia. Madrid: Consejo Superior de Investigaciones Científicas, 1944.

Migne, J. P. *Patrologiae Cursus Completus: Series Latina.* 221 vols. Paris: Garnieri Fratres, 1844–64.

Miquel Rosell, Francisco. *Regesta de letras pontíficas del Archivo de la Corona de Aragón.* Madrid: Cuerpo de Archiveros, Bibliotecarios y Arqueologos, 1948.

Molina, Tirso de. *Historia general de la Ordén de Nuestra Señora de las Mercedes.* 2 vols. Edited by Manuel Penedo Rey. Madrid: Provincia de la Merced de Castilla, 1973.

Molina Grande, María Concepción. *Colección de documentos para la historia del reino de Murcia: Documentos de Enrique IV.* Murcia: Academia Alfonso X el Sabio, 1988.

Molina Molina, Ángel Luis. *Colección de documentos para la historia del reino de Murcia: Documentos de Pedro I.* Murcia: Academia Alfonso X el Sabio, 1978.

Muntaner, Ramon. *Chrònica.* 2 vols. Edited by Marina Gustà. Barcelona: Edicions 62, 1979.

Münzer, Jerónimo. *Viaje por España y Portugal.* Edited and translated by Ramón Alba. Madrid: Ediciones Polifemo, 1991.

Muñoz y Romero, Tomás. *Colección de fueros municipales y cartas pueblas de los reinos de Castilla, León, Corona de Aragón y Navarra.* Madrid: Impr. de Don J. M. Alonso, 1847.

Parsons, Sister Wilfrid. *Saint Augustine: Letters, Volume II (83–130).* New York: Cima, 1953.

Poggibonsi, Fra Niccolo de. *A Voyage beyond the Seas, 1346–1350.* Edited and translated by T. Bellorini and E. Hoade. Jerusalem: Franciscan Press, 1945.

Possideus. *Vita Augustini.* Edited and translated by F. R. Hoare in *The Western Fathers: Being the Lives of SS. Martin of Tours, Ambrose, Augustine of Hippo, Honoratus of Arles, and Germanus of Auxerre* (New York: Sheed and Ward, 1954).

Powers, James, ed. and trans. *The Code of Cuenca: Municipal Law on the Twelfth-Century Castilian Frontier.* Philadelphia: University of Pennsylvania Press, 2000.

Pulgar, Fernando del. *Crónica de los reyes católicos por su secretario Fernando del Pulgar.* 2 vols. Edited by Juan de Mata Carriazo. Madrid: Espasa-Calpe, 1943.

Rodríguez Llopis, Miguel. *Documentos para la historia medieval de Moratalla.* Murcia: Academia Alfonso X el Sabio, 1988.

Rodríguez Molina, José, et al. *Colección diplomática del archivo municipal de Jáen, siglos XIV–XV.* Jaén: Excelentisimo Ayuntamiento de Jaén, 1985.

Rodríguez Moñino, Antonio, ed. *Cancionero de romances (Anvers, 1550)*. Madrid: Editorial Castalia, 1967.

Rohricht, R. "Lettres de Ricolde de Monte Croce." In *Archives de l'Orient Latin* 2 (1884): 258–96.

Rosell y López, Cayetano. *Crónica de los reyes de Castilla*. In *Biblioteca de autores españoles* 3 vols. Madrid: Ediciones Atlas, 1953.

Rubio Vela, Agustín. *Epistolari de la Valencia medieval*. 2 vols. Valencia: Institut de Filologia Valenciana, 1985–98.

Salicrú i Lluch, Roser. *Documents per a la història de Granada del regnat d'Alfons el Magnànim (1416–1458)*. Barcelona: Consell Superior d'Investigaciones Científiques, Institució Milà i Fontanals, 1999.

Sánchez Parra, María Pilar. *Crónica anónima de Enrique IV de Castilla, 1454–1474*. 2 vols. Madrid: Ediciones de la Torre, 1991.

Sancho y Vicens, A. "Documentos sobre cautivos." *Boletín de la Sociedad Arqueologica Luliana* 28 (1939–43): 547–55.

Sbaraglia, Giovanni G. *Bullarium Franciscanum Romanorum Pontificum*. 7 vols. Rome: Typis Sacrae Congregrationis de Propaganda Fide, 1759.

Schaff, Philip, and Henry Wace. *A Select Library of Nicene and Post Nicene Fathers of the Christian Church—Second Series*. 14 vols. New York: Christian Literature, 1890–1900.

Tintó Sala, Margarita. *Cartas del baile general de Valencia, Joan Mercader, al rey Fernando de Antequera*. Valencia: Consejo Superior de Investigaciones Cientificas, 1979.

Torres Fontes, Juan. *Colección de documentos para la historia del reino de Murcia*. Murcia: Nogués, 1963.

———. *Colección de documentos para la historia del reino de Murcia: Documentos de Fernando IV*. Murcia: Nogués, 1980.

Ubieto Arteta, Antonio. *Colección diplomática de Cuellar*. Segovia: n.p., 1961.

Valera, Mosen Diego de. *Crónica de los reyes católicos*. Edited by Juan de Mata Carriazo. Madrid: J. Molina, 1927.

Veas Arteseros, Francisco. *Colección de documentos para la historia del reino de Murcia: Documentos del siglo XIV*. 2 vols. Murcia: Academia Alfonso X el Sabio, 1985–90.

Vergara, Sebastian de. *Vida y milagros de el thaumaturgo Español Moyses Segundo, redemptor de cautivos, abogado de los felices partos, Sto. Domingo Manso, abad Benedictino, reparador de el Real Monasterio de Silos*. Madrid: Imprenta de los Herederos de Francisco del Hierro, 1736.

Vich y Salom, Juan. *Documenta Regni Majoricarum (Miscelanea)*. Palma de Majorca: Imp. Amengual y Muntaner, 1945.

Ximena Jurado, Martín de. *Catálogo de los obispos de las iglesias catedrales de Jaén y anales eclesiásticos de este obispado*. Edited by José Rodríguez Molina and María José Osorio Pérez. Granada: Servicio de Publicaciones de la Universidad de Granada, 1991.

Zurita, Jerónimo. *Anales de la Corona de Aragón*. 9 vols. Edited by Ángel Canellas López. Zaragoza: Institución "Fernando el Católico," 1974.

SECONDARY SOURCES

Al-'Abbadi, Ahmad Mujtar. *El reino de Granada en la época de Muhammad V.* Madrid: Instituto de Estudios Islámicos, 1973.

Alemany, M. José. "Milicias cristianas al servicio de los sultanes musulmanes del Al Magreb." In *Homenaje a Don Francisco Codera,* edited by Eduardo Saavedra, 133–69. Zaragoza: M. Escar, 1904.

Altisent, Agustín. *L'almoina reial a la corte de Pere de Ceremoniós: Estudi i edició dels manuscrits de l'almoiner fra Guillem Deude, monjo de Poblet (1378–1385).* Poblet: Abadia de Poblet, 1969.

Argente del Castillo Ocaña, Carmen. "Los cautivos en la frontera entre Jaén y Granada." In *Relaciones exteriores del reino de Granada,* edited by Cristina Segura Graiño, 211–25. Almeria: Instituto de Estudios Almerienses, 1988.

Arié, Rachel. *El reino Nasrí de Granada (1232–1492).* Madrid: Editorial Mapfre, 1992.

———. "Remarques sur l'alimentation des Musulmans d'Espagne au cors du bas Moyen Âge." *Cuadernos de estudios medievales* 2–3 (1974–75): 299–312.

Arnold, T. W. *The Preaching of Islam: A History of the Propagation of the Muslim Faith.* New York: AMS, 1974.

Arribas Palau, Mariano. "Los benimerines en los pactos concertados entre Aragón y Granada. "In *Actas, primer congreso de estudios árabes e islámicos,* 179–88. Cordova: Comite Permanente del Congreso de Estudios Árabes e Islámicos, 1962.

———. *Intercambios de embajadas entre Abu Said Utman III de Marruecos y Fernando I de Aragón.* Tetuan: Editora Marroquí, 1956.

———. *Musulmanes de Valencia apresados cerca de Ibiza en 1413.* Tetuan: Impr. del Majzen, 1955.

———. *Las treguas entre Castilla y Granada firmadas por Fernando I de Aragón.* Tetuan: Editora Marroquí, 1956.˙

Atiya, A. S. "An Unpublished 14th-Century Fatwâ on the Status of Foreigners in Mamlûk Egypt and Syria." In *Studien zur Geschichte und Kultur des Nahen und Fernen Ostens Paul Kahle,* edited by Willi Heffening and Willibald Kirfel, 55–68. Leiden: E. J. Brill] 1935.

Backman, Clifford. *The Decline and Fall of Medieval Sicily: Politics, Religion, and Economy in the Reign of Frederick III, 1296–1337.* Cambridge: Cambridge University Press, 1995.

Bakare-Yusuf, Bibi. "The Economy of Violence: Black Bodies and the Unspeakable Terror." In *Gender and Catastrophe,* edited by Ronit Lentin, 171–83. London: Zed, 1997.

Balard, Michael. "Coastal Shipping and Navigation in the Mediterranean." In *Cogs, Caravels, and Galleons: The Sailing Ship, 1000–1650,* edited by Robert Gardiner, 131–38. London: Conway Maritime Press, 1994.

Bang, Frederick B. "The Role of Disease in the Ecology of Famine." In *Famine: Its Causes, Effects, and Management,* edited by John R. K.

Robson, 61–75. New York: Gordon and Breach Science Publishers, 1981.

Barber, Malcolm. *The Military Orders: Fighting for the Faith and Caring for the Sick.* London: Ashgate, 1994.

Baron, Salo Wittmayer. *A Social and Religious History of the Jews.* 18 vols. New York: Columbia University Press, 1952.

Batlle i Gallart, Carmen, and Montserrat Casas i Nadal. "La caritat privada i les institucions benefiques de Barcelona (Segle XIII)." In *La pobreza y la asistencia a los pobres en la Cataluña medieval,* edited by Manuel Riu, 1:117–90. Barcelona: Consejo Superior de Investigaciones Científicas, 1980.

Ben Driss, Abdelghaffar. "Los cautivos entre Granada y Castilla en el siglo XV según las fuentes Árabes." In *Actas del Congreso: La frontera oriental Nazarí como sujeto histórico (s. XIII–XVI),* edited by Pedro Segura Artero, 301–10. Almeria: Instituto de Estudios Almerienses, 1997.

———. "La frontera Granadino-Castellana en la primera mitad del siglo XV." In *Estudios de frontera: Alcalá la Real y el Arcipreste de Hita,* edited by Francisco Toro Ceballos and José Rodríguez Molina, 41–48. Jaén: Diputación Provincial de Jaén, Area de Cultura, 1996.

Bennassar, Bartolome. *Los cristianos de Alá.* Madrid: Nerea, 1989.

———. "L'Europe devant l'Inquisition: Le cas des renégats." In *Glaubensprozesse—Prozesse des Glaubens?* edited by Titus Heydenreich and Peter Blumenthal, 33–42. Tubingen: Stauffenburg Verlag, 1972.

———. "Frontières religieuses entre Islam et Chrétienté: L'experience vecue par les renégats." In *Las frontieres religieuses en Europe de XV e au XVII e siecle,* edited by Robert Sauzet, 71–78. Paris: J. Vrin, 1992.

Bensch, Stephen. "From Prizes of War to Domestic Merchandise: The Changing Face of Slavery in Aragón." *Viator* 25 (1994): 63–93.

Bisson, T. N. The Medieval Crown of Aragon. Oxford: Clarendon, 1986.

Blackburn, Robin. *The Making of New World Slavery: From the Baroque to the Modern, 1492–1800.* London: Verso, 1997.

Blum, Jerome. *The End of the Old Order in Rural Europe.* Princeton, N.J.: Princeton University Press, 1978.

Bolton, Brenda. "'Perhaps You Do not Know?': Innocent III's Approach to the Release of Captives." In *La liberazione dei "captivi" tra Cristianità e Islam. Oltre la crociata e il ǧihād: Tolleranza e servizio umanitario,* edited by Giulio Cipollone, 457–63. Vatican City: Archivio Segreto Vaticano, 2000.

Boswell, John. *The Royal Treasure: Muslim Communities under the Crown of Aragón in the Fourteenth Century.* New Haven, Conn.: Yale University Press, 1977.

Bradley, Keith R. "*Servus Onerosus:* Roman Law and the Troublesome Slave." *Slavery and Abolition* 11 (1990): 135–57.

Braudel, Fernand. *The Mediterranean and the Mediterranean World in the Age of Philip II.* 2 vols. Translated by Siân Reynolds. New York: Harper and Row, 1966.

Bresc, Henri. "Course et piraterie en Sicile (1250–1450)." *Anuario de estudios medievales* 10 (1980): 751–58.

Brett, Edward Tracy. *Humbert of Romans: His Life and Views of Thirteenth-Century Society.* Toronto: Pontifical Institute of Mediaeval Studies, 1984.

Brodman, James. "The Mercedarian Order and the Problem of Royal Patronage during the Reign of James I." In *Jaime I y su época, Vols. 3–5,* edited by Engracia Alsina Prat et al., 3:71–76. Zaragoza: Institución Fernando el Católico, 1979.

———. "Military Redemptionism and the Castilian Reconquest." *Military Affairs* 44 (1980): 24–27.

———. "Municipal Ransoming Law on the Medieval Spanish Frontier." *Speculum* 60, no. 2 (1985): 318–30.

———. "The Origins of Hospitallerism in Medieval Catalonia." In *Iberia and the Mediterranean World of the Middle Ages,* edited by Larry Simon, 290–302. Leiden: E. J. Brill, 1995.

———. "Ransomers or Royal Agents: The Mercedarians and the Aragonese Crown in the 14th Century." In *Iberia and the Mediterranean World of the Middle Ages,* edited by P. E. Chevedden, D. J. Kagay, and P. G. Padilla, 239–52. Leiden: E.J. Brill, 1996.

———. *Ransoming Captives in Crusader Spain: The Order of Merced on the Christian Islamic Frontier.* Philadelphia: University of Pennsylvania Press, 1986.

———. "The Rhetoric of Ransoming: A Contribution to the Debate over Crusading in Medieval Iberia." In *Tolerance and Intolerance: Social Conflict in the Age of Crusades,* edited by Michael Gervers and James Powell, 41–52. Syracuse, N.Y.: Syracuse University Press, 2001.

———."The Trinitarian and Mercedarian Orders: A Study of Religious Redemptionism in the Thirteenth Century." PhD dissertation, University of Virginia, 1974.

———. "What Is a Soul Worth? Pro Anima Bequests in the Municipal Legislation of Reconquest Spain." *Medievalia et humanistica* 20 (1994): 15–23.

Bromley, David G. "The Social Construction of Contested Exit Roles: Defectors, Whistleblowers, and Apostates." In *The Politics of Religious Apostasy: The Role of the Apostates in the Transformation of Religious Movements,* edited by David G. Bromley, 19–48. Westport, Conn.: Praeger, 1998.

Brownmiller, Susan. *Against Our Will: Men, Women, and Rape.* New York: Simon and Schuster, 1975.

Brunschvig, Robert. "Abd." In *Encyclopedia of Islam,* 2nd ed., 1:24–40. Leiden: E. J. Brill, 1960.

———. "Documents inedits sur les relations entre la couronne d'Aragon et la Berbérie orientale au XIVe siècle." *Annales de l'Institut d'Estudes Orientales* 2 (1936): 235–65.

Buckle, Colin. *Weather and Climate in Africa.* Essex, Eng.: Longman, 1996.

Bulliet, Richard. *Conversion to Islam in the Medieval Period: An Essay in Quantitative History.* Cambridge, Mass.: Harvard University Press, 1979.

Bunes Ibarra, Miguel Ángel de. *La imagen de los musulmanes y del norte de África en la España de los siglos XVI y XVII: Los caracteres de una hostilidad.* Madrid: Consejo Superior de Investigaciones Científicas, 1989.

Burns, Robert. "Canon Law and the Reconquista: Convergence and Symbiosis in the Kingdom of Valencia under Jaume the Conqueror (1213–1276)." In *Proceedings of the Fifth International Conference of Medieval Canon Law,* edited by Stephan Kuttner and Kenneth Pennington, 387–424. Vatican City: Biblioteca Apostolica Vaticana, 1980.

———. "Christian Islamic Confrontation in the West: The 13th-Century Dream of Conversion." *American Historical Review* 76 (1971): 1386–434.

———. *The Crusader Kingdom of Valencia: Reconstruction on a Thirteenth-Century Frontier.* 2 vols. Cambridge, Mass.: Harvard University Press, 1967.

———. *Muslims, Christians, and Jews in the Crusader Kingdoms of Valencia.* Cambridge: Cambridge University Press, 1984.

———. "Renegades, Adventurers, and Sharp Businessmen: The 13th-Century Spaniard in the Cause of Islam." *Catholic Historical Review* 58 (1972): 341–66.

———. "Social Riots on the Christian-Moslem Frontier (Thirteenth-Century Valencia)." *American Historical Review* 66 (1961): 378–400.

Buxó Massaguer, Sofía Ana. "Iconografía de la pobreza en la pintura catalana de los siglos XII–XV." In *La pobreza y la asistencia a los pobres en la Cataluña medieval,* edited by Manuel Riu, 2:49–79. Barcelona: Consejo Superior de Investigaciones Científicas, 1980–82.

Cabanes Catalá, María Luisa. *Correspondencia entre el "consell" de Valencia y las tierras Alicantinas en el siglo XIV.* Alicante: Instituto de Cultura Juan Gil-Albert, 1995.

Cabanes Pecourt, María D. "El 'Llibre Negre' del Archivo General del Reino de Valencia." *Ligarzas* 2 (1970): 139–73.

Cabestany i Fort, Joan Ferran, and Salvador Claramunt. "El 'Plat des Pobres' de la parroquia de Santa María del Pi de Barcelona (1401–1428)." In *A pobreza e a assistência aos pobres na península ibérica durante a Idada Média,* 157–218. Lisbon: Imprensa Nacional, Casa da Moeda, 1973.

Cabrera Muñoz, Emilio. "Cautivos cristianos en el reino de Granada durante la segunda mitad del siglo XV." In *Relaciones exteriores del reino de Granada,* edited by Cristina Segura Graiño, 227–36. Almeria: Instituto de Estudios Almerienses, 1988.

Canellas, Ángel. "Aragón y la empresa del estrecho en el siglo XIV: Nuevos documentos del Archivo Municipal de Zaragoza." *Estudios de la edad media de la Corona de Aragón* 2 (1946): 7–73.

Capmany y de Monpalau, Antonio de. *Memorias históricas sobre la marina, comercio y artes de la antigua ciudad de Barcelona.* 3 vols. Barcelona: Cámara Oficial de Comercio y Navegación de Barcelona, 1962.

Card, Claudia. "Rape as a Weapon of War." *Hypatia* 11 (1996): 5–18.

Cariñena i Balaguer, Rafael, and Andrés Díaz i Borràs. "Corsaris valencians i esclaus barbarescs a les darriers del segle XIV: Una subhasta d'esclaus a València el 1385." *Estudis castellonencs* 2 (1984–85): 439–56.

Carle, María del Carmen. "La servidumbre en las *Partidas.*" *Cuadernos de historia de España* 12 (1949): 105–19.

Carriazo, Juan de Mata. "Relaciones fronterizas entre Jaén y Granada en el año 1479." *Revista de archivos, nibliotecas y museos* 61 (1955): 23–51.

Cenival, Pierre de. "L'église chretienne de Marrakesh au XIIIe Siecle." *Hesperis* 7 (1927): 69–83.

Charouiti Hasnaoui, Milouda. "Esclavos y cautivos según la ley islámica: Condiciones y consequencias." In *De l'esclavitud a la llibertat: Esclaus i lliberts a l'edat mitjana,* edited by Maria Teresa Ferrer i Mallol and Josefina Mutgé Vives, 1–18. Barcelona: Consell Superior d'Investigacions Científiques, 2000.

Chazan, Robert. *Barcelona and Beyond: The Disputation of 1263 and Its Aftermath.* Berkeley: University of California Press, 1992.

Chiffoleau, Jacques. *La comptabilité de l'au-delà: Les hommes, la mort et la religion dans la région d'Avignon à la fin du Moyen Âge (vers 1320–vers 1480).* Rome: Ecole Française de Rome, 1980.

Cipollone, Giulio. *Cristianità-Islam: Cattività e liberazione in neme di dio. Il Tempo di Innocenzo III, dopo "il 1187."* Rome: Editrice Pontificia Università Gregoriana, 1992.

———. "Esclavitud y liberación en la frontera." In *Estudios de frontera: Alcalá la Real y el Arcipreste de Hita,* edited by Francisco Toro Ceballos and José Rodríguez Molina, 59–97. Jaén: Diputación Provincial de Jaén, Area de Cultura, 1996.

———, ed. *La liberazione dei "captivi" tra Cristianità e Islam. Oltre la crociata e il ǧihād: Tolleranza e servizio umanitario.* Vatican City: Archivio Segreto Vaticano, 2000.

———. "L'ordo Trinitatis et captivorum: Il suo insediamento nelle baleari (XIII–XIV)." *Congres d'historia de la Corona d'Aragó* (1989): 169–78.

———. "L'ordre de la Sainte Trinité et de la rédemption des captifs (1198): Les Trinitaires dans le Midi." *Cahiers de Fanjeaux* 18 (1983) 135–56.

Claramunt, Salvador. "Dos aspectes de l'alimentació medieval: Dels canonges a les *Miserabiles Personae.*" In *Alimentació i societat a la Catalunya medieval,* 167–72. Barcelona: Consell Superior d'Investigaciones Científiques, 1988.

Clissold, Stephen. *The Barbary Slave.* London: P. Elek, 1977.

Colley, Linda. *Captives.* New York: Pantheon, 2002.

Constable, Olivia Remi. "Muslim Spain and Mediterranean Slavery: The

Medieval Slave Trade as an Aspect of Muslim-Christian Relations."
In *Christendom and Its Discontents: Exclusion, Persecution, and
Rebellion, 1000–1500*, edited by Scott L. Waugh and Peter D. Diehl,
264–84. Cambridge: Cambridge University Press, 1996.
———. *Trade and Traders in Muslim Spain: The Commercial
Realignment of the Iberian Peninsula, 900–1500*. Cambridge:
Cambridge University Press, 1994.
Coope, Jessica A. "Religious and Cultural Conversion to Islam in Ninth-
Century Umayyad Córdova." *Journal of World History* 4 (1993): 47–68.
Cossío, Jóse María de. "Cautivos de Moros en el siglo XIII." *Al-Andalus* 7
(1942): 49–112.
Cruz Hernández, Miguel. *El Islam de Al-Andalus: Historia y estructura
de su realidad social*. Madrid: Agencia Espannñola de Cooperación
Internacional, Instituto de Cooperación con el Mundo Arabe, 1992.
Darnton, Robert. "A Bourgeois Puts His World in Order: The City as
a Text." In *The Great Cat Massacre and Other Episodes in French
Cultural History*, 107–43. New York: Basic Books, 1985.
Davis, David Brion. *The Problem of Slavery in Western Culture*. Ithaca,
N.Y.: Cornell University Press, 1966.
———. *Slavery and Human Progress*. New York: Oxford University
Press, 1984.
Davis, Natalie Z. "The Sacred and the Body Social in Sixteenth-Century
Lyon." *Past and Present* 90 (1981): 40–70.
Davis, Robert. *Christian Slaves, Muslim Masters: White Slavery in the
Mediterranean, the Barbary Coast, and Italy, 1500–1800*. New York:
Palgrave Macmillan, 2003.
Díaz Borrás, Andrés. *El miedo al Mediterráneo: La caridad popular
valenciana y la redención de cautivos bajo poder Musulmán, 1323–
1539*. Barcelona: Consejo Superior de Investigaciones Científicas, 2001.
———. "Notas sobre los primeros tiempos de la atención valenciana a
la redención de cautivos cristianos." *Estudis catellonencs* 3 (1986):
337–54.
———. "La organización de la caridad redentiva en la ciudad de Valencia
a finales del siglo XIV." In *Estudios de frontera: Alcalá la Real y
el Arcipreste de Hita*, edited by Francisco Toro Ceballos and José
Rodríguez Molina, 157–75. Jaén: Diputación Provincial de Jaén, Area
de Cultura, 1996.
———. *Los orígenes de la piratería islámica en Valencia: La ofensiva
musulmana trecentista y la reacción cristiana*. Barcelona: Consejo
Superior de Investigaciones Científicas, 1993.
Díaz Plaja, Fernando. *La vida cotidiana en la España musulmana*.
Madrid: EDAF, 1993.
Dillard, Heath. *Daughters of the Reconquest: Women in Castilian Town
Society, 1100–1300*. New York: Cambridge University Press, 1984.
Dockes, Pierre. *Medieval Slavery and Liberation*. Translated by Arthur
Goldhammer. London: University of Chicago Press, 1982.
Dossat, Yves. "Les ordres de rachat, les Mercédaires." In *Assistance et*

charité, edited by Edouard Privat, 365–87. Toulouse: Center d'Etudes Historiques de Fanjeaux, 1978.

Douglas, Mary. *Natural Symbols*. London: Pantheon, 1970.

———. *Purity and Danger: An Analysis of the Concepts of Pollution and Taboo*. 1966. Reprint, London: Routledge, 1995.

Drost Beattie, Pamela. "'Pro Exaltatione Sanctae Fidei Catholicae': Mission and Crusade in the Writings of Ramon Llull." In *Iberia and the Mediterranean World of the Middle Ages*, edited by Larry Simon, 113–29. Leiden: E. J. Brill, 1995.

Dufourcq, Charles E. "Catalogue chronologique et analytique du registre 1389 de la chancellerie de la Couronne d'Aragon, intitule 'Guerre Sarracenorum, 1367–1386' (1360–1386)." *Miscelanea de textos medievales* 2 (1974) 65–166.

———. "Chrétiens et Musulmans durant les derniers siècles du Moyen Âge." *Anuario de estudios medievales* 10 (1980): 207–25.

———. *L'Espagne catalane et le Maghrib aux XIIIe et XIVe siècles*. Paris: Presses Universitaires de France, 1966.

———. "Las relations de la Peninsule Ibérique de l'Afrique du Nord au XIVe siècle." *Anuario de estudios medievales* 7 (1970–71): 39–65.

———. *La vie quotidienne dans les ports méditerranéens au Moyen Âge (Provence-Languedoc-Catalogne)*. Paris: Hachette, 1975.

Dunbabin, Jean. *Captivity and Imprisonment in Medieval Europe*. New York: Palgrave Macmillan, 2002.

Dyck, Andrew R. *A Commentary on Cicero, "De Officiis."* Ann Arbor, Mich.: University of Michigan Press, 1996.

Dyer, Christopher. *Standards of Living in the Later Middle Ages: Social Changes in England*. Cambridge: Cambridge University Press, 1984.

Echániz Sans, María. "La alimentación de los pobres asistidos por la *Pia Almonia* de la catedral de Barcelona según el libro de cuentas de 1283–1284." In *Alimentació i societat a la Catalunya medieval*, 173–261. Barcelona: Consell Superior d'Investigaciones Científicas, 1988.

Echevarría, Ana. *The Fortress of Faith: The Attitude towards Muslims in 15th-Century Spain*. Leiden: E. J. Brill, 1999.

Eltis, David. *The Rise of African Slavery in the Americas*. Cambridge: Cambridge University Press, 2000.

Epalza, Mikel de. *Fray Anselm Turmeda y su polémica Islamo-Cristiana: Edición, traducción y estudio de la Tuhfa*. 2nd ed. Madrid: Hiperión, 1994.

Epstein, Steven. *Wills and Wealth in Medieval Genoa, 1150–1250*. Cambridge, Mass.: Harvard University Press, 1984.

Escobar Camacho, José Manuel. "Advocaciones y devociones populares en la Córdova bajomedieval a través de las mandas testamentarias." In *Religiosidad popular en España*, 1:297–305. Madrid: Ediciones Escurialenses, 1997.

———. "La práctica de la caridad en Palma del Rio (siglos XIV y XV)." In *Actas I Coloquio de Historia de Andalucía: Andalucía medieval*, 353–67. Cordova: Monte de Piedad y Caja de Ahorros de Córdoba, 1978.

Ferrer i Mallol, Maria Teresa. *La frontera amb l'Islam en el segle XIV: Cristians i Sarraïns al País Valencià.* Barcelona: Consell Superior d'Investigacions Científiques], 1988.

———. *Organizació i defensa d'un territori fronterer: La governació d'Oriola en el segle XIV.* Barcelona: Consell Superior d'Investigacions Científiques, 1990.

———. "La redempció de captius a la Corona Catalano-Aragonesa (segle XIV)." *Anuario de estudios medievales* 15 (1985): 237–97.

———. *Els sarraïns de la Corona Catalano-Aragonesa en el segle XIV: Segregació i discriminació.* Barcelona: Consell Superior d'Investigacions Científiques, 1987.

Fisher, A. G. B., and H. G. Fisher. *Slavery and Muslim Society in Africa.* London: Doubleday, 1970.

Forey, Alan J. "The Military Orders and the Ransoming of Captives from Islam." *Studia monastica* 33 (1991): 259–79.

———. "The Military Orders and the Spanish Reconquest in the 12th and 13th Centuries." *Traditio* 40 (1984): 197–234.

———. "The Order of Mountjoy." *Speculum* 46 (1971): 250–66.

Friedman, Ellen. "Christian Captives at 'Hard Labor' in Algiers, 16th to 18th Centuries." *International Journal of African Historical Studies* 13 (1980): 616–32.

———. "The Exercise of Religion by Spanish Captives in North Africa." *Sixteenth-Century Journal* 6 (1995): 19–34.

———. *Spanish Captives in North Africa in the Early Modern Age.* Madison: University of Wisconsin Press, 1983.

———. "Trinitarian Hospitals in Algiers: An Early Example of Health Care for Prisoners of War." *Catholic Historical Review* 66 (1980): 551–64.

Friedman, Yvonne. *Encounter between Enemies: Captivity and Ransom in the Latin Kingdom of Jerusalem.* Leiden: E. J. Brill, 2002.

———. "The Ransom of Captives in the Latin Kingdom of Jerusalem." In *Autour de la Premiere Croisade,* edited by Michael Balard, 177–89. Paris: Publications de la Sorbonne, 1996.

———. "Women in Captivity and Their Ransom during the Crusader Period." In *Cross Cultural Convergences in the Crusader Period,* edited by Michael Goodich, Sophia Menache, and Sylvia Schein, 75–87. New York: P. Lang, 1995.

Galan Sánchez, Ángel. *Los Mudejares del reino de Granada.* Granada: Universidad de Granada, Diputación Provincial de Granada, 1991.

García Antón, José. "Cautiverios, canjes y rescates en la frontera entre Lorca y Vera en los ultimos tiempos Nazaries." In *Homenaje al Professor Juan Torres,* 1:547–59. Murcia: Academia Alfonso X el Sabio, 1987.

García de la Borbolla, Ángeles. "Santo Domingo de Silos y las milagrosas redenciones de cautivos en tierras andalusíes (siglo XIII)." In *La liberazione dei "captivi" tra Cristianità e Islam. Oltre la crociata e il ğihād: Tolleranza e servizio umanitario,* edited by Giulio Cipollone, 539–48. Vatican City: Archivio Segreto Vaticano, 2000.

García Fernández, Manuel. "La defensa de la frontera de Granada en el reinado de Alfonso XI de Castilla, 1312–1350." In *Relaciones exteriores del reino de Granada*, edited by Cristina Seguro Graiño, 37–54. Almeria: Instituto de Estudios Almerienses, 1989.

García Herrero, María del Carmen. *Las mujeres de Zaragoza en el siglo XV*. 2 vols. Zaragoza: Ayuntamiento de Zaragoza, 1990.

Gari i Siumell, José. *Historia de las redenciones de cautivos cristianos*. Barcelona: Imprenta de los Herederos de la Viuda Pla, 1873.

Gazulla, Faustino. "Moros y Cristianos: Los cautivos de la frontera." *Boletín de la Sociedad Castellonense de Cultura* 11 (1930): 94–107, 201–10.

———. *La Orden de Nuestra Señora de la Merced: Estudios historiocríticos (1218–1317)*. Barcelona: Gili, 1934.

Geremek, Bronislaw. *Poverty: A History*. Oxford: Blackwell, 1994.

Gilchrist, John. "The Medieval Canon Law on Unfree Persons." *Studia gratiana* 19 (1976): 276–301.

Giménez Soler, Andrés. "La Corona de Aragón y Granada." In *Boletín de la Real Academia de Buenas Letras de Barcelona* 19 (1905): 101–34; 20 (1905): 186–224; 21 (1906): 295–324; 22 (1906): 333–65; 23 (1906): 450–76; 24 (1906): 485–96; 26 (1907): 49–91; 27 (1907): 146–80; 28 (1907): 200–25; 29 (1908): 271–98; 30 (1908): 342–75.

———. "El corso en el Mediterráneo en los siglos XIV y XV." In *Archivo de investigaciones históricas* 1 (1911): 149–79.

Goitein, S. D. *A Mediterranean Society: The Jewish Communities of the Arab World as Portrayed in the Documents of the Cairo Geniza*. 5 vols. Berkeley: University of California Press, 1967–88.

———. "Slaves and Slavegirls in the Cairo Geniza Records." *Arabica* 9 (1962): 1–20.

González Hurtebise, Eduardo. *Libros de tesorería de la casa real de Aragón*. 2 vols. Barcelona: Tip. L. Benaiges, 1911.

Gozalbes Busto, Guillermo. "Redenciones mercedarias en la frontera granadina en el siglo XV." In *Estudios de frontera: Alcalá la Real y el Arcipreste de Hita*, edited by Francisco Toro Ceballos and José Rodríguez Molina, 239–48. Jaén: Diputación Provincial de Jáen, Area de Cultura, 1996.

Gozalbes Cravioto, Enrique. "La liberación de los últimos cautivos cristianos de Granada (1482–1492)." In *La liberazione dei "captivi" tra Cristianità e Islam. Oltre la crociata e il ǧihād: Tolleranza e servizio umanitario*, edited by Giulio Cipollone, 749–65. Vatican City: Archivio Segreto Vaticano, 2000.

Grassoti, Hilda. "Para la historia del botín y de las parias en León y Castilla." *Cuadernos de historia de España* 39–40 (1964): 43–132.

Gual, Miguel. "La asistencia a los pobres en la corte de Pedro IV, El Ceremonioso." In *A pobresa e a assistência aos pobres na península Ibérica durante la idade Media*, 1:455–81. Lisbon: Imprensa Nacional, Casa da Moeda, 1973.

Guillén Robles, F. *Málaga musulmana: Sucesos, antigüedades, ciencias*

222

2222222

y letras malagueñas durante la edad media. 1880. Reprint, Málaga: Editorial Arguval, 1994.

Guilleré, Christian. "Assistance et charité à Gérone au début du XIVème siècle." In *La pobreza y la asistencia a los pobres en la Cataluña medieval,* edited by Manuel Riu, 1:191–204. Barcelona: Consejo Superior de Investigaciones Científicas, 1980.

Guilmartin, John F. *Gunpowder and Galleys: Changing Technology and Mediterranean Warfare at Sea in the Sixteenth Century.* London: Conway Maritime Press, 1974.

Guiral Hadziiossif, Jacqueline. *Valence: Port méditerranéen au XVe siècle (1410–1525).* Paris: Publications de la Sorbonne, 1986.

Hamilton, Earl J. *Money, Prices, and Wages in Valencia, Aragón, and Navarre, 1351–1500.* Philadelphia: Porcupine, 1975.

Hasnaoui, Milouda. "La ley islámica y el rescate de los cautivos según las fetwas de al-Wanšarīsī e Ibn Tarkāt." In *La liberazione dei "captivi" tra Cristianità e Islam. Oltre la crociata e il ǧihād: Tolleranza e servizio umanitario,* edited by Giulio Cipollone, 549–58. Vatican City: Archivio Segreto Vaticano, 2000.

Heers, Jacques. *Esclavos y sirvientes en las sociedades mediterráneas durante la edad media.* Valencia: Institució Valenciana d'Estudis i Investigacio, 1989.

———. "Les nations maritimes et le transport des hommes (guerriers, pelerins, marchands, esclaves) en Méditerranée de l'an mil l'an 1500 environ." In *Trasporti e sviluppo economico: Secoli XIII–XVIII,* edited by Anna Vannini Marx, 33–60. Florence: F. Le Monnier, 1986.

———. "Le royaume de Granade et la politique merchande de Gênes en Occident (XVe siècle)." In *Société et économie à Gênes (XIVe–XVe siècles).* Aldershot, Eng.: Variorum Reprints, 1979.

Hillgarth, J. N. *The Problem of a Catalan Mediterranean Empire.* London: Longman, 1975.

Hinojosa Montalvo, José. "Confesiones y ventas de cautivos en la Valencia de 1409." *Ligarzas* 3 (1971): 113–27.

———. "Crevillente: Una comunidad mudéjar en la governación de Orihuela en el siglo XV." In *Actas del IV Simposio Internacional de Mudejarismo: Economía,* 307–17. Teruel: Instituto de Estudios Turolenses de la Excma, Diputación Provincial de Teruel, 1992.

———. "La esclavitud en Alicante a fines de la edad media." In *Les sociétés urbaines en France Méridionale et en Péninsule Ibérique au Moyen Âge,* 373–92. Paris: CNRS, 1991.

———. "Piratas y corsarios en la Valencia de principios del siglo XV (1400–1409)." *Cuadernos de historia* 5 (1975): 93–116.

Hodgson, Marshall G. S. *The Venture of Islam: Conscience and History in a World Civilization.* 3 vols. Chicago: University of Chicago Press, 1974.

Hoffer, L. John. "Starvation." In *Modern Nutrition in Health and Disease,* 8th ed., edited by Maurice E. Shils et al., 927–49. Philadelphia: Lea and Febiger, 1994.

Hopkins, J. F. P. *Medieval Muslim Government in Barbary.* London: Luzac, 1958.

Housley, Norman. "Pope Clement V and the Crusades of 1309–10." *Journal of Medieval History* 8 (1982): 29–43.

Ivars Cardona, Andreu. *Dos creuades valenciano-mallorquines a les costes de Berberia, 1397–1399.* Valencia: Imprenta de Olmos y Luján, 1921.

Johnston, Mark. "Ramon Llull and the Compulsory Evangelization of Jews and Muslims." In *Iberia and the Mediterranean World of the Middle Ages,* edited by Larry Simon, 3–37. Leiden: E. J. Brill, 1995.

Jordan, William C. *The Great Famine: Northern Europe in the Early Fourteenth Century.* Princeton, N.J.: Princeton University Press, 1996.

Julien, Charles-André. *History of North Africa.* Edited by C. C. Stewart. Translated by John Petrie. New York: Praeger, 1970.

Kaminsky, Howard. "From Lateness to Waning to Crisis: The Burden of the Later Middle Ages." *Journal of Early Modern Europe* 4 (2000): 85–125.

Karras, Ruth M. *Slavery and Society in Medieval Scandinavia.* New Haven, Conn.: Yale University Press, 1988.

Kedar, Benjamin Z. *Crusade and Mission: European Approaches toward the Muslims.* Princeton, N.J.: Princeton University Press, 1984.

———. "Multidirectional Conversion in the Frankish Levant." In *Varieties of Religious Conversion in the Middle Ages,* edited by James Muldoon, 190–99. Gainesville, Fla.: University of Florida Press, 1997.

———. "Muslim Conversion in Canon Law." In *Proceedings of the 6th International Congress of Medieval Canon Law,* edited by Stephan Kuttner and Kenneth Pennington, 321–32. Vatican City: Biblioteca Apostolica Vaticana, 1985.

Kempers, Bram. "Icons, Altarpieces, and Civic Ritual in Siena Cathedral, 1100–1530." In *City and Spectacle in Medieval Europe,* edited by Barbara A. Hanawalt and Kathryn L. Reyerson, 89–136. Minneapolis: University of Minnesota Press, 1994.

Khadduri, Majid, and Herbert J. Liebesny. *Origin and Development of Islamic Law.* Washington, D.C.: AMS, 1955.

Khalilieh, Hassan S. *Islamic Maritime Law: An Introduction.* Leiden: E. J. Brill, 1998.

Klingshirn, William. *Caesarius of Arles: The Making of a Christian Community in Late Antique Gaul.* Cambridge: Cambridge University Press, 1994.

———. "Charity and Power: Caesarius of Arles and the Ransoming of Captives in Sub-Roman Gaul." *Journal of Roman Studies* 75 (1985): 183–203.

Koningsveld, P. S. van. "Muslim Slaves and Captives in Western Europe during the Late Middle Ages." *Islam and Christian Muslim Relations* 6 (1995): 5–23.

Ladero Quesada, Miguel Ángel. "La esclavitud por guerra a fines del siglo XV: El caso de Málaga." *Hispania* 27 (1967): 63–88.

Lagardère, Vincent. *Histoire et société en occident musulman au Moyen Âge: Analyse du Miyǎr D'Al-Wanšrisī*. Madrid: Casa de Velázquez, 1995.

Lappin, Anthony. *The Medieval Cult of Saint Dominic of Silos*. Leeds: Maney Publications for the Modern Humanities Research Association, 2002.

Le Blevec, Daniel. "Le rachat des provençaux captifs au XIVe siècle." In *Islam et Chrétiens du Midi (XIIe–XIVe s.)*, 157–68. Toulouse: E. Privat, 1983.

Levtzion, Nehemiah. "Conversion under Muslim Domination: A Comparative Study." In *Religious Change and Cultural Domination*, edited by David N. Lorenzen, 19–38. Mexico City: Colegio de México, 1981.

———. "Toward a Comparative Study of Islamization." In *Conversion to Islam*, 1–23. New York: Holmes and Meier, 1979.

Levy, Ernst. "*Captivus Redemptus.*" *Classical Philology* 38 (1943): 159–76.

Lewis, Archibald. "Northern European Sea Power and the Straits of Gibraltar, 1031–1350 A.D." In *Order and Innovation in the Middle Ages: Essays in Honor of Joseph R. Strayer*, edited by William C. Jordan et al., 139–64. Princeton, N.J.: Princeton University Press, 1976.

Little, Donald. "Christians in Mamlûk Jerusalem." In *Christian Muslim Encounters*, edited by Yvonne Yazbeck Haddad and Wadi Zaidan Haddad, 210–20. Gainesville, Fla.: University of Florida Press, 1995.

Livi Bacci, Massimo. *Population and Nutrition: An Essay on European Demographic History*. Cambridge: Cambridge University Press, 1991.

Lofland, John, and Norman Skonovd. "Conversion Motifs." *Journal for the Scientific Study of Religion* 20 (1981): 373–85.

Lomax, Derek. *The Reconquest of Spain*. London: Longman, 1978.

López Alonso, Carmen. *La pobreza en la España medieval: Estudio histórico social*. Madrid: Centro de Publicaciones, Ministerio de Trabajo y Seguridad Social, 1986.

López Dapeña, Asunción. "Cautiverio y rescate de Don Juan Manrique, capitán de la frontera castellana (1456–1457)." *Cuadernos de estudios medievales* 12–13 (1984): 243–53.

López de Coca Castañer, José Enrique. "Institutions on the Castilian-Granadan Frontier, 1369–1482." In *Medieval Frontier Societies*, edited by Robert Bartlett and Angus MacKay, 127–50. Oxford: Clarendon, 1989.

López de Meneses, Amada. "Correspondencia de Pedro el Ceremonioso con la soldanía de Babilonia." *Cuadernos de historia de España* 20 (1959): 293–337.

López Elum, Pedro. "Apresamiento y venta de Moros cautivos en 1441 por 'acaptar' sin licensia." *Al-Andalus* 34 (1969): 329–79.

López Pérez, María Dolores. *La Corona de Aragón y el Magreb en el siglo XIV (1331–1410)*. Barcelona: Consejo Superior de Investigaciones Científicas, 1995.

———. "Las relaciones diplomáticas y commerciales entre la Corona de Aragón y los estados Norteafricanos durante la baja edad media." *Anuario de estudios medievales* 20 (1990): 149–69.

———. "Sobre la guerra y la paz: El acuerdo entre Tremecén y la Corona de Aragón (1362)." *Anuario de estudios medievales* 29 (1999): 527–45.

Lourie, Elena. "Anatomy of Ambivalence: Muslims under the Crown of Aragón in the Late Thirteenth Century." In *Crusade and Colonization: Muslims, Christians, and Jews in Medieval Aragón.* Aldershot, Eng.: Variorum Reprints, 1990.

———. "A Society Organized for War: Medieval Spain." *Past and Present* 35 (1966): 54–76.

Lovejoy, Paul E. *Transformations in Slavery: A History of Slavery in Africa.* Cambridge: Cambridge University Press, 1983.

MacKay, Angus. "The Ballad and the Frontier in Late Medieval Spain." *Bulletin of Hispanic Studies* 53 (1976): 15–33.

Malausséna, P. "Promissio redemptionis: Le rachat des captifs chrétiens en pays musulman a la fin de XIVe siècle." *Annales du Midi* 80 (1968): 255–81.

Marmon, Shaun. "Concubinage, Islamic." In *Dictionary of the Middle Ages,* 3:527–29. New York: Scribners, 1983.

———. "Domestic Slavery in the Mamluk Empire: A Preliminary Sketch." In *Slavery in the Islamic Middle East,* edited by Shaun Marmon, 1–23. Princeton, N.J.: Markus Wiener, 1999.

Martínez Carrillo, María de los Llanos. "Rescate de cautivos—commercio de esclavos: Murcia, siglos XIV–XV." *Estudios de historia de España* 2 (1989): 35–64.

Martínez Martínez, María. "La cabalgalda: Un medio de vida en la frontera Murciano-Granadina (siglo XIII)." *Miscelánea medieval murciana* 13 (1986): 49–62.

Martínez Ortiz, José. "Gentes de Teruel en una expedición marítima contra piratas en respuesta al saqueo de Torreblanca." *Boletín de la Sociedad Castellonense de Cultura* 58 (1982): 79–91.

Masía de Ros, Ángeles. *La Corona de Aragón y los estados del norte de África: Política de Jaime II y Alfonso IV en Egipto, Ifriquia y Tremecén.* Barcelona: Instituto Español de Estudios Mediterráneos, 1951.

Mas Latrie, M. L. *Traités de paix et de commerce et documents divers concernant les relations des Chrétiens avec les Arabes de l'Afrique Septentrionale au Moyen Âge.* Paris: H. Plon, 1865.

McCormick, Michael. *Eternal Victory: Triumphal Rulership in late Antiquity, Byzantium, and the Early Medieval West.* Cambridge: Cambridge University Press, 1986.

Melero Fernández, María Inez. "La redención de cautivos y el hospital de Santiago de Toledo." In *Homenatge a la memoria del Profesor Dr. Emilio Sáez,* 273–86. Barcelona: Centre d'Estudis Medievals de Catalunya, 1989.

Meyerson, Mark. *The Muslims of Valencia in the Age of Fernando and*

Isabel: Between Coexistence and Crusade. Berkeley: University of California Press, 1991.

———. "Prostitution of Muslim Women in the Kingdom of Valencia: Religious and Sexual Discrimination in a Medieval Plural Society." In *The Medieval Mediterranean's Cross Cultural Contacts*, edited by M. J. Chiat and K. L. Reyerson, 87–96. St. Cloud, Minn.: North Star, 1988.

———. "Slavery and Solidarity: Mudejars and Foreign Muslim Captives in the Kingdom of Valencia." *Medieval Encounters* 2 (1996): 286–343.

Millán Rubio, Joaquín. *La Orden de Nuestra Señora de la Merced (1301–1400).* Rome: Instituto Histórico de la Orden de la Merced, 1992.

Miret i Sans, Joaquim. "La esclavitud en Cataluña." *Revue hispanique* 41 (1917): 1–109.

Mitjà, Marina. "L'orde de la Merce en crisi en el regnat de Joan I." *Cuadernos de archeologia e historia de la Ciudad* 9 (1966): 61–89.

Molina Molina, Ángel Luis. *La vida cotidiana en la Murcia bajomedieval.* Murcia: Academia Alfonso X el Sabio, 1987.

Molina Molina, Ángel Luis, and Amparo Bejarano Rubio. "Actitud del hombre ante la muerte: Los testamentos murcianos de finales del siglo XV." *Miscelánea medieval murciana* 12 (1985) 185–202.

Mollat, Michele. "Essai d'orientation pour l'etude de la guerre de course et la piraterie (XIIIe–XVe s.)." *Anuario de estudios medievales* 10 (1980): 743–49.

Mott, Lawrence V. *Sea Power in the Medieval Mediterranean: The Catalan-Aragonese Fleet in the War of the Sicilian Vespers.* Gainesville, Fla.: University of Florida Press, 2003.

Muir, Edward. *Ritual in Early Modern Europe.* Cambridge: Cambridge University Press, 1997.

Munro, Dana C. "The Western Attitude toward Islam during the Period of the Crusades." *Speculum* 6 (1931): 329–43.

Murray, Gordon. *Slavery in the Arab World.* New York: New Amsterdam, 1989.

Nieto Soria, José Manuel. *Ceremonias de la realeza: Propaganda y legitimación en la Castilla Trastámara.* Madrid: Nerea, 1993.

Nirenberg, David. *Communities of Violence: Persecution of Minorities in the Middle Ages.* Princeton, N.J.: Princeton University Press, 1996.

———. "Religious and Sexual Boundaries in the Medieval Crown of Aragón." In *Christians, Muslims, and Jews in Medieval and Early Modern Spain,* edited by Mark Meyerson and Edward D. English, 141–60. Notre Dame, Ind.: University of Notre Dame Press, 1999.

O'Callaghan, Joseph. *A History of Medieval Spain.* Ithaca, N.Y.: Cornell University Press, 1975.

Origo, Iris. "The Domestic Enemy: The Eastern Slaves in Tuscany in the 14th and 15th Century." *Speculum* 30 (1955): 321–66.

Osiek, Carolyn. "The Ransom of Captives: Evolution of a Tradition." *Harvard Theological Review* 74 (1981): 365–86.

Padilla, Paul G. "The Transport of Muslim Slaves in 15th-Century Valencia." In *Iberia and the Mediterranean World in the Middle Ages,* edited by Paul Chevedden et al., 379–94. Leiden: E. J. Brill, 1996.

Passmore, Reginald, et al. *Handbook of Human Nutritional Requirements*. Geneva: World Health Organization, 1974.

Patterson, Orlando. *Slavery and Social Death: A Comparative Study*. Cambridge, Mass.: Harvard University Press, 1992.

Pescador del Hoyo, María del Carmen. "Cómo fué de verdad la toma de Granada: A la luz de un documento inédito." *Al-Andalus* 20 (1955): 283–344.

Piles Ros, Leopoldo. *Apuntes para la historia económico social de Valencia durante el siglo XV*. Valencia: Ayuntamiento de Valencia, 1969.

———. *Estudio documental sobre el bayle general de Valencia, su autoridad y jurisdicción*. Valencia: Instituto Valenciano de Estudios Históricos, 1970.

———. "Un factor económico específico: La liberación de esclavos a comienzos del siglo XV en Valencia." In *IV Simposio Internacional de Mudejarismo: Economía*, 281–92. Teruel: Instituto de Estudios Turolenses de la Excma, Diputación Provincial de Teruel, 1992.

Pipes, Daniel. *Slave Soldiers and Islam: The Genesis of a Military System*. New Haven, Conn.: Yale University Press, 1981.

Piponnier, Françoise, and Perrine Mane. *Dress in the Middle Ages*. Translated by Caroline Beamish. New Haven, Conn.: Yale University Press, 1997.

Porras Arboledas, Pedro A. "Las relaciones entre la ciudad de Jaén y el reino de Granada: La paz y la guerra según los libros de actas de 1480 y 1488." *Al-Qantara* 11 (1988): 29–45.

Porres Alonso, Bonifacio. *Libertad a los cautivos: Actividad redentora de la orden Trinitaria*. 2 vols. Córdova and Salamanca: Secretariado Trinitario, 1998.

Poston, Larry. *Islamic Dawah in the West: Muslim Missionary Activity and the Dynamics of Conversion to Islam*. New York: Oxford University Press, 1992.

Powers, James. *A Society Organized for War: The Iberian Municipal Militias in the Central Middles Ages, 1000–1284*. Berkeley: University of California Press, 1988.

Pryor, John H. *Geography, Technology, and War: Studies in the Maritime History of the Mediterranean, 649–1571*. Cambridge: Cambridge University Press, 1988.

Pueyo Colomina, Pilar. "*Litterae 'pro captivis'* en los registros de Pedro de la Jugie y Guillermo de Aigrifeuille, arzobispos de Zaragoza (años 1346–1349)." *Memoria ecclesiae* 11 (1997): 355–66.

Puig y Puig, Sebastián. *Episcopologio de la sede Barcinonense*. Barcelona: Biblioteca Balmes, 1929.

Rambo, Lewis. *Understanding Religious Conversion*. New Haven, Conn.: Yale University Press, 1993.

Ramos y Loscertales, José Maria. *El cautiverio en la Corona de Aragón durante los siglos XIII, XIV y XV*. Zaragoza: Publicaciones del Estudio de Filología de Aragón, 1915.

Ribera, Manuel Mariano. *Real patronado de los serenísimos señores reyes de España en la real y militar orden de Nuestra Señora de la Merced redempción de cautivos cristianos.* Barcelona: Pablo Campins Impressor, 1725.

Richters, Annemiek. "Sexual Violence in Wartime. Psycho-Sociocultural Wounds and Healing Processes: The Example of the Former Yugoslavia." In *Rethinking the Trauma of War,* edited by Patrick J. Bracken and Celia Petty, 112–28. London: Free Association, 1998.

Riu, Manuel. "La ayuda a los pobres en la Barcelona medieval: El 'plat dels pobres vergonyants' en la parroquía de Santa María del Mar." In *A pobreza e a assistência aos pobres na Península Ibérica durante la idade média,* 2:783–811. Lisbon: Imprensa Nacional, Casa da Moeda, 1973.

Robson, J. A. "The Catalan Fleet and Moorish Sea Power, 1337–1344." *English Historical Review* 74 (1959): 386–408.

Roca Traver, Francisco. "Un siglo de vida mudejar an la Valencia medieval: 1238–1338." *Estudios de edad media de la Corona de Aragón* 5 (1952): 115–208.

———. "El tono de vida en la Valencia medieval." *Boletín de la Sociedad Castellonense de Cultura* 58 (1982): 239–309, and 59 (1983): 1–81.

Rogers, Everett M. *Diffusion of Innovations.* 3rd ed. New York: Free Press, 1983.

Rosenthal, Joel. *The Purchase of Paradise: Gift Giving and the Aristocracy, 1307–1485.* London: Routledge and K. Paul, 1972.

Rotberg, Robert I., and Theodore K. Rabb, eds. *Hunger and History: The Impact of Changing Food Production and Consumption Patterns on Society.* Cambridge: Cambridge University Press, 1983.

Rubino, A. *Lineamenti di spiritualita mercedaria.* Rome: F. Santarelli, 1975.

Rubio Vela, Agustín. *Pobreza, enfermedad y asistencia hospitalaria en la Valencia del s. XIV.* Valencia: Institución Alfonso el Magnánimo, 1984.

Ruiz, Teófilo F. "Festivités, couleurs et symboles du pouvoir en Castile au XVe siècle: Les célébrations de mai 1428." *Annales: ESC* 46 (1991): 521–46.

———. *From Heaven to Earth: The Reordering of Castilian Society, 1150–1350.* Princeton, N.J.: Princeton University Press, 2004.

———. "Unsacred Monarchy: The Kings of Castile in the Late Middle Ages." In *Rites of Power: Symbolism, Ritual, and Politics since the Middle Ages,* edited by Sean Wilentz, 109–44. Philadelphia: University of Pennsylvania Press, 1985.

Russell-Wood, A. J. R. "Before Columbus: Portugal's African Prelude to the Middle Passage and Contribution to the Discourse on Race and Slavery." In *Caribbean Slavery in the Atlantic World,* edited by Verene Shepherd and Hilary McD. Beckles, 134–68. Princeton, N.J.: Marcus Weiner, 2000.

———. "Iberian Expansion and the Issue of Black Slavery: Changing Portuguese Attitudes." *American Historical Review* 83 (1978): 16–42.

Ruxton, F. H. *Mâliki Law: Being a Summary from French Translations of the Mukhta.sar of Sîdî Khalîl.* Westport, Conn.: Hyperion, 1980.
Ruzafa García, Manuel. "La frontera de Valencia con Granada: La ruta terrestre (1380–1440)." In *Andalucía entre Oriente y Occidente (1236–1492),* edited by Emilio Cabrera Muñoz, 659–72. Córdova: Servicio de Publicaciones de la Excma, Diputación Provincial de Córdoba, 1988.
Ryder, Alan. *Alfonso the Magnanimous: King of Aragon, Naples, and Sicily, 1396–1458.* Oxford: Clarendon, 1990.
Sáinz de la Maza Lasoli, Regina. "Los Mercedarios en la Corona de Aragón durante la segunda mitad del siglo XIV." *Miscellanía de textos medievals* 4 (1988): 221–99.
Salicrú i Lluch, Roser. "Cartes de captius cristians a les presons de Tunis del regnat de Ferran d'Antequera." *Miscellanía de textos medievals* 7 (1994): 549–90.
———. "The Catalano-Aragonese Commercial Presence in the Sultanate of Granada during the Reign of Alfonso the Magnanimous." *Journal of Medieval History* 27 (2001): 289–312.
———. "En busca de una liberación alternativa: Fugas y apostasía el la Corona de Aragón bajomedieval." In *La liberazione dei "captivi" tra Cristianità e Islam. Oltre la crociata e il ğihād: Tolleranza e servizio umanitario,* edited by Giulio Cipollone, 703–13. Vatican City: Archivio Segreto Vaticano, 2000.
———. *Esclaus i propietaris d'esclaus a la Catalunya del segle XV: L'assegurança contra fugues.* Barcelona: Consell Superior d'Investigacions Científiques, 1998.
———. *El sultanat de Granada i la Corona d'Aragó, 1410–1458.* Barcelona: Consell Superior d'Investigaciones Científiques, 1998.
Sánchez, Diego. "Dos conversiones interesantes." *Al-Andalus* 9 (1944): 507–12.
Sánchez Albornoz, Claudio. *España, un enigma histórico.* 2 vols. Buenos Aires: Editorial Sudamericana, 1956.
Sánchez Herrero, José. "La acción benéfica de las cofradías durante los siglos XIV al XVII: La redención de cautivos y la dotación de doncellas para el matrimonio." In *Religiosidad popular en España,* 1:163–91. Madrid: Ediciones Escurialenses, 1997.
Sánchez Martínez, Manuel. "En torno a la piratería Nazarí entre 1330–1337." In *Andalucía entre Oriente y Occidente (1236–1492),* edited by Emilio Cabrera Muñoz, 431–61. Córdova: Servicio de Publicaciones de la Excma, Diputación Provincial de Córdoba, 1988.
Sancho, P. A. "La redención de cautivos por los frailes Trinitarios." *Boletín de la Sociedad Arqueologica Luliana* 8 (1900): 336.
Sarlach, Josep M. "Els orígens de l'orde de la Mercè." *Acta historica et archaeologica medievalia* 9 (1988): 189–201.
Saunders, A. C. de C. M. *A Social History of Black Slaves and Freedmen in Portugal: 1441–1555.* Cambridge: Cambridge University Press, 1982.
Scarry, Elaine. *The Body in Pain: The Making and Unmaking of the World.* New York: Oxford University Press, 1985.

Schacht, Joseph. *An Introduction to Islamic Law.* Oxford: Clarendon, 1964.

Schein, Sylvia. *Fideles Crucis: The Papacy, the West, and the Recovery of the Holy Land, 1274–1314.* Oxford: Clarendon, 1991.

Schutz, Yves, and Eric Jéquier. "Energy Needs: Assessment and Requirements." In *Modern Nutrition in Health and Disease,* 8th ed., edited by Maurice E. Shils et al., 101–11. Philadelphia: Lea and Febiger, 1994.

Seifert, Ruth. "The Second Front: The Logic of Sexual Violence in Wars." *Women's Studies International Forum* 19 (1996): 35–43.

Semple, Ellen C. *The Geography of the Mediterranean Region: Its Relation to Ancient History.* London: Constable, 1932.

Sersen, William John. "Stereotypes and Attitudes towards Slaves in Arabic Proverbs: a Preliminary View." In *Slaves and Slavery in Muslim Africa,* edited by John Ralph Willis, 1:92–105. London: F. Cass, 1985.

Sevillano Colom, Francisco. "Demografía y esclavos del siglo XV en Mallorca." *Boletín de la Sociedad Arqueologica Luliana* 34 (1973): 160–97.

Shatzmiller, Maya. *Labor in the Medieval Islamic World.* Leiden: E. J. Brill, 1994.

———. "Marriage, Family, and the Faith: Women's Conversion to Islam." *Journal of Family History* 21 (1996): 235–66.

Simonet, Francisco Javier. *Historia de los mozárabes de España: Deducida de los mejores y más auténticos testimonios de los escritores cristianos y árabes.* Amsterdam: Oriental, 1967.

Sixto Iglesias, Ricardo. "Emigrantes musulmanes y cautivos norteafricanos en Valencia." In *VI Simposio Internacional de Mudejarismo,* 357–64. Teruel: Centro de Estudios Mudéjares, Instituto de Estudios Turolenses, 1995.

Smith, Jane I. "Old French Travel Accounts of Muslim Beliefs concerning the Afterlife." In *Christian Muslim Encounters,* edited by Yvonne Yazbeck Haddad and Wadi Zaidan Haddad, 221–41. Gainesville, Fla.: University of Florida Press, 1995.

Smith, Robert. "Fourteenth-Century Population Record of Catalonia." *Speculum* 19 (1944): 494–501.

Spufford, Peter. *Handbook of Medieval Exchange.* London: Royal Historical Society, 1986.

Stella, Alessandro. "*Herrado en el rostro con una S y un clavo:* L'homme-animal dans l'Espagne des XVᵉ–XVIIIᵉ siècles." In *Figures de l'esclave au Moyen Âge et dans le monde moderne,* edited by Henri Bresc, 147–63. Paris: Editions L'Harmattan, 1996.

Taylor, Bruce. *Structures of Reform: The Mercedarian Order in the Spanish Golden Age.* Leiden: E. J. Brill, 2000.

Thornton, John. *Africa and Africans in the Making of the Modern World, 1400–1680.* Cambridge: Cambridge University Press, 1992.

Throop, Palmer A. *Criticism of the Crusade: A Study of Public Opinion and Crusade Propaganda.* Amsterdam: Swets and Zeitlinger, 1940.

Toro Ceballos, Francisco, and José Rodríguez Molina, eds. *Estudios de frontera: Alcalá la Real y el Arcipreste de Hita*. Jaén: Diputación Provincial de Jaén, Area de Cultura, 1996.

Torres Balba, Leopoldo. "La acrópolis musulmana de Ronda." *Al-Andalus* 9 (1944): 449–80.

———. "Las mazmorras de la Alhambra." *Al-Andalus* 9 (1944): 198–218.

Torres Delgado, Cristobal. "Liberación de cautivos en el reino de Granada, siglo XV." *En la España medieval* 3 (1982):639–51.

———."El Mediterraneo Nazarí: Diplomacia y piratería, siglos XIII–XIV." *Anuario de estudios medievales* 10 (1980): 227–35.

Torres Fontes, Juan. "Los alfaqueques castellanos en la frontera de Granada." In *Homenaje a Don Agustín Millares Carlos*, 2:99–116. Madrid: Caja Insular de Ahorros de Gran Canaria, 1975.

———. "El concepto concejil murciano de limosna en el siglo XV." In *A pobresa e a assistência aos pobres na Península Ibérica durante la idade media*, 2:839–71. Lisbon: Imprensa Nacional, Casa da Moeda, 1973.

———. "La frontera de Granada en el siglo XV y sus repercusiones en Murcia y Orihuela: Los cautivos." In *Homenaje a Don José Maria Lacarra de Miguel*, 4:191–211. Zaragoza: Anubar, 1977.

———. "La hermandad de moros y cristianos para el rescate de cautivos." In *Actas del Ier Simposio Internacional de Mudejarismo*, 499–508. Madrid: Consejo Superior de Investigaciones Científicas, 1981.

———. "La intromisión granadina en la vida murciana (1448–1452)." *Al-Andalus* 27 (1962): 105–45.

———."Notas sobre los fieles de rastro y alfaqueques murcianos." *Miscelanea de estudios árabes y hebraicos* 10 (1961): 89–105.

Torres Fontes, Juan, et al. *La expansión peninsular y Mediterránea (c. 1212–c. 1350)*. 2 vols. Madrid: Espasa-Calpe, 1990–91.

Turner, Victor. *From Ritual to Theater: The Human Seriousness of Play*. New York: Performing Arts Journal Publications, 1982.

Turner, Victor, and Edith Turner. "Locality and Universality in Medieval Pilgrimages." In *Image and Pilgrimage in Christian Culture: An Anthropological Perspective*, 172–202. New York: Columbia University Press, 1978.

———. "Pilgrimage as a Liminoid Phenomenon." In *Image and Pilgrimage in Christian Culture: An Anthropological Perspective*, 1–39. New York: Columbia University Press, 1978.

Udina Martorell, Federico. "Las relaciones entre Tunez y la Corona de Aragón en el segundo tercio del siglo XIV." *Anuario de estudios medievales* 10 (1980): 337–40.

Ullman, Chana. *The Transformed Self: The Psychology of Religious Conversion*. New York: Plenum, 1989.

Unali, Anna. *Mariners, pirates i corsaris catalans a l'època medieval*. Translated by. Maria Antònia Oliver. Barcelona: Institut Municipal d'Història, 1986.

Ursano, Robert, and James Rendell. "The Prisoner of War." In *War Psychiatry*, edited by Franklin D. Jones et al., 431–55. Washington, D.C.: U.S. Office of the Surgeon General, 1995.

U.S. Naval Oceanographic Office. *Sailing Directions (enroute) for the Western Mediterranean—Pub No. 131*. Washington, D.C., 1971.

Van Gennep, Arnold. *The Rites of Passage*. Translated by Monika B. Vizedom and Gabrielle L. Caffee. Introduction by Solon Kimball. Chicago: University of Chicago Press, 1960.

Van Kleffens, E. N. *Hispanic Law until the End of the Middle Ages*. Edinburgh: Edinburgh University Press, 1968.

Vásquez Núñez, Guillermo. *Manual de historia de la Orden de Nuestra Señora de la Merced*. 2 vols. Toledo and Madrid: Editorial Catolica Toledana, 1931–36.

———. *Mercedarios ilustres*. Barcelona: Edita Revista Estudios, 1966.

Veas Arteseros, Francisco de Asis, and Juan Francisco Jiménez Alcázar. "Notas sobre el rescate de cautivos en la frontera de Granada." In *Actas del Congreso La Frontera Oriental Nazarí como Sujeto Histórico (s. XIII–XVI)*, 229–36. Almeria: Instituto de Estudios Almerienses, 1997.

Verlinden, Charles. "Aspects quantitatifs de l'esclavage méditerranéen au bas Moyen Âge." *Anuario de estudios medievales* 10 (1980): 769–90.

———. *The Beginnings of Modern Colonization*. Translated by Y. Freccero. Ithaca, N.Y.: Cornell University Press, 1970.

———. *L'esclavage dans l'Europe médiévale*. 2 vols. Brugge: De Tempel, 1955.

———. "Medieval Slavers." In *Economy, Society, and Government in Medieval Italy: Essays in Memory of Robert L. Reynolds*, edited by David Herlihy et al., 1–14. Kent, Ohio: Kent State University Press, 1969.

Vidal Castro, Francisco. "El cautivo en el mundo islámico: Visión y vivencia desde el Otro Lado de la frontera Andalusí." In *Estudios de frontera II: Actividad y vida en la frontera*, edited by Francisco Toro Ceballos and José Rodríguez Molina, 771–823. Jaén: Diputación Provincial de Jaén, Area de Cultura, 1998.

Vinyoles i Vidal, María Teresa. *La vida quotidiana a Barcelona vers 1400*. Barcelona: R. Dalmau, 1985.

Webster, Jill. *Els Menorets: The Franciscans in the Realm of Aragon, from St. Francis to the Black Death*. Toronto: Pontifical Institute of Mediaeval Studies, 1993.

Weigert, Gideon. "A Note on Hudna: Peace Making in Islam." In *War and Society in the Eastern Mediterranean, 7th–15th Centuries*, edited by Yaacov Lev, 399–405. Leiden: E. J. Brill, 1997.

Weiss, Gillian Lee. "From Barbary to France: Processions of Redemption and Early Modern Cultural Identity." In *La liberazione dei "captivi" tra Cristianità e Islam. Oltre la crociata e il ǧihād: Tolleranza e servizio umanitario*, edited by Giulio Cipollone, 789–805. Vatican City: Archivio Segreto Vaticano, 2000.

Willis, John Ralph, ed. *Slaves and Slavery in Muslim Africa*. 2 vols. London: F. Cass, 1985.

Wright, Nicholas. "'Pillagers' and 'Brigands' in the Hundred-Years War." *Journal of Medieval History* 9 (1983): 15–24.

———. "The Ransom of Non-combatants during the Hundred-Years War." *Journal of Medieval History* 17 (1991): 323–32.

Zika, Charles. "Hosts, Processions, and Pilgrimages: Controlling the Sacred in Fifteenth-Century Germany." *Past and Present* 118 (1988): 25–64.

INDEX

Captives & Their Saviors in the Medieval Crown of Aragon was designed and typeset in Trump Mediaeval by Kachergis Book Design of Pittsboro, North Carolina. It was printed on 60-pound Natures Natural and bound by Thomson-Shore of Dexter, Michigan.